Suspended Futures

SERIES | RACE AND EDUCATION

Series edited by H. Richard Milner IV

OTHER BOOKS IN THIS SERIES

Urban Preparation
Chezare A. Warren

Justice on Both Sides
Maisha T. Winn

Truth Without Tears
Carolyn R. Hodges and Olga Welch

Millennial Teachers of Color
Edited by Mary E. Dilworth

Culturally Responsive School Leadership
Muhammad Khalifa

Science in the City
Bryan A. Brown

Race, Sports, and Education
John N. Singer

Start Where You Are, But Don't Stay There, Second Edition
H. Richard Milner IV

The Chicana/o/x Dream
Gilberto Q. Conchas and Nancy Acevedo

Restorative Justice in Education
Maisha T. Winn and Lawrence T. Winn

Teachers of Color Resisting Racism and Reclaiming Education
Rita Kohli

Stuck Improving
Decoteau J. Irby

Jim Crow's Pink Slip
Leslie T. Fenwick

Not Paved for Us
Camika Royal

Equality or Equity
Jeffrey M. R. Duncan-Andrade

Racial Opportunity Cost
Terah Venzant Chambers

Race and Culturally Responsive Inquiry in Education
Edited by
Stafford L. Hood
Henry T. Frierson
Rodney K. Hopson
Keena N. Arbuthnot

#BlackEducatorsMatter
Edited by Darrius A. Stanley

Radical Brown
Margaret Beale Spencer
Nancy E. Dowd

The Big Lie About Race in America's Schools
Edited by Royel M. Johnson and Shaun R. Harper

How Schools Make Race
Laura C. Chávez-Moreno

Suspended Futures

Transforming Racial Inequities in School Discipline

RICHARD O. WELSH

HARVARD EDUCATION PRESS
CAMBRIDGE, MASSACHUSETTS

Paperback ISBN 9781682539767

Library of Congress Cataloging-in-Publication Data is on file.

Published by Harvard Education Press,
an imprint of the Harvard Education Publishing Group

Harvard Education Press
8 Story Street
Cambridge, MA 02138

Cover by Dave Kessler Design

The typefaces in this book are Sabon LT Std and Myriad Pro.

For the Founder.

I love you. I miss you. I thank you for your guidance. My scholarship reflects your parenting and mentorship. I will never forget one of your last words of encouragement you shared that serves as the North Star of my research.

"Make the work unquestionable."

Lloyd Allan Welsh

March 12, 1951–November 19, 2023

For Mama Welsh.

My precious Granma. I will forever treasure our conversations and hold dear all the lessons you instilled.

Be wise and not foolish.

Hurt no man and let no man hurt you.

Be strong and of good spirit.

Jane Elizabeth Welsh

July 31, 1926–May 8, 2024

For Solomon and Amina Welsh.

Your father loves you more than you will ever know. You inspire me more than you will ever know.

Speak the truth.

And speak it well.

Cost it what it will.

Contents

Foreword

H. RICHARD MILNER IV

Several years ago, I witnessed a teacher in an underserved school demonstrate what appeared to be deep frustration with students because they did not form a line outside of the restroom straight enough to the teacher's satisfaction. The teacher had walked the students to the restroom and water fountain, and the students had been directed "many times in the past" on what was expected before walking back to their classroom as a group. These young people appeared to be giving their best effort to satisfy their teacher's expectation but struggled to make the line straight enough for some reason. After speaking briefly to the principal at the school who observed the interaction as well and had much more knowledge about this teacher, students, and school, I concluded the following: (a) the teacher and administrator cared about their students but worried they lacked the skills and ability to follow directions well; (b) most of the students at the school were Black and lived below the poverty line; (c) students at the school were not succeeding on the state's standardized test; and (d) students were being suspended for noncompliance and fighting at very high rates.

Meanwhile, I recall an experience in a well-resourced school where a group of students ran out the cafeteria down the hallway headed to their classroom. Like my experience described above in the poorly resourced school, these students (who appeared to be around the same age as those I observed in the underresourced school) were being directed to head back into their classroom—one group after having finished using the restroom and the other after finishing their lunch. Seconds after the students ran past me in the hallway in the well-resourced school, their teacher appeared. The teacher walked swiftly but confidently behind the students and posed a question to me: "Did my students almost bump into you?" Not wanting the students to get into trouble, I simply replied, "No, it is fine." The teacher then expressed how the students had lots of energy and that they would eventually slow down when walking down the hallway. What I heard most from this teacher's assessment of the students was that the students were "developing."

Later, I spoke to the head of the school about what I observed and the teacher's response to students running down the hallway after lunch. The head of the school was not surprised at all and reified the notion that the school recognized that when students disobeyed or did not follow rules that they are in developmental stages; students were not expected to already and always get it right. What is most important to consider in the two examples I just described—one in the poorly resourced school and the other in the highly resourced school—is that educators and students are working in systems that perpetuate ideas and ideals about student learning and development. Thus, my point is not to criticize the practice of the teacher in the poorly resourced school for being disgusted with students' inability to form a straight line (yet) as they headed back to the classroom. My point is also not to praise the teacher in the highly resourced school for viewing students as developmental beings and not vilifying them for running down the hallway. Instead, my point here is to stress that students and educators respond to challenges in schools based on the overall ethos of a school: culture, expectations, norms, and worldviews of leadership and other adults who make important decisions on behalf of young people.

In this way, it is essential for any of us interested in reducing school suspensions and expulsions to study these issues at a macro level as well as a micro level in so far as these issues run in confluence. But why is it that students in the highly resourced school are allowed to develop, while those in the underresourced school are viewed as those who should already be developed?

Richard Welsh has written a powerhouse book, *Suspended Futures: Transforming Racial Inequities in School Discipline*, one that I will assign and recommend to those who care about education for years to come. Frankly, this is the book I wish I was assigned as a preservice teacher. This book is surely to be a difference-maker in the work of teachers, school administrators, counselors, researchers, theorists, and interventionists interested in and committed to understanding how pushout practices—those that are often framed as discipline practices—harm and undermine what education should and could accomplish in schools across the United States.

I invite readers to critically engage the text as Welsh details "the why" of racial disparities related to pushout, suspension, and expulsion. As Welsh explains what we know about the genesis and reasons for "suspended futures," he shares a new and expanded strategy for how to disrupt and transform patterns that have had detrimental effects for too many inside and outside of education. Indeed, from my view, I recommend this book in the absolute highest terms because so many minoritized students experience (a) missed instructional time due to suspension and expulsion; (b) subjective infraction that can lead to harsh punishment and consequences; and (c) classroom-level pushout due to noncompliance. While the issues explored in this book are broad and systemic, as Welsh details, we also know how important classroom teachers are in this complex maze of suspension and expulsion. Most infractions in schools begin at a classroom level and are for student noncompliance—not because of student physical threats to themselves or others.

Suspended Futures breaks new and expanded grounds. It is solidly and methodically researched, framed by years of careful empirical research. Moreover, Welsh advances a robust and deep knowledge about what it takes to transform districts, schools, and classrooms to be more inclusive, caring, understanding, and supportive of young people who refuse to conform to rules and expectations that feel demeaning and reductive to them. Brilliantly and effectively framed as a human and civil rights issue, Welsh has taken the often inside-of-education debated issues of office referral, suspension, and expulsion into a broader discourse for policy makers, parents, and community members to engage. Indeed, as teachers are "stuck between a rock and hard place," as Welsh describes in this book, we need to build a cadre of supporters who dare to work with educators to transform educational systems not well designed for some students—particularly those of color, those with a disability, and those who live below the poverty line. This is the book we need; I am ready to witness and participate in Welsh's collective call to transform education as we know it.

H. Richard Milner IV
Cornelius Vanderbilt Professor of Education
Vanderbilt University

The Urgency of Inequality in School Discipline

Inequities in educational opportunities are as American as apple pie. And school discipline is a key cog in the cycle of generational educational and subsequential economic inequality.

School discipline has evolved into one of the most contentious and polarizing topics in education—and for good reason. Educational stakeholders across the political and ideological spectrum are increasingly concerned with how student behavior is perceived and responded to in schools. One of the primary ways that instructional time is stolen in K–12 education is through exclusionary discipline such as office discipline referrals (ODRs), suspensions, referrals to alternative schools, and expulsions.[1] It is hard to digest the research and not wonder whether how students are disciplined in America's schools depends more on the color of their skin than the content of their character or the nature of their misbehavior.

The quest to reduce racial inequities in students' disciplinary outcomes is an important educational equity and social justice issue. District and school leaders are seemingly caught between a rock and a hard place. Teachers and parents are demanding safe schools. Equity advocates highlight persistent racial inequality in exclusionary discipline and the growing evidence of the school-to-prison pipeline. A handful of surveys and even more popular media articles have pointed to an uptick in student misbehavior as students settle back into in-person learning after the disruption of the COVID-19 pandemic. For instance, the School Pulse Panel, a monthly survey instituted by the National Center for Education Statistics to measure the impacts of COVID-19 on education, asked about student behavior in the May 2022 survey. Eighty-four percent of principals agreed or strongly agreed that students' behavioral development has been negatively impacted by the pandemic.[2] Furthermore, 56 percent of principals reported increases in disruptive student misconduct, 48 percent reported increased disrespect of teachers and staff, and 33 percent reported an increase in fights or physical attacks.[3] Interaction and engagement issues are fueling more fights and disciplinary infractions in schools.[4] New infractions, namely vaping and cell phone use, are on the rise.[5] There is an ongoing mental health crisis among students.[6] Teachers and principals are fleeing classrooms and schools due to the supposed mounting chaos in public schools. In New York City Public Schools, in the 2022–2023 school year relative to the 2021–2022 school year, there was a more than 10 percent increase in suspensions.[7] The increasing overall prevalence of exclusionary discipline (the rates at which students receive disciplinary consequences) in the postpandemic era has been accompanied by widening racial disparities. Black students continue to be significantly more likely than their White peers to be excluded from classrooms and schools for perceived misbehavior.[8]

The strategic focus on improving student behavior as the sole path to resolving the school discipline crisis is misplaced and, frankly, has not moved the needle toward educational equity. School discipline is at an inflection point. Although the overall use of exclusionary discipline has declined in recent years, racial disparities in disciplinary outcomes have persisted across districts in the United States.[9] From federal and state policy makers to teachers in classrooms, the question of how to address student behavior (without the use of exclusion) remains largely unanswered. And it is not for lack of trying. How can district and school leaders disrupt persistent and longstanding racial inequality in school discipline? That is the question this book addresses. The urgency of the question has been heightened with changes in student behavior in the aftermath of the COVID-19 pandemic. We are stuck in punitive sands as racial disparities in students' disciplinary outcomes remain persistent. We need a better plan.

THE SCHOOL DISCIPLINE CRISIS

Charleston pastor Reverend Matthew Watts described school discipline as the "most significant unaddressed issue in the state of West Virginia and nationally."[10] I tend to agree with him, but I may be biased given that I have devoted the past decade or so of my life researching school discipline and partnering with district and school leaders to disrupt discipline disparities.

Discipline disparities are much more than simple discrepancies in how students are treated. They reflect the unjust environments and processes in America's schools that violate students' rights. In September 2023, prominent civil rights attorney Ben Crump joined a case against the Baltimore City Schools. The attorney highlighted that, "It's not enough for me simply to fight for our children's lives when they are killed by biased policing. It's just as horrific when you think about our children being killed softly, slowly, every day in an unsympathetic, uncaring school system that believes in just passing them along to get along." In his trademark articulate manner, the attorney got to the heart of the school discipline crisis: "I think it's even more than a civil rights issue. It's a human rights issue."[11]

The school discipline crisis—persistent differences in how White and Black students are disciplined—is not about how well these students behave but the consequential differences in how teachers, assistant principals, and principals perceive and respond to students' behavior. Black students are disproportionately removed from classrooms and receive harsher punishment than their peers for similar transgressions. There is emerging consensus on appropriate and commensurate consequences for misbehavior, but "appropriate" should apply equally to Black and White students. This is not the case in too many of America's schools. There are multifaceted differences in how Black and White students are treated and punished in schools from who is referred to the office and for what infractions to who is ultimately suspended or receive multiple disciplinary consequences in a given school year. We should care about racial inequities in school discipline because of the prevalence of exclusionary discipline (which entails the rates of exclusion from classrooms and schools, including suspensions and expulsions), the multilayered disparities in students' disciplinary outcomes (e.g., culturally based discretionary decisions made by teachers and principals, unwarranted severity for small or infrequent infractions, differences in consequences across Black and White students for similar infractions), and the adverse impact of exclusionary discipline on student achievement and adult outcomes.[12]

We should all be appalled and ashamed of how schools punish students. It is a crisis of (sadly and frustratingly) epic and immense proportions—not only because of the disproportionalities along racial and other lines but also because of the far-reaching impacts of exclusionary discipline. Getting suspended matters for the lives and livelihoods of students, particularly Black lives in the United States.

Black Students Are Disciplined Differently in Schools

Whether it is for not following the dress code or being loud, Black students are referred to the office, suspended, expelled, or sent to alternative schools more than any other student group. The age at which students are excluded from classrooms starts as early as prekindergarten and stretches until grade twelve. The disparities are systematic and start as early as prekindergarten: Black preschool students accounted for 43 percent of students receiving one or more out-of-school suspension (OSS) but made up only 18.2 percent of total preschool enrollment.[13]

In 2017–2018, Black students represented 15.1 percent of total K–12 enrollment, yet Black students represented 38.8 percent of expulsions, 38.2 percent of students who received one or more OSS, and 31.4 percent of one or more in-school suspension (ISS).[14] According to the Civil Rights Data Collection, "Black boys received both in-school suspensions (20.1%) and out-of-school suspensions (24.9%) at rates more than three times their share of total student enrollment (7.7%)—the largest disparity across all race/ethnicity and sex groupings."[15] A 2024 report by the United States Government Accountability Office (GAO) found that

> Among girls, Black girls faced more and harsher forms of discipline than other girls and had the highest rates of exclusionary discipline, such as suspensions and expulsions. According to GAO's analysis of the most recent Department of Education data before the pandemic, in school year 2017–18, Black girls comprised 15 percent of all girls in public schools but received almost half of suspensions and expulsions. Further, GAO's analysis of school year 2017–18 infraction or behavior data showed that Black girls received harsher punishments than White girls even when the infractions that prompted disciplinary action were similar. For example, Black girls had higher rates of exclusionary discipline compared to White girls for similar behaviors such as defiance, disrespect, and disruption. The data also show that in every state in the U.S., Black girls are disciplined at higher rates. When they also had a disability, exclusionary discipline rates of Black girls grew larger.[16]

Disparities in school discipline are largely driven by the unequal punishment of Black students. Similar to Victor Valley Union High School District in San Bernardino County, California (which was deemed noncompliant with Title VI due to its pattern of disciplining Black students more often and more harshly than White students), several districts across the United States are guilty of civil rights offenses.[17] In particular, the civil rights of Black students are being violated when they receive more frequent and harsher punishment than their White peers for similar infractions, when they are unfairly punished for subjective offenses such as incivility and insubordination and when they are disproportionately removed from classrooms.[18] Whether from the GAO using national data or from individual states and districts exploiting longitudinal and infraction-level data, the theoretical debate of whether discipline disparities are caused by Black students misbehaving more is increasingly being settled by mounting empirical evidence. For instance, sociologists Jayanti Owens and Sara McLanahan examined the drivers of racial disparities in suspensions and expulsions and found that the differential treatment and support of students with similar behaviors accounted for the majority of disparities in exclusionary discipline.[19] Subjective offenses, or infractions that are largely dependent on the discretion in the disciplinary decisions of teachers and school administrators, are of particular concern.[20] As such, the path forward in school discipline requires creating structures that foster inclusion rather than exclusion and disrupting the deficit language and the criminalization of Black students that permeate schools.

Differential treatment (differential selection and differential processing) is the crux of the school discipline crisis. Differential selection pertains to the referral process and disproportional likelihood of Black students being referred to the office, whereas differential processing refers to the adjudication of ODRs and captures the phenomenon of Black students receiving harsher punishment than their peers for similar disciplinary infractions.[21] As argued by urban education expert Rich Milner, contemporary school discipline can be characterized as punishment for Black students whose behavior is misaligned with White educators' behavioral and academic expectations.[22] I contend that the inequitable application of discretion in disciplinary decisions is partly a function of bias and anti-Black racism. There are growing concerns about race and bias in school discipline among not only teachers but also school leaders.[23] And there is mounting evidence of bias and discrimination along racial lines in school discipline.[24] Consider ODRs. Previous research has used infraction-level data to examine different facets of racial inequality in whether some students receive ODRs and others do not for similar infractions.[25] There are significant differences in the referral rates of Black and White students.[26] For instance, school discipline expert Russell Skiba and colleagues found that Black students were more likely to be referred to the office than White students, and education policy researchers Gary Ritter and Kaitlin Anderson found that Black students had a higher risk of receiving an ODR for subjective infractions.[27]

Discipline Disparities Matter for K–12 Outcomes and Beyond

Discipline disparities are a primary example of how issues of race and inequality collide to shape the schooling opportunities and life trajectories of Black and Brown children. The deleterious impact of exclusion from classrooms and schools starts with missing instructional time. And then it metastasizes into low achievement, high school dropout, involvement in juvenile and criminal justice systems, and adult incarceration. Overall, racial disparities in who is referred to the office and ultimately suspended are eroding the foundation of educational opportunity in public schools.

Disparities in exclusionary discipline are robbing students of color of precious instructional time.[28] In a 2020 report, "Lost Opportunities: How Disparate School Discipline Continue to Drive Differences in the Opportunity to Learn," Daniel Losen and Paul Martinez highlighted that during the 2015–2016 school year, 11,392,474 days of instruction were lost due to OSSs. Black boys and girls lost the bulk of this instructional time.[29] For instance, at the secondary level, Black students lost 103 days per 100 students enrolled compared to 21 days per 100 students enrolled for their White peers.

These discipline disparities matter. Millions of lost instructional days due to suspensions are linked to lower student achievement and adverse adult outcomes for Black students. Scholars have contended that the racial, income, and gender disparities in students' disciplinary outcomes widen achievement gaps.[30] A robust literature has linked exclusionary discipline to worse achievement and adult outcomes.[31] There is also growing empirical evidence of the school-to-prison pipeline because exclusionary discipline increases the likelihood of contact with the juvenile justice system and adult incarceration.[32] For instance, education researcher Lucy Sorensen and colleagues found that school principal propensity to remove students from school (i.e., harsher school discipline) is associated with lower levels of misbehavior in schools but also with more juvenile crime and reduced high school graduation rates for the student bodies.[33] Exclusionary discipline harms the health of students.[34] A 2024 report from the Centers for Disease Control and Prevention highlighted the prevalence of unfair disciplinary practices (as reported by students), the link between exclusionary discipline and a variety of health risks and declared that "school discipline is an urgent public health problem."[35]

In addition, there is also the collateral damage or spillover effects of exclusionary discipline. Stated differently, suspensions also affect nonsuspended students in schools.[36] Recent evidence highlighted that Black students who witness their Black peers receiving suspensions for minor infractions feel threatened and expect unfair treatment.[37] Scholars Juan Del Toro and Ming-Te Wang highlighted that for Black students in predominantly Black classrooms, classmates' suspensions were particularly predictive of students' defiant interactions.[38]

SCHOOL DISCIPLINE REFORMS ARE CHALLENGED BY GROWING TOXICITY

The politics of school discipline are growing more toxic over time. School discipline has also evolved as a teacher labor market issue. The empathy associated with the pandemic is dissipating. The anti-Blackness in society manifested in extrajudicial killings of George Floyd and Breonna Taylor is fading from memories. There is increasing polarization in school discipline policy and reforms. The discourse on school discipline is dripping with racism and anti-Blackness. Indeed, the discourse is growing more adrift from empirical evidence. Some scholars (read: misguided souls) have even called for the reform of zero tolerance and a cessation of the march toward to educational equity.[39] The "equity" camp and the "law and order" camp are becoming ships in the night. As shockingly displayed in a news story questioning why Metro Nashville Public Schools suspension and expulsion rates were holding steady, "law and order" stakeholders will question why discipline rates are stagnant or, God forbid, declining.[40] If rates of ODRs and suspensions decline, are students "getting away with it"? The locus of the debate seems to have distinctly moved from doing what's best for students to catering to the adults in schools and the biases of society in the name of law and order.

The growing toxicity of school discipline politics is pitting students against teachers, teachers against school leaders, and teachers and their professional association—in tandem with parents—against the reduction of racial inequality in school discipline. Advocates of punitive school discipline often cite teachers' welfare as the reason for needing harsh punishment. Additional teacher discretion is often characterized as necessary for an orderly classroom, but it is also a pathway to racial inequality in school discipline. It is truly a sad and sordid day if teachers and parents are less committed to fostering child development for all students, and more concerned about stagnant rates of exclusion rather than the persistence of racial inequities in students' disciplinary outcomes.

The Politics of School Discipline Are Growing Toxic

Often, the conversation on school discipline is polarizing and gets framed in binary terms. There are seemingly two camps on how to approach school discipline. Either you're for a punitive approach or a restorative approach. Either students should be suspended all the time or not at all. Either you are for law and order and three strikes or against all school exclusion at the expense of a safe and productive learning environment. There is a bit more nuance when we consider the empirical evidence on school discipline.

As highlighted by educational researchers NaYoung Hwang and Thurston Domina (who found that math achievement increases when classmates were suspended for disruptive behavior), "suspensions, when used appropriately, can improve the academic achievement of nonsuspended students, particularly for students from vulnerable populations."[41] Moreover, in such a racialized topic, the research evidence may be overshadowed by biases, ideology, and personal experiences.

One of the sources of polarization in school discipline is disagreement about the root causes of discipline disparities, the genesis of disciplinary infractions, and the progression of disciplinary consequences. One would get vastly different responses to the query, "Why, really are Black students suspended more than White students?"[42] And these responses tend to vary systematically based on one's worldview and political orientation. Is it because Black students misbehave more? Is it because of poverty? Despite a robust school discipline literature, there is manufactured disagreement on what the issue in school discipline really is and whether student behavior or practices in schools by educators need to change to disrupt inequality in who is referred to the office and suspended. Additionally, there is an ongoing conflation of school discipline (racial inequities in punishment) with school safety (keeping students and staff safe in schools).

The variation in how discretion is applied to address perceived misbehavior is at the core of the school discipline crisis. Consider for a moment, suspend your disbelief, and allow me to leverage a robust school discipline literature to impress upon you that student behavior is not the issue driving discipline disparities. Black students are not misbehaving more in schools, thus warranting higher rates of exclusionary discipline. Rather, this book shows that a wealth of studies have dismissed this conservative refuge.

There is also a demand for punishment that accompanies school discipline discourse. Similar to teachers, some parents—such as those at a Minnesota high school in January 2024, where physical altercations involving adults and students resulted in school closure—are clamoring for zero tolerance discipline policies.[43] Parents in some districts such as San Diego Unified School District are declaring school discipline policy broken as students evade consequences for bad behavior.[44] The carceral DNA of the American ethos, reminiscent of the demand for a pound of flesh in *The Merchant of Venice*, is manifesting in school discipline disparities.[45] Parents want action, and students should be adequately punished—appropriate time for appropriate crime. Trapped in the carceral spiral, restorative and nonpunitive approaches to school discipline are branded (read: mischaracterized) as soft and without consequences. School discipline is not preparation for the criminal justice system. When did suspensions become "doing time"?

As the argument goes, there is no valid reason why the majority of well-behaved students (read: White students) should be held hostage by the disruptive behavior of a handful of students (read: students of color, generally; Black students, particularly). It seems that too many people in the United States—through the disciplinary system in public schools—are more interested and invested in the incarceration rather than the education of Black youth. Indeed, the criminalization of Black students is at the root of calls for harsher school discipline policies. The misguided sentiment is that if students are not suspended or expelled, they escape consequences for their criminal activity. A popular argument of the law-and-order approach to school discipline is the protection of instructional time of peers of misbehaving students. A nonpunitive approach essentially wastes time and resources on these criminals who are robbing their orderly compatriots (read: White students) from an orderly learning environment. This ignores the undertones that some students' (read: White students) instructional time and educational opportunity are a priority to those of others. It is as if Black students are only entitled to three-fifths of a quality education. Contrary to the misguided notion that discipline is restoring order, the limited but growing evidence is pointing to a communal toll that arises when disciplinary consequences are dispensed.

The real issue at hand—Black students being punished differently—seems to be forgotten on the implicit assumption that some students' learning and instructional time is more prioritized than that of others. Conservative positions typically advocate for strict enforcement of discipline policy—if students break the rules, they ought to be held responsible (read: punished). Yet whether or not discipline policy and the rigidity of enforcement are applied consistently across students receives far less attention. One cannot ignore the demographic mismatch in schools, the history of racial animus, White fragility, White supremacy, and anti-Blackness that pervades American society. Teachers are largely middle-class White women. The students most frequently and severely punished are Black boys and girls.

School Discipline as a Teacher Retention Issue

School discipline is now firmly on the radar of teachers' unions nationwide and growing increasingly prominent in teacher labor market discussions. School discipline challenges are being increasingly linked to teachers leaving classrooms, and the protection of teachers is motivating changes in school discipline policies. Teachers are leaving the profession, citing violence and student behavioral issues as one of the primary reasons for leaving the classroom.[46] Punitive discipline is now being openly rationalized and justified by teacher recruitment and retention. Politicians are beginning to blame school discipline as the reason why teachers exit teaching. As the story goes, the deteriorating behavior of students is jeopardizing the safety of teachers in classrooms. Fortunately, the trend is concerning, but not absolute. For example, in November 2023, striking teachers in Portland cited the high suspension rates of Black and Native students as a point of contention.

Consider the case of Kentucky. "Every one of them said, 'I'm leaving'—some in their 30s, some in their 40s—'I'm leaving because I'm scared of the kids,'" he said. "'And I know central office won't back me up.'"[47]

These are the words a Republican lawmaker in Kentucky said were relayed to him by teachers leaving the classroom, citing the lack of school discipline. "Scared of the kids." White teachers are leaving classrooms in droves because they are scared of violent students of color who have lost their respect for authority.

Teachers are calling for additional discretion in disciplinary decisions and strict enforcement of school discipline policies. Teachers are increasingly voicing their frustration about the lack of accountability and consequences for student behavior.[48] This has worsened in the aftermath of the pandemic. Thus, new student codes of conduct and policy changes are increasingly pitting students against teachers in the name of providing greater protections to teachers, which we see in Tennessee's Teacher's Discipline Act. Teachers are increasingly demanding that disruptive students are punished. In Louisiana, an advisory group, "Let Teachers Teach," was tasked with "protecting" teachers' time and reducing disruptions in classrooms. This teacher panel prioritized student behavior and discipline as one of its six focus areas and offered a slew of recommendations, including the removal of "ungovernable" students and modifying accountability policies such that schools with high suspension rates are not held to account.[49] These are indeed polarizing times, for the direction and disposition of teachers and their unions will undoubtedly stoke disciplinary tensions and pit teachers not only against students but also against school administrators.[50]

States such as Alabama, Arizona, and West Virginia are approving bills to give teachers even more discretion in the disciplinary process. In these states, in the name of protecting the precious White women in classrooms, legislators are taking power away from principals (another group of largely White middle-class females) and stoking tensions and discontent among teachers and school leaders. In Arizona, the school superintendent encouraged lawmakers to penalize districts that don't pursue teachers' school discipline complaints. It is interesting that teacher retention has been linked to school discipline, but the conversation about teacher preparation and professional capacity (or lack thereof) and the connections to discipline disparities has been largely muted. Interesting. Legislators want to protect teachers through additional discretion. But what about the school leaders? And what about expanding the professional capacity of educators?

School discipline is such an important and complex topic that it has birthed an uncommon alliance between Republican lawmakers and teachers' unions across several states. Republican politicians are tripping over themselves to "protect teachers." In Utah, "teacher empowerment" bills such as SB137 are predicated on "giving teachers more control of their classroom environments." In Oklahoma, the state superintendent rode in on his white horse armed with the "Discipline Reform Plan" to "protect teachers." Teachers' perception of feeling unsafe seemingly trumps the belonging and educational experiences of Black students in schools.

Teachers are crying out for support. Surveys of teachers' mental health in the aftermath of the pandemic are concerning and highlight the need for support: 48 percent of public school teachers and 32 percent of private school teachers report their mental health has a negative impact on their work.[51] Findings from the 2024 State of the American Teacher survey indicated that managing student behavior was the top source of job related stress (for both 2023 and 2024).[52] The object of teachers' ire should be on carceral disciplinary systems and inadequate preparation in classroom management and relationship building rather than the behavior of developing children. If we agree that valuing and supporting teachers is key to disrupting discipline disparities, the operative question is how do we do it? Teachers need better tools and resources to effectively manage their diverse classrooms. As such, supporting teachers is central to disrupting discipline disparities. Too often, disciplinary practices become a vehicle for educators' anti-Blackness.

THE NEED FOR COORDINATION AND STRATEGY IN SCHOOL DISCIPLINE REFORM

The path to transforming racial inequities in school discipline faces two major roadblocks: the "why" and "how" of reforms. Albeit for vastly different reasons, from safety to equity concerns, there is a growing consensus on the need for school discipline reforms. Most district and school leaders are stuck on the "how." For the moment, let's assume there is a firm and humane will to reduce racial inequality in exclusionary discipline (an assumption that is fully tenuous at worst and certainly questionable at best). We are struggling to find the way. Something needs to be done about the disproportionate rates at which Black students—Black girls, Black boys, Black boys with disabilities—are excluded from classrooms and schools.

Discipline reform is scattershot, and individual policy and program changes are insufficient to reduce racial inequality in school discipline.[53] The response to school discipline disparities has been a hodgepodge of policy and program changes without a clear strategic direction and a lack of alignment between key actors (district leaders, school administrators, and teachers). There is an urgent need for stronger connective tissues between district and school leaders—two key actors in the disruption of discipline disparities. There is a need for strategy to align and coordinate the many moving parts in schools and districts that feed inequities in students' disciplinary outcomes. The policies and practices of schools will need to be in sync with the policies and practices of districts. A central premise of this book is that the confrontation of racial inequities in school discipline lacks strategy and coordination, and this partly explains the largely mixed results of decades of reforms.

"Zero tolerance has not worked. We are pushing out our most vulnerable populations, students with disabilities and students of color. We need to come up with better, proactive ways to keep them in school," said John Inglish, the former chair of the Oregon School Discipline Advisory Council. "The end goal shouldn't be punishment, the end goal should be fostering accountability."[54]

"If you're really trying to affect systemic change at a district level, it's going to take you three to five years. It's a marathon, not a sprint," Inglish said. "You've got to have superintendents, building principals, assistant principals, teachers, and counselors, all with that same common vision."

He should know, as Oregon has embarked upon the road to transforming school discipline with mixed results. Using a voluntary sample of 401 K–5 schools that implemented Positive Behavioral Interventions and Supports (PBIS) in Oregon, Nishioka and colleagues found that there was "a significant shift in the post policy years from exclusionary to nonexclusionary discipline" for most students, but not African American students. An earlier study highlighted that the short-term decline in the use of exclusionary discipline trended upward in later years.[55]

We Gotta Coordinate

An overlooked dimension of school discipline reforms is the coordination among district and school leadership. Superintendents and the folks in the central office need to be on the same page and rowing in the same direction as principals and assistant principals. This is often not the case as district and school leaders carry varying opinions about the contributors and solutions of inequities in school discipline. And there is no unifying framework, taxonomy, or shared playbook to harmonize the efforts of superintendents and principals in the fight against racial inequality in school discipline. Without the buy-in and support of principals and assistant principals, any directive or discipline reform posited by superintendents and directors of support toward transforming school discipline is akin to a raisin in the sun.

We need coordination to win, and sustain wins, in school discipline. And by wins, I mean the reduction of differences in students' disciplinary outcomes. There is dissonance in the decision-making in schools and districts that needs to be resolved to disrupt discipline disparities. There are valid questions on whether the key actors are aligned in vision and goals in the disruption of discipline disparities.

We Gotta Strategize

There is a need for a strategic framework for school discipline reforms. I contend that districts and schools grappling with the school discipline crisis have not fully leveraged the vast research literature to plot a strategy from measuring disparities (and distinguishing prevalence from disparities) and determining areas of greatest need for intervention to assessing the efficacy of reforms. Strategy in school discipline reform requires the alignment of contributors to solutions of discipline disparities. Strategy in school discipline needs a framework that allows practitioners to put the wealth of insights from the school discipline research literature into action. When determining policies, programs, and initiatives to invest in to reduce discipline disparities, district and school leaders should consider research and evidence-based practices and interventions. But where do they find such insights? These insights are not readily available at their fingertips.

Schools' and districts' limited resources also necessitate a clear strategy. Resources are scarce, which means actors must target areas of greatest need to achieve the largest potential bang for buck. Not all schools and teachers contribute equally to discipline disparities in districts. As such, it is not the most effective use of scarce resources to apply a carte blanche approach to transforming school discipline. Strategy in school discipline is essential.

A NEW DAWN

The need for a new dawn in school discipline arises from decades-long disparities in suspensions and expulsions. Disproportionate discipline is one the enduring inequities in America's public education system. The crux of the school discipline crisis is not the overall prevalence of exclusionary discipline but rather that certain students (read: Black students) get punished more often and more severely than others without a just cause. There have been fits and bouts of progress toward reducing discipline inequities. While a notable share of districts and schools have experienced success in reducing overall suspensions, most districts and schools have failed to disturb the inequality in exclusionary discipline that bedevils the schooling system in the United States. There is an urgent need for a new way forward in school discipline.

What This Book Does and Who It Is For

Why have school discipline reforms reduced rates but not narrowed disparities in students' disciplinary outcomes? Is it the students' or the adults' behavior in schools that is driving discipline disparities? Furthermore, what is the path to reducing racial inequality in school discipline? This book answers these questions and more.

Suspended Futures: Transforming Racial Inequities in School Discipline responds to the persistence of racial disparities in exclusionary discipline with a new strategic direction and a multifaceted evidence-based framework to facilitate the disruption of discipline disparities. Drawing on a synthesis of prior literature reviews and empirical studies in the robust school discipline literature as well as original analysis of recent waves of national data from the Civil Rights Data Collection (CRDC) and administrative data from New York City Public Schools, the book establishes the need for a comprehensive framework by illustrating the decline in prevalence yet persistent disparities in exclusionary discipline in the past decade nationwide, the mixed results of school discipline reforms, and the importance of school-level factors such as school personnel and school climate in discipline disparities.

The book presents the Transforming School Discipline Strategic Framework, an approach intended to spark change in the disciplinary process in classrooms and schools. The Transforming School Discipline Strategic Framework is a research-based strategic framework intended to strengthen the alignment of causes and solutions to discipline disparities and improve the coordination between key decision-makers in disciplinary systems. It is a thought partner for district and school leaders trying to solve the school discipline dilemma. The combination of policy, program, and personnel changes aligned with the mechanisms driving discipline disparities requires a unifying framework given that the path to solving the school discipline dilemma does not run through a singular program or policy but instead lies in a comprehensive strategic approach aligned with contributors to racial inequities in exclusionary discipline.

Suspended Futures: Transforming Racial Inequities in School Discipline argues for a shift from a student-focused to educator-focused approach to school discipline reforms commensurate with the contributors to racial inequality in school discipline. An educator-focused approach addresses the structure of schooling that drives disparities in the disciplinary process, rather than student-related factors, as the main contributor to racial inequality in school discipline. Instead of focusing on what we can do to help the behavior of students, the framework asks what we can do to help educators so that the adults in schools can better help students. The book posits that current interventions largely aimed at modifying student rather than adult behavior have fallen short in reducing racial disparities in school discipline. School discipline disparities are a structural failure. A key plank of the renewed strategy for school discipline reform is shifting from blaming to supporting teachers and school administrators. It is the broken structures of schools that are fueling discipline disparities rather than the behavior of students. Thus, in a Shakespearean twist, the reduction of suspensions is more reliant on changing adult behavior rather than student conduct. The path to disrupting discipline disparities is not predicated on expecting less from students, but expecting more of the adults in the school building whose job is to the prepare the next generation of just and well-thinking citizens. In other words, it's the adults, stupid.

I wrote this book for practitioners, rather than an academic audience that cares about practice. This book is for superintendents, directors of behavior and student support services, principals, and assistant principals earnestly seeking to disrupt discipline disparities. Every superintendent should get this book for principals in their district to align, collaborate, learn, and disrupt discipline disparities. Likewise, every principal should get this book for teachers in their school. This book is for leaders who are committed to disrupting a dysfunctional disciplinary system that manifests in racial disproportionalities. *Suspended Futures: Transforming Racial Inequities in School Discipline* charts a direction from philosophical shifts to evidence-based practices to ultimately restore the instructional time Black students lose to exclusion. The book provides a common language for practitioners to discuss school discipline challenges and solutions, and offers strategies and insights for disruptive decision-makers as well as personnel in schools that can effectively reduce disparities in students' disciplinary outcomes. However, this book will be of interest to everyone who touches and is touched by disciplinary systems in schools and to educational stakeholders (parents, community activists, and school board members) interested in social justice issues, such as the school-to-prison pipeline.

This book is a call to action and a strategic playbook for disruptive decision-makers. It is foremost for the people in the district offices and schools who ultimately make the decisions that either fertilize the soils of inequities or plant the seeds of hope and progress. These decisions about district and school policies and practices matter for the disciplinary experiences of students, particularly Black students. The book takes a step in ensuring that decisions and practices in disciplinary systems are shaped more by empirical evidence than by anecdotes, biases, and opinions.

I want to persuade district and school leaders that there is a path to reducing discipline disparities that involves leveraging their experiential knowledge and tapping into the vast evidence-based repository of studies and reports. I want to impress upon superintendents, directors of student supports, principals, and assistant principals that their decisions matter for discipline disparities. And these decisions, if more rooted in empirical evidence, can be disruptive and transform school discipline.

Ultimately, my hope is that this book restores dignity in disciplinary decisions and decorum in the discipline debate and, most importantly, instruction and inclusion for Black students in public schools. In the forthcoming chapters, I hope to impress upon you the scope, magnitude, and urgency of the school discipline crisis. The goal, however, is not to leave you with a sense of despair, but inspiration on a path forward.

UNDERSTANDING AND TRANSFORMING SCHOOL DISCIPLINE

The book starts with taking stock of the national school discipline landscape and the efficacy of current reforms to disrupt racial inequality in school discipline. Chapter 1 describes trends in the prevalence of and disparities in students' disciplinary outcomes and discusses the emerging literature on the effectiveness of alternative approaches. Drawing on multiple data sources including four waves of CRDC data (2011–2012, 2013–2014, 2015–2016, and 2017–2018), studies and reports from districts nationwide, and recent literature reviews, chapter 1 introduces readers to the depth of the school discipline crisis and explains why school discipline reforms are not disrupting racial inequality in exclusionary discipline.

Chapter 2 presents the Transforming School Discipline Strategic Framework. The framework is an analytic tool to describe the prevalence and disparities in exclusionary discipline, connect disparities to the mechanisms that produce racial inequality, and align salient mechanisms in the disciplinary process with evidence-based interventions intended to disrupt discipline disparities. The chapter describes and explains the sequential steps of the disruption of discipline disparities.

The Transforming School Discipline Strategic Framework in chapter 2 is rationalized and complimented by the original research in chapters 3 through 5. Chapters 3 through 5 draw on a rich dataset from New York City to investigate the relationship between school personnel, school climate, and school discipline. Chapter 3 illustrates the contribution of school personnel to discipline disparities and why starting with the adults in schools is the key to solving the school discipline dilemma. Chapter 4 illustrates the contribution of school climate to discipline disparities and why setting the right climate is a prerequisite to disrupting racial inequality in school discipline. Chapter 5 discusses the need for an "asset-based" approach to reduce discipline disparities and explores inclusive disciplinary environments at the district and school level.

Suspended Futures: Transforming Racial Inequities in School Discipline concludes with a call for greater investments in school discipline reforms and school discipline data collection and analysis. I also imagine a schooling system with limited to no racial inequality in school discipline and what that may mean for inequality in schooling and society.

MY WHY

The why of the work is perhaps the most fun, joyful, and inspiring segment of what can be riveting (read: painfully long) school board meetings—when young students of color excel, are centered, shine bright, and are uplifted by schools. The applause in the awards and recognition at the start of these school board meetings, coupled with the smiles on the faces of the supporting village in the audience and the joy and slight bewilderment on the part of the students, encapsulate the why of the work to dismantle discipline disparities, the quest of this book. Black achievement and excellence warrant a standing ovation in contemporary American society. Black students have a right to unbridled and unchained joy in public schools that is often suspended.

My journey into fatherhood deeply shaped and impacted my foray into school discipline. The serendipity of discovering the phenomena of school discipline while writing my dissertation on student mobility at the same time and space when my son was born is not lost on me. I'm a Black father with a Black son and a Black daughter. This is central to my positionality and how I enter school discipline. The apples of my eyes are vulnerable to the school discipline crisis.

I have not taught or led a public school or district in the United States (or in my birthplace, Jamaica). I've been a tenure-track or tenured professor at predominantly White institutions in the Northeast and the South. My experiential entry into school discipline is through various research–practice partnerships with district and school leaders. Through thought partnerships, I get to visit district offices and schools regularly. I get to have frank and insightful conversations on the contributors and solutions to racial inequality in exclusionary discipline. I get to do school walkthroughs, sit in on classes, and observe lunches and dismissals. Through my district and school partners, I have been embedded in the disciplinary process in districts and schools. And this has allowed me to connect the insights of a robust school discipline literature to the lived experiences of those on the school discipline frontlines.

I was never sent to the office or suspended as I did my K–12 schooling in Jamaica. I did fight in first form (the equivalent of ninth grade). I was sent to Mrs. Johnson, our feared dean of discipline. I was assigned a disciplinary consequence: afterschool detention. However, unlike too many other Black boys, my disciplinary consequence was not a gateway to adverse achievement and adult outcomes.

My scholarship and this book are rooted in reimagining a different way and a different vision of schooling. My goal is to create a welcoming, inclusive, and inspiring schooling environment for my children and children who look like them. My hope is that this book advances the discourse (and disruptive action) on making the vision of educational equity a reality.

Stuck in Punitive Sands

In 1969, one of the first demands made by Black students in New York City (NYC) was no more automatic suspensions.[1] More than a half century later, in 2021, NYC students were making a similar cry, underscoring the conditions of Black students and the urgency of this demand.[2]

We are stuck in punitive sands. In 2024, sadly, the disciplinary experiences of Black students remain a pressing educational equity concern. Reducing racial inequality in exclusionary discipline is a pivotal plank of improving K–12 education systems. However, districts and schools nationwide are grappling with the challenge of how to reduce racial disparities in students' disciplinary outcomes. Disparities in the disciplinary outcomes of Black students and their peers have remained persistent over time despite myriad school discipline reforms. To be clear, school discipline reforms have reduced the overall use of exclusionary discipline, but the disproportionate use of office discipline referrals (ODRs) and suspensions on Black students compared to their White counterparts remains a lingering challenge. This raises important questions about a misalignment of problems and solutions in school discipline.

This chapter details the scope of the school discipline crisis and why discipline disparities seem impervious to reform efforts. The chapter is divided into three main sections. First, using four waves of data on districts nationwide from the Civil Rights Data Collection (CRDC) (2011–2012 through 2017–2018) and data from the New York City Public Schools (NYCPS), I provide an empirical portrait of the school discipline landscape across districts in the United States and describe the salient trends in the prevalence of and disparities in students' disciplinary outcomes. Next, drawing on recent literature reviews and empirical studies published in the past decade, I interrogate the effectiveness of alternative approaches to exclusionary discipline.[3] Finally, I conclude the chapter with a discussion of why school discipline reforms are not disrupting racial inequality in exclusionary discipline. The chapter provides readers with answers to three foundational questions in the school discipline debate: (a) What is the extent of disparities in students' disciplinary outcomes? (b) Are alternative approaches to exclusionary discipline reducing racial inequality in school discipline? (c) Why aren't school discipline reforms benefiting Black students? As such, the chapter provides a richer understanding of how the tentacles of anti-Blackness in society may manifest in racial inequality in exclusionary discipline in schools. The microscopic focus on the experiences of Black educators, students, and families situated within an *anti-Blackness in school discipline* theoretical framework reveals a layered and nuanced system of anti-Blackness saturating the disciplinary process in K–12 schools.[4]

HISTORY REPEATING ITSELF

When I reflect on the nature of the school discipline crisis, there is an eerie feeling of history repeating itself. History shapes the students and teachers in today's classroom and how teachers respond to different student's behavior. *Brown v. Board of Education* is a monumental historical moment in fomenting the school discipline crisis. There may have been suspensions prior to the ruling as some scholars have suggested.[5] Yet others have highlighted the marked increase in the proportion of Black students being excluded from schools via suspensions in the implementation of desegregation in the 1960s and 1970s.[6] Suspended futures are illustrated by decades of evidence of racial disparities in students' disciplinary outcomes. Simply put, discipline disparities are not a modern-day phenomenon. These enduring disparities can be partly explained by history. A history of slavery, a history of *Brown v. Board*, a history of zero tolerance, and many other historical moments and processes that continues to shape punishment and educational opportunity in the twenty-first century.

In October 1974, two decades after the groundbreaking *Brown v. Board* ruling in 1954, a landmark report drew attention to a phenomenon that has evolved into (and remains) one of the biggest racial justice issues in public education. The Children's Defense Fund (CDF) report *Children Out of School in America* found that roughly two million students were not enrolled in schools, and data from five states (Arkansas, Maryland, New Jersey, Ohio, and South Carolina) highlighted that "during the 1972–73 school year, at least 153,904 children were suspended at least once for over 575,000 school days or 3,200 school years" with half of the 402 districts suspending 5 percent or more of their Black students.[7] In chapter 5 of the report, "School Discipline and Its Exclusionary Impact on Students," the authors articulately stated the historical and contemporary conundrum:

"We favor discipline and order with schools. But we question the current methods used to achieve these goals. We do not believe the answer to children's discipline problems lies in denying them schooling. Worse is the denial of schooling without any semblance of fairness, for a wide range of reasons, some indefensible and others unnecessary."[8] The report drew attention to racial discrimination in the use of suspensions and made visible the "hidden weapon" of suspensions as "neither the federal, state, nor local governments had any idea how many children were suspended or why."[9]

A follow-up report in 1975, *School Suspensions: Are They Helping Children?*, further expounded on the school discipline crisis with data from 2,862 districts from the Office for Civil Rights and found that over a million students were suspended with more than four million school days lost (more than 22,000 school years), indicating that "the vast majority of school suspensions in CDF's survey were for nondangerous, nonviolent offenses which do not have a seriously disruptive effect on the educational process."[10] The 1975 report also underscored racial inequality in school discipline: "No one is immune from suspension, but Black children were suspended at twice the rate of any other ethnic group. Nationally, if they had been suspended at the same rate as Whites, nearly 50 percent or 188,479 of the Black children suspended would have remained in school. Although Black children accounted for 27.1 percent of the enrollment in districts reporting to OCR, they constituted 42.3 percent of the racially identified suspensions."[11] In truth, these reports likely spotlighted a disturbing trend that accelerated in the aftermath of the landmark *Brown v. Board* decision: the exclusion of Black students from classrooms and schools and the robbery of their instructional time (and educational opportunity).[12]

And the more things change, the more they remain the same. As I detail below, recent data from the CRDC (2011–2012 through 2017–2018) provide a longitudinal view of the disciplinary experiences of K–12 students in the past decade and eerily resemble the trends highlighted by the CDF reports from the 1970s. Moreover, recent research on differential processing—Black students receiving harsher punishment for similar disciplinary infractions—is quite congruent with accounts of school discipline in the 1970s.[13] Indeed, the 1975 CDF report posited:

> Some will claim that disproportionate suspension of Black children simply reflects their disproportionate misbehavior. We reject this view. All the evidence we have seen: our survey data: our analysis of OCR data and school district suspension reports: interviews with school officials, parents, children and community groups: and review of the investigations and literature of other groups on school discipline makes plain that disproportionate suspension of

Blacks reflect a pervasive school intolerance for children who are *different*. . . . The fact is that many school districts treat Black children differently from White children.[14]

The school discipline crisis is both historical and contemporary. Indeed, the breadth and depth of the disparities in students' disciplinary experiences and outcomes are underlined by the alarming and vexing fact that the CDF reports from decades ago accurately capture the state of school discipline in today's schools. It is as if time has stood still, and Black children today face the same predicament as their peers from yesteryear.

THE STATE OF SCHOOL DISCIPLINE: TRENDS IN SUSPENSIONS

One of the central questions in school discipline research and policy discourse is the extent and variation of suspensions across districts and states in the United States. Why focus on suspensions? Because suspensions are the major pathway to exclusion from classrooms and schools. Suspensions, of which there are two main types—in-school suspensions (ISSs) and out-of-school suspensions (OSSs)—are the most frequently occurring disciplinary consequence.[15] Discipline disparities start with ODRs, which are then converted into suspensions.[16] When students are referred to the office, there are a range of possible resolutions including student and parent conference. However, most ODRs are resolved with suspensions. Thus, although there are a handful of possible pathways, suspensions are the most frequent pathway though which school discipline results in school exclusion.[17]

Students receive exclusionary discipline for both low-level (e.g., tardiness and disruption) and high-level (e.g., fighting and terroristic threats) offenses.[18] Subjective offenses, or infractions that are largely dependent on the discretion in the disciplinary decisions of teachers and school administrators, are of particular concern.[19] ODRs are disciplinary decisions made primarily by teachers, whereas suspensions are decisions primarily made by school administrators.[20] As such, ODRs provide some indication of how teachers may be responding to perceived misbehavior in classrooms and teachers' bias in their decision to report certain infractions for specific students, whereas suspensions capture how school leaders make decisions on ODRs and may also reflect similar biases of school administrators.[21]

The Overall and Disproportionate Use of Suspensions

Table 1.1 illustrates the prevalence of OSSs by decade from the 1970s through the 2020s. Research using national school discipline data indicates that there was an increase in OSS from the 1970s to the 2010s with

TABLE 1.1 Trends in OSS (%) by decade

	1970s	*1980s*	*1990s*	*2000s*	*2010s*	*2020s[a]*
Overall	4.0	5.1	6.8	7.0	5.7	1.3
Black	6.0	9.6	12.9	14.4	14.0	2.3
Native American	2.8	4.7	7.1	7.6	8.1	1.3
Latinx	2.7	4.6	6.5	6.5	5.2	0.8
White	3.1	4.0	5.5	4.9	3.8	1.4
Asian	1.1	2.6	3.2	2.8	2.1	0.3

Source: Rates for 1970s to 2010s are from Leung-Gagne et al. 2022 based on separate CRDC reports in each decade: https://learningpolicyinstitute.org/media/3885/download?inline&file=CRDC_School_Suspension_REPORT.pdf.

Note: Table estimates are based on number of OSSs overall and by race divided by number of students overall and of each race for the United States. Rates are averaged by decade. Due to changes in CRDC methodology between decades, comparisons are indicative only.

[a]Rates for 2020s are based only on 2020–2021 estimates from CRDC 2023: https://www2.ed.gov/about/offices/list/ocr/docs/crdc-discipline-school-climate-report.pdf. (Note that these estimates are impacted by COVID and school closures and may not be comparable to previous decades.)

a decrease in recent decades.[22] In the early 1970s, less than 5 percent of students were suspended.[23] The overall prevalence of OSSs has slightly increased over time. By 2009–2010, suspension rates were nearly twice that of the 1970s, with roughly 7 percent of students being suspended. Notwithstanding, the 2010s in some regard represent a suspension peak. In the past decade, overall suspension rates have declined from 7 percent in 2009–2010 to 5 percent in 2017–2018.[24] Trends in OSS rates across student race paint a different picture from the consideration of overall prevalence. The suspension rates of Black students have increased over time from 6 percent in 1973 to 16 percent in 2009–2010 to 12 percent in 2017–2018. Thus, suspension rates for Black students have doubled from the 1970s to the 2010s, even though the overall rates of OSS went from 3.1 to 3.8 percent over the corresponding period.[25] The suspension rates of White students slightly increased from 3.1 percent in the 1970s to 3.8 percent in the 2010s. This illustrates why overall rates of exclusionary discipline may remain stable (or even decline), yet racial disparities in disciplinary outcomes persist.

There Are Multiple Suspension Types

Although OSS typically receives the bulk of the research and policy, there are multiple suspension types and OSS may not be the most widely used suspension. Even though millions of students receive ISSs nationwide, researchers have largely overlooked ISSs due in part to data limitations. The lion's share of empirical studies examining school discipline patterns focus on OSS, and few studies have focused on ISS or differentiated between the two suspension types.[26] For instance, in its most recent release, the Institute of Education Sciences tables presented data from the 2017–2018 wave on OSS and expulsion across states.[27]

Table 1.2 illustrates ISS and OSS prevalence and disparities, by region and student race. In the decade prior to the onset of the COVID-19 pandemic (2012–2018), nationwide, the overall ISS rate (5.42 percent) has been roughly equal to the OSS rate (5.08 percent).

Attention to both suspension types is essential to investigating the disciplinary process in schools and highlighting the scope of the prevalence of and disparities in school discipline. Solely focusing on OSS risks underestimating the extent of exclusionary discipline. ISS may act as a substitute for OSS as schools shift away from OSS and rely more on ISS (students still miss instructional time, albeit in the school building).[28] Furthermore, little is known about the content and variation of ISS environments within and across districts as well as within and across states.

ISS Is a Southern Thing

There are also instructive differences in the use of suspensions across states and regions in the United States. Using 2011–2012 data on suspensions and expulsions nationwide, education policy scholars Edward Smith and Shaun Harper found that Black students were suspended more frequently than their peers and discipline disparities were most visible in southeastern states, where nearly half of all Black suspensions occurred.[29] Figure 1.1 presents a map of ISS and OSS prevalence between 2012 and 2018.

As table 1.2 illustrates, there is notable variation in disciplinary outcomes across regions in the United States. In the past decade, the ISS rate in the South (9.46 percent) was the highest suspension rate across both suspension types and regions. The ISS rate of the South is roughly double that of the West (3.70 percent), Midwest (4.72 percent), and Northeast (3.61 percent) regions. An opposite trend regarding the prevalence of suspension types occurred in the West and to a lesser extent in the Northeast. In the West, the OSS rate is about 2 percentage points higher than the ISS rate. In the South, the overall ISS rate is more than 3 percentage points higher than that of the OSS rate.

TABLE 1.2 ISS and OSS prevalence and disparities, by region and student race

	ISS					*OSS*				
	(1)	*(2)*	*(3)*	*(4)*	*(5)*	*(6)*	*(7)*	*(8)*	*(9)*	*(10)*
	National	*South*	*West*	*Midwest*	*Northeast*	*National*	*South*	*West*	*Midwest*	*Northeast*
(A) Prevalence of ISS and OSS										
Overall rate	5.42	9.46	3.70	4.72	3.61	5.08	6.32	5.88	4.67	3.68
Black rate	9.80	15.36	5.96	8.88	7.95	9.62	10.19	9.64	9.92	8.44
Latinx rate	5.58	8.26	3.81	5.33	4.45	5.01	5.00	4.95	5.22	4.70
Asian rate	1.74	2.07	1.79	1.09	2.46	1.80	1.07	3.59	1.03	2.38
Pacific Islander rate	3.50	4.94	0.73	1.78	1.69	3.94	2.91	1.27	1.45	1.82
Multirace rate	6.75	11.60	4.06	6.18	4.85	7.01	8.12	6.55	7.37	5.62
White rate	4.77	8.14	3.48	4.25	3.12	4.35	5.34	5.01	4.12	3.13
(B) Disparities in ISS and OSS										
Black-White RRR	2.05	1.89	1.71	2.09	2.55	2.21	1.91	1.92	2.41	2.70
Latinx-White RRR	1.17	1.01	1.09	1.25	1.43	1.15	0.94	0.99	1.27	1.50
Multirace-White RRR	1.42	1.43	1.17	1.45	1.55	1.61	1.52	1.31	1.79	1.80

Notes: Regions as classified by the National Center for Education Statistics (NCES). "South" includes Alabama, Arkansas, Delaware, District of Columbia, Florida, Georgia, Kentucky, Louisiana, Maryland, Mississippi, North Carolina, Oklahoma, South Carolina, Tennessee, Texas, Virginia, West Virginia. "West" includes Alaska, Arizona, California, Colorado, Hawaii, Idaho, Montana, Nevada, New Mexico, Oregon, Utah, Washington, Wyoming. "Midwest" includes Illinois, Indiana, Iowa, Kansas, Michigan, Minnesota, Missouri, Nebraska, North Dakota, Ohio, South Dakota, Wisconsin. "Northeast" includes Connecticut, Maine, Massachusetts, New Hampshire, New Jersey, New York, Pennsylvania, Rhode Island, Vermont. RRR is the Relative Risk Ratio, which is the Black or Latinx or Multirace rate divided by the White rate.

FIGURE 1.1 (a) ISS and (b) OSS prevalence, 2012–2018

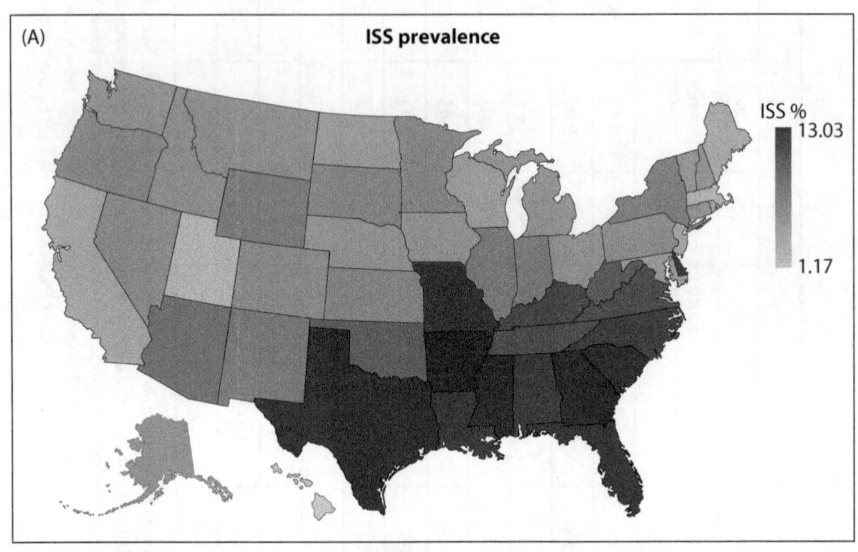

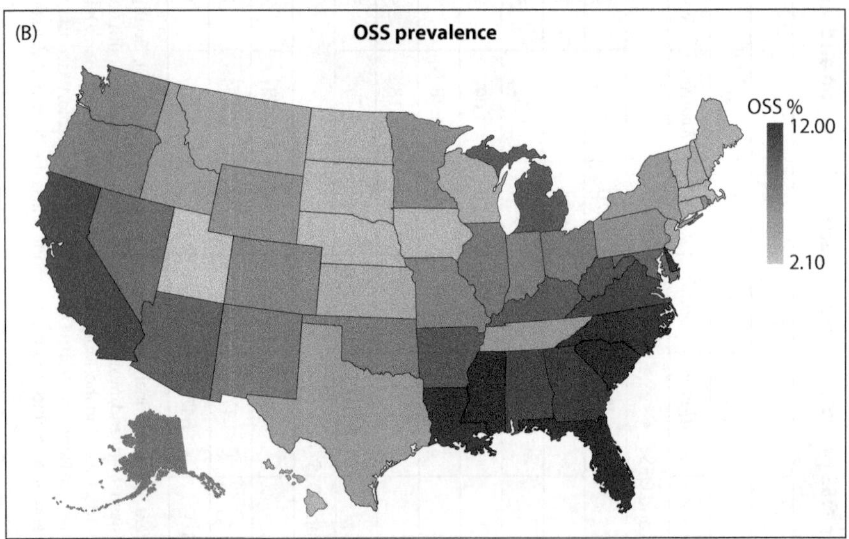

Source: Powered by Bing © GeoNames, Microsoft, TomTom

Note: Shade colors are not consistent across maps. Each shade is relative to the mean within each map.

Similar to ISS, the prevalence of OSS in the South is concerning. Indeed, school discipline in the South is an urgent education policy and equity issue. While OSS rates varied between regions of the country, this variance was less extreme than the variance in ISS rates between regions. OSS rates are highest in the South, but rates of OSS in the South are markedly lower than rates of ISS in the South. In contrast, OSS is more prevalent than ISS in the West and, to a lesser extent, the Northeast. Black and Latinx ISS rates are highest in the South. These students have notably higher ISS rates than OSS rates only in this region of the country. The Black ISS rate in the South (15.36 percent) is the highest suspension rate across suspension types and regions. Among Latinx students, the ISS rate in the South (8.26 percent) is markedly higher (roughly at least 3 percentage points higher) than suspension rates (ISS or OSS) in other regions. The South—a place of racial and socioeconomic animus—is also where the punitive spaces flourish as evidenced by the highest prevalence and disparities in both suspension types. As such, reducing the prevalence of ISS *and* OSS in the South is a national school discipline goal.

Black Students Have Received the Most Suspensions for Decades

Since the 1970s, Black students have always had the highest rates of suspensions out of all student groups. Between the 1970s and 2010s, the Black suspension rate increased faster than that of any other student group. As such, racial disparities in suspensions widened. In 1975, the Black OSS rate was just over 6 percent, and the White rate was roughly 3 percent.[30] Thus, in the 1970s, Black students were suspended at twice the rate of White students. Fast forward a few decades and the disparities have remained and worsened. The 2010s marked the only period of decline in the Black suspension rates. From 2010 to 2018, the Black OSS rate declined from 15.7 to 11.9 percent.[31] However, all other student groups also experienced declines in OSS, hence the persistence of racial disparities in suspensions. In 2015, after a period of decline in the overall suspension rates, the Black OSS rate of 11.9 percent was still roughly four times that of the White OSS rate of 3.3 percent. Thus, in the 2010s, Black students were suspended at roughly four times the rate of White students. Essentially, racial inequality in school discipline has increased over the decades, with Black students suspended at markedly higher rates relative to their peers.

Notably, across all regions in the past decade, Black suspension rates, regardless of suspension type, have been the highest of all student groups. The Black ISS rate (9.80 percent) is the highest overall rate of any student group nationwide. The rate at which Black students receive an ISS is roughly five times the rate of Asian students and double the rate of White students. Similar trends exist in OSS rates. In the past decade, nationally, the rate at which Black students are placed in OSS (9.62 percent) is higher than the OSS rate for any other racial or ethnic group. The rate at which Black students receive OSS is roughly five times the rate of Asian students (1.80 percent) and double the rate of White students (4.35 percent).

In the West and Northeast, OSS rates for Black and Latinx students are higher than ISS rates. In the Midwest, the Black OSS rate is higher than the Black ISS rate, whereas Latinx OSS and ISS rates are roughly equal.

In sum, Black students experience the highest rates of both ISS and OSS of any racial or ethnic group across all four regions. The exclusion of Black children via school discipline is not confined to a pocket of the United States. It is a national pandemic (though some regions are more concerning than others). Moreover, the disproportionate exclusion of Black students has remained consistent over time. This provides the rationale for why the objective of school discipline reform ought to be the reduction in racial inequality in exclusionary discipline, especially for Black students, rather than simply reducing suspensions.

Black–White Disparities Are the Most Significant and Have Remained Consistent over Time

In the past decade, Black–White disparities in both ISS and OSS have constituted the largest racial disparities nationwide and in each region. As Table 1.2 shows, nationwide from 2012–2018, Black students were roughly twice as likely to be suspended (whether ISS or OSS) than their White peers (Black–White RRR around 2). The Black–White disparities in both ISS and OSS from the decade prior to the COVID-19 pandemic is a replica of the inequities revealed by the CDF reports in the 1970s. We are stuck in punitive sands. The Latinx–White disparities remain notably lower than the Black–White disparities. It is important to note that racial discipline disparities slightly declined between 2012 and 2018. However, the Black–White discipline gap has persisted and is still large, whereas the Latinx–White gap had almost entirely disappeared by 2018. There was one exception to the slight decline in racial disparities between 2012 and 2018: Multirace–White disparities in both ISS and OSS.

Another key consideration in the school discipline crisis is the variation in suspension disparities across regions. Black–White disparities in ISS are highest in the South followed by the Midwest. While ISS disparities seem to be most concentrated in the South and the Midwest, Black–White disparities in OSS are more evenly distributed across the country. For instance, states such as Alabama, Nevada, and Michigan have some of the highest disparities and are in different regions. Unlike the South, the Black–White disparities in OSSs in the Midwest, Northeast, and West are higher than the Black–White disparities in ISSs, on average. Overall, significant racial disparities in the use of ISS are predominantly confined to the South, whereas in other parts of the country, OSSs remain the suspension type manifesting larger racial disparities. Of note, Alabama has some of the highest Black–White disparities in suspensions, both ISS and OSS.

The School Discipline Crisis Persists after the Pandemic

Emerging post-pandemic school discipline trends mirror those of pre-COVID-19 and underscore the urgency of the school discipline crisis. Racial disparities in school discipline have returned with a vengeance as students have settled into in-person learning after the COVID-19 pandemic. And Black students continue to shoulder the burden of the structural flaws in the approach to school discipline across the nation. Analysis of the 2020–2021 data from CRDC reveals similar trends in school discipline prior to the pandemic such as (a) disparities as early as preschool (Black preschool children accounted for 17 percent of preschool enrollment but 31 percent of children who received one or more OSS), (b) more ISS than OSS (786,600 students received one or more ISS compared to 638,700 students receiving one or more OSS), (c) racial disparities persist (Black boys were roughly twice as likely as white boys to receive an OSS and Black girls were nearly twice as likely to receive an ISS or OSS than White girls), and (d) suspensions result in lost instructional time (students receiving one or more OSS missed more than 2 million school days).[32]

Racial inequality in school discipline is also being reported across states and districts in the aftermath of the pandemic. For instance, in North Carolina, the Southern Coalition for School Justice 2022–2023 Racial Equity Report Cards highlighted that Black students were roughly four times more likely to receive a short-term suspension than White students.[33] In the 2022–2023 year, Black female and male students in Ohio were six and 4.3 times more likely to be suspended or expelled than their White peers, respectively.[34] OSS rates may have even increased in some urban districts. A 2024 report by the Council of Great City Schools found an increase in OSS rates with notable jumps in Black and Hispanic female OSS rates when comparing 2018–2019 and 2022–2023 school years.[35] In New York City, administrators issued 5.5 percent more superintendent suspensions (i.e., lasting five or more days) and 0.8 percent fewer principal suspensions (i.e., fewer than five days) in fall 2023 compared to fall 2022—an overall increase of 0.6 percent.[36] These numbers are a 7 percent increase from fall 2019, the last semester pre-COVID.

SCHOOL DISCIPLINE IN NYCPS: A MICROCOSM OF THE NATIONAL LANDSCAPE

The school discipline landscape in New York City (NYC), characterized by persistent racial disparities in suspensions despite a shift away from exclusionary discipline, is emblematic of the challenge of racial inequality in school discipline facing districts nationwide. Within the past decade, the NYC Department of Education has implemented a series of reforms aimed at reducing the use of suspensions in NYC schools.

Similar to numerous districts, NYC has shifted away from exclusionary discipline through programmatic investments in restorative justice (RJ).[37] Beginning in 2015, the NYCPS began to promote RJ and social-emotional learning (SEL) approaches to address nonviolent forms of misbehavior.[38] As part of this citywide initiative, the city initially allocated $47 million dollars toward staff training on restorative disciplinary practices and mental health supports. In addition, with the appointment of former schools chancellor Richard Carranza in 2018, antibias training for teachers and administrators and culturally responsive education became further embedded in the fabric of NYCPS education policy reforms.

NYC, like other districts, has also made several changes to their code of conduct, such as prohibiting suspensions in lower grades for subjective offenses.[39] Subsequent to 2012, suspensions were no longer assigned for level 1 and 2 infractions (minor offenses) due to previous suspension reforms taking effect.[40] Several other school discipline policy changes were implemented in tandem with programmatic initiatives, including a firm requirement that principals obtain written approval from the NYCPS central office to suspend a student for infractions considered of lower severity.

Declining Prevalence, Persistent Disparities

Figure 1.2 presents suspension rates across student race/ethnicity spanning pre-COVID and post-COVID school years for middle and high schools (grades 6–12). There is a noticeable decline in prevalence over time for all students. In 2012, roughly 8 percent of students in NYC's middle and high schools were suspended at least once during the academic year, compared

FIGURE 1.2 Suspension rates in New York City Public Schools across student race/ethnicity (grades 6–12)

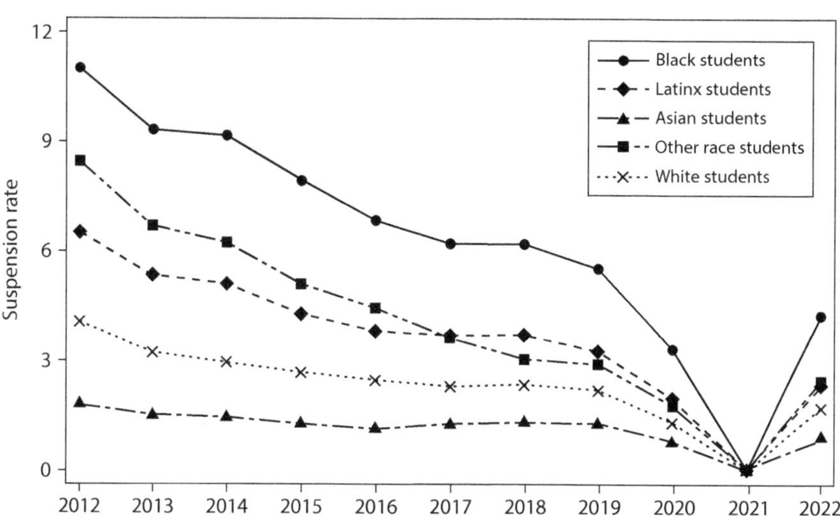

Note: Authors' calculations made using NYCPS data. Sample restricted to schools serving grades 6 through 12.

to 5 percent in 2018. During the school closure period amid the COVID-19 pandemic, there were virtually no suspensions. There has been a rebound in the rates of suspension in the aftermath of the pandemic, where the prevalence of suspensions is approaching prepandemic levels, using the 2018–2019 school year. Throughout the past decade, there have been persistent racial disparities in both ODRs and suspensions. The gap between Black students and their peers was largely unchanged over time; Black students received ODRs and suspensions at about twice the rate as other students. In the pre-COVID era, suspension rates have dropped, but racial disparities persist. Despite a decline in overall suspensions and African American students' suspension rates (from 11 percent in 2012 to 6 percent in 2018 in NYC), racial disparities have persisted as Black students were suspended at higher rates relative to other students.[41] These patterns are not unique to NYCPS. Discipline disparities are a challenge faced by many other urban districts throughout the United States.

Intersectional Lens Illuminates the Plight of Black Students

One of the original tenets of critical race theory (CRT) is intersectionality.[42] Intersectionality is rooted in the notion that a single individual may inhabit multiple marginalized identities (e.g., race/ethnicity, socioeconomic status, limited English proficiency). Intersectionality theory posits that multiple identities influence experiences and discrimination in society.[43] When multiple marginalized identities intersect, the likelihood of discrimination and oppression increases. In essence, social identities are interdependent.[44] Intersectionality provides a theoretical understanding of how categorizations of difference (e.g., race, class, gender, ability) converge and overlap, resulting in a complex and intersecting experience of oppression among individuals. School discipline is an educational equity issue that necessitates an intersectionality lens to magnify the discipline disadvantage in schools. Black youth are socially positioned by a wide range of other characteristics (culture, gender, disability, and ability) that intersect and influence their experiences with exclusionary discipline.[45]

Table 1.3 presents ODR and suspension rates across the intersectional identities of Black students. In NYCPS, between 2012 and 2019, for the overall sample, the ODR rate is 11.9 percent and the suspension rate is

TABLE 1.3 ODRs and suspension rates (%) across the intersectional identities of Black students

	ODR rate		*Suspension rate*	
Student group	*Mean*	*Standard deviation*	*Mean*	*Standard deviation*
All students	11.92	0.59	5.09	0.92
Black	18.52	0.63	8.63	1.32
Black male	21.51	0.79	10.26	1.67
Black female	15.41	0.54	6.93	0.99
Black low SES	20.64	0.71	9.71	1.33
Black not low SES	14.21	0.72	6.42	1.31
Black in temporary housing	23.89	1.37	11.69	1.85
Black not in temporary housing	18.05	0.68	8.35	1.36
Black receiving SPED	25.98	0.99	12.60	1.81
Black not receiving SPED	16.52	0.71	7.57	1.30

Note: SES = socioeconomic status; SPED = special education services.

5.1 percent. Disaggregated by student race, Black students have by far the highest ODR (18.5 percent) and suspension (8.6 percent) rates. The overall Black rates are higher than the overall male and low-income rates, but lower than the overall special education status (SPED) rates. Among all student intersectional identities (across race, gender, socioeconomic status, temporary housing, and SPED), the group with the highest discipline rates is Black male students receiving SPED, with an ODR rate of 27.9 percent and a suspension rate of 13.7 percent. This is more than double the ODR and suspension rates for all students. Black male students are referred to the office and suspended at higher rates than Black female students. The Black male ODR and suspension rates are higher than the overall average for Black students, whereas the opposite is true for female students. Black students receiving SPED have one of the highest ODR rates, at 25.98 percent, more than double the overall ODR rate. Similarly, low socioeconomic status Black students are referred and suspended more compared to their more advantaged Black peers. Black males receiving SPED have slightly higher ODR and suspension rates than Black females receiving SPED, although these two groups have the highest rates of exclusionary discipline within Black students. In sum, there are a handful of categories within Black students in which the ODR rate is above 20 percent, nearly twice that of all students: Black male (21.51 percent), Black low socioeconomic status (20.64 percent); Black receiving special education (25.98 percent); Black male receiving special education (27.90 percent); and Black female receiving special education (22.25 percent).[46]

It is important to consider how students being persistently disciplined (i.e., receiving more than one ODR and/or more than one suspension in a year) is related to their intersectional identity.[47] Again, Black male SPED students are the clear outliers. Although Black male SPED students represent only 3 percent of all students, they account for 2 percent of students who did not receive an ODR, 8 percent of students who received one ODR, and 10 percent of students who were persistently referred. They also make up 7 percent of students who received an ODR but not a suspension, 9 percent of students who received a suspension, and 10 percent of students who were persistently suspended. The plight of persistently disciplined students is substantially worse for Black students than other racial groups, across gender and SPED status. While these results are consistent across all middle and high school grade levels, Black male and Black male SPED students are most persistently referred and suspended in grades 7, 8, 9, and 10, with particularly high rates in grade 7 for persistent referrals and grade 9 for persistent suspensions.[48]

There are also large and statistically significant differences in likelihood of receiving an ODR and suspension by student intersectional identity. The odds of receiving an ODR are about 7.9 times higher for Black male SPED students compared to White female non-SPED students. The odds of receiving a suspension are about 12.2 times higher for Black male SPED students compared to White female non-SPED students. Among male students, the odds of receiving an ODR are about 2.1 times higher for Black students compared to White students, whereas the odds of receiving a suspension are approximately 2.5 times higher for Black students. Finally, among Black students, the odds of receiving an ODR or suspension are approximately 1.6 times higher for male students compared to female students.[49]

UP THE DOWN ESCALATOR? THE EFFECTIVENESS OF SCHOOL DISCIPLINE REFORMS

What Have States, Districts, and Schools Done in Response to Discipline Disparities?

States, districts, and schools are experimenting with an array of policy and programmatic changes. School discipline reforms can be grouped into the 3Ps—policy, program, and personnel changes.

One of the starting points for districts addressing disparities in students' disciplinary outcomes is updating the student code of conduct or the procedures for the sequence from perceived misbehavior to disciplinary consequences. As part of the settlement with the US Department of Education in response to the violation of Black students' civil rights through the use of exclusionary discipline, the Victor Valley Union High School District agreed to revise its school discipline policies as a key step to rectify inequitable discipline practices.[50] Several states and districts have prohibited suspensions in elementary grades or for certain disciplinary infractions such as truancy or subjective offenses and lower-level infractions.[51] Nearly half of all states plus Washington, DC, have such laws.[52] In 2018, eleven states enacted a bill related to exclusionary discipline and/or alternative discipline practices. Legislation includes restrictions on the use of exclusionary discipline, providing guidance for and encouraging the use of alternative methods, and reporting requirements.[53] A more recent report found that at least fifteen states and the District of Columbia limit the use of suspensions and expulsions based on grade level, thirty-seven states include alternatives to suspensions in discipline policy, thirty-nine states require reporting on suspension and expulsion rates, and twenty-two states require disaggregated data reporting by race, ethnicity, gender, and other student groups.[54] Districts such as LAUSD, Philadelphia, and NYC have also made several changes to their code of conduct and discipline policies, such as prohibiting suspensions in lower grades and banning suspensions for subjective offenses (e.g., willful defiance and certain types of nonviolent behavior), to disrupt racial inequality in school discipline.[55]

The use of popular school-level, nonexclusionary programs, such as RJ and Positive Behavioral Interventions and Supports (PBIS), has expanded considerably in the past decade in the United States.[56] A 2020 analysis by the Center on Gender Justice and Opportunity at Georgetown Law found that "21 states and the District of Columbia have enacted legislation supporting the use of RJ in schools."[57] A March 2024 EdWeek Research Center survey illustrated that almost half of educators are using RJ more than they did prior to the pandemic in the 2018–2019 school year.[58] Encouragingly, survey respondents also reported less use of both in-school and out-of-school suspensions. The addition of personnel is a category of school discipline reform often referenced by district and school leaders.[59] Admittedly, the empirical evidence on how personnel changes affect students' disciplinary outcomes is thinner than evidence on program and policy changes. Nevertheless, districts such as Oakland and LAUSD have made investments in personnel to reduce inequities in school discipline.

Is It Working?

Despite myriad efforts at the federal, state, and district levels, discipline disparities seem immune to school discipline reforms. The evidence suggests that policy changes are necessary but not sufficient to disrupt discipline disparities.[60] Moreover, bans typically target OSS yet ISS is equally prevalent (though emerging evidence suggests that there is no substitution toward ISS or uptick in ISS rates).[61] A select number of program-based approaches show promise of not only reducing overall rates but disproportionalities. With a handful of notable exceptions, discipline reforms have not improved the lot of Black students in most need of reprieve from exclusion.

Changes in school discipline policy (at both the state and district levels) have led to a reduction of suspensions or the general use of exclusionary discipline, but racial disparities remain persistent. In Arkansas, Black students had a decrease in ODRs following a policy prohibiting suspensions for truancy.[62] Similar to Arkansas, in Rhode Island, OSS was first prohibited for attendance-related infractions and then for disruption-specific infractions. Banning OSS for attendance-specific infractions markedly lowered OSS as well as Black–White and Latinx–White disparities whereas the ban on disruption-specific infractions did not change OSS or reduce disparities.[63] Evidence from Maryland indicates that a ban on OSS in early grades (PK–2) led to a decline in the frequency and length of suspensions, yet disparities persisted.[64] In Oregon, Nishioka and colleagues found that the number of ODRs increased, especially for Black students, after a 2015 policy reform that limited the use of exclusionary discipline in elementary schools.[65] This is congruent with an earlier study highlighting that the short-term decline in the use of exclusionary discipline trended upward in later years.[66]

Results for policy changes at the district-level are similar to the findings from state-level policy changes. Evidence from Los Angeles, Philadelphia, and NYC illustrates that school discipline policy changes typically result in reduction in prevalence of exclusionary discipline, but disparities remain.[67] In Los Angeles, in response to the combination of prohibiting suspensions for willful defiance and the implementation of RJ, districtwide school suspensions and days lost as a result of suspensions decreased, but discipline disparities remained.[68] Similarly, in New York City, a change in the code of conduct reduced the risk of first suspensions but increased the risk of second suspensions disproportionately for marginalized students.[69] In Philadelphia, the rates of OSS for classroom disorder were reduced following the implementation of a change in discipline code of conduct; however, racial disparities remained stable.[70] A study of four California districts that banned suspensions for willful defiance found that "while these policies decreased willful defiance out-of-school suspension rates by around 69%, they did not reduce overall out-of-school suspension rates. In fact, the policies significantly increased out-of-school suspension rates among Black students, particularly in schools with a small share of Black teachers. Taken together, the results suggest that the willful defiance suspension bans failed to address implicit and explicit biases in California schools."[71]

Similar to policies, the emerging evidence indicates that the implementation of RJ and PBIS results in a decline in the overall use of exclusionary discipline in most cases and a reduction in discipline disparities in fewer instances.[72] The effectiveness of programs varies across contexts. PBIS and RJ result in decreases in overall ODRs. Evidence from Denver and Oakland indicates that RJ resulted in a schoolwide decline in ODRs.[73] In Denver, the implementation of RJ resulted in a decrease in OSS, but racial disparities persisted.[74] Using randomized controlled trials in Pittsburgh, Augustine and colleagues found that the implementation of RJ resulted in a decrease in the number of suspensions and number of days lost to suspensions, especially for Black students.[75] Notably, there was a slight decrease in discipline disparities in elementary schools but not in middle and high schools. The implementation of PBIS is associated with decreases in ODRs.[76] Studies have found that PBIS is also associated with decreases in the use of suspensions.[77]

School discipline policy and program changes have not improved the disciplinary experiences and outcomes of Black students. Several studies raise doubts about school discipline reforms to differentially benefit the disciplinary outcomes of the students most affected by racial inequities in school discipline.[78] Alternative approaches to exclusionary discipline are benefiting White students more than Black students. School discipline expert Anne Gregory and colleagues found that although there was a lower overall likelihood of receiving exclusionary discipline (incident rate) in restorative practices (RPs) (RPs "include proactive practices to inculcate conflict resolution skills and strengthen community bonds [for example, through community-building circles] and responsive practices to resolve conflicts and repair relationships [for example, through mediation and harm-repair circles]"[79]) schools, RP did not benefit male students, Black students, and students with disabilities more than female, White, and Hispanic students and students without disabilities; thus, discipline disparities persisted in intervention schools.[80] Similarly, sociologist Miles Davison and colleagues found that RJ led to a marked decline in overall suspensions; however, White students benefited most from RJ, whereas Black students' disciplinary outcomes remained fairly stable, thus widening racial disproportionality.[81] In a systematic literature review, school discipline expert Rebecca Cruz and colleagues found "limited evidence that available programs reduce discipline disparities and that common programs may function as a protective factor for White and female students while failing to do so for marginalized students."[82] Similar to Cruz and colleagues' findings of benefits of programs for White students, education researcher Vicki Nishioka and colleagues found that there was "a significant shift in the post policy years from exclusionary to nonexclusionary discipline" for most students but not African American students.[83] Education researcher Rui Wang found that in four districts in California that implemented a willful defiance suspension ban (WDB), "Despite receiving OSS at much higher rates before adoption, Black students benefited less from WDBs than White and Hispanic students. Particularly, WDBs increased nonwillful defiance OSS rates for Black students by around 26%, which contributed to increases in overall OSS rates. There were no significant changes in overall OSS rates for White and Hispanic students following the implementation of WDBs. Students' behavior changes could not explain such heterogeneity in treatment effects by race."[84]

WHY SCHOOL DISCIPLINE REFORMS ARE NOT DISRUPTING RACIAL INEQUALITY IN STUDENTS' DISCIPLINARY OUTCOMES

Based on the prevailing empirical evidence, I contend that there are four main reasons why school discipline reforms have not reduced stubborn disparities in students' disciplinary outcomes. These are (a) overlooked and rampant anti-Blackness in American society and schools that manifest in discipline disparities; (b) the absence of cultural responsiveness and the presence of race-neutral reform approaches; (c) a misalignment between alternative approaches and the contributors to racial inequality in school discipline, namely the predominant focus on fixing student behavior rather than supporting educators; and (d) implementation challenges accompanying school discipline reforms.

Anti-Blackness in School Discipline

Although several scholars have drawn attention to the historical context of school exclusion and anti-Blackness in school discipline,[85] I maintain that we (educational stakeholders and researchers) have been slow to recognize and name the urgent criticality of anti-Blackness in school discipline.

As Black Critical Theory scholars Michael Dumas and kihana miraya ross poignantly highlighted in their seminal article " 'Be Real Black for Me': Imagining BlackCrit in Education":

> Understanding this distinction between a theory of racism and a theory of blackness (in an anti-Black world) is key: whereas the former may invoke Black examples, and even rely on Black experience of racism in the formation of its tenets, only critical theorization of blackness confronts the specificity of *anti-blackness*, as a social construction, as an embodied lived experience of social suffering and resistance, and perhaps most importantly, as an antagonism, in which the Black is a despised thing-in-itself (but not person for herself or himself) in opposition to all that is pure, human(e), and White (Gordon, 1997; Wilderson, 2010).[86]

School discipline is one of the primary ways in which racism and anti-Blackness manifest in schools. Blackness—Black bodies, Black minds, and Black souls—is being punished in classrooms on a daily basis. Discipline disparities are manifestations of anti-Blackness in schools and a deficit in the structure of schooling to cultivate genius and joy for Black children.[87] As such, discipline disparities are more of an indictment on the behavior of adults in schools and structural deficiencies that influence the educational experiences of Black children rather than of students who are manifesting their genius.

Racism continues to be a disputed notion in the United States even though any well-thinking individual would not have to delve deeply into historical and contemporary American society to discover racism. In many ways, anti-Blackness, harking back to the days of chattel slavery, is the soil in which the seeds of America's strange fruits are rooted. Anti-Blackness remains a raw and open wound that has hamstrung the nation's fight against inequality of all varieties. Anti-Blackness in the United States has withstood the test of time and transcended generations. Why, then, would one find it hard to believe that the tentacles of anti-Blackness in American society are manifested in racial inequality in students' disciplinary outcomes in schools?

Schools are the sites where three societies clash and collide: the society of yesterday, through the upbringing and experiences of adults in school; the society of today, through the context and content of how learning takes place; and the society of the future, through the learning and long-term outcomes of the students being molded. As sociologist Amanda Lewis highlighted, schools are race-making and race-made.[88] It is through the prism of society that the ills of school discipline should be viewed. Anti-Blackness and racism in society can trickle into schools. Thus, it is plausible, even likely and happening right in front of our eyes, that race, in the vitriol of anti-Blackness, manifests in the disciplinary process in schools in insidious ways.

The erasure of Blackness and the permanence of anti-Blackness in society are translated into racial inequality in school discipline that largely afflicts Black students. In many ways, school discipline has morphed into a twenty-first century segregation tool with exclusionary disciplinary practices preparing Black students for their role (read: predicament) in an increasingly carceral society. I contend that the same anti-Blackness that is ubiquitous in society is present in schools and manifested in differences in students' disciplinary outcomes. The discipline disparities are a symptom of the dismissal and punishment of Black presence in schools. I assert that discipline disparities will seem immortal until the mortality of anti-Blackness in society and schools is stared squarely in the eyes and confronted with an equivalent fervor and aggressiveness that characterize the manifestation of anti-Blackness in school discipline. As such, the path to reducing racial inequality in school discipline starts with grappling with the manifestation of anti-Blackness in school discipline.

In his April 2024 presidential address, president of the American Educational Research Association, Tyrone Howard, asked us, "Why do Black children suffer the most?" It appears that schools have become prisons for some and places of prosperity for others. And the color a student's skin, rather than the content of their character, determines whether schools prepare students for prison or prosperity. The system of haves and have-nots created through exclusionary discipline is reminiscent of the gap in economic outcomes, such as homeownership. The criminalization of Blackness in schools reinforces historical inequities and is a harbinger of the discriminatory future students of color will have to endure in the United States.

Schooling Reflects Society

Anti-Blackness permeates American society. In the midst of Whiteness and White supremacy, Blackness is a crime in appearance rather than the conduct of Black people. What's happening in the criminal justice system, politics, sports, and everyday life in American society is happening in schools, but without the media coverage and attendant critique to expose anti-Blackness. There are abundant examples of anti-Blackness in contemporary American society to remind us that anti-Blackness is not a historical vestige but a contemporary menace.

In August 2023, a conviction of a Black man was overturned because it was determined that his rights were violated by a federal judge who declared, "This guy looks like a criminal to me."[89] The judge blamed his blatant display of anti-Blackness on being upset at delays in the case.

Consider the case of Tennessee representatives Justin Pearson, Justin Jones, and Gloria Johnson—the "Tennessee Three."[90] In April 2023, the three Democratic representatives all protested and advocated for gun safety laws in the aftermath of a dastardly school shooting at a private Christian school in Nashville. In actions eerily similar to differential processing in school discipline (where Black students receive harsher punishment than their White peers for similar behavior), the Republican-led House of Representatives voted to expel Pearson and Jones, yet Representative Johnson was spared expulsion. All three committed the same disciplinary infraction, but there were different consequences for the two Black males and the White female. Take the case of Paramore and Allison Russell. Both were 2024 Grammy winners from the great state of Tennessee. For whatever reasons, the White group, Paramore, was elevated and honored by the state's House of Representatives, whereas the Black, queer, immigrant performer, Allison Russell, was snubbed.[91] These acts of anti-Blackness happen all the time in American life. And it is not farfetched that a similar dynamic has taken root in public schools.

In 2024, in the early rounds of the NCAA women's tournament, the University of Utah basketball team made the trip to Coeur d'Alene, Idaho, to experience March Madness. Instead, they witnessed unforgettable anti-Blackness that made me wonder if we had time traveled to the 1950s or perhaps the 1800s.[92] Yet time has not healed the gaping and everlasting wound of racism and anti-Blackness in the United States. The team went to dinner only to be serenaded by the N-word complemented by threatening and menacing dispositions—the "we don't like your kind around here" type vibes. The Utah team—shocked, appalled, and traumatized—bolted town and was followed by the University of California Irvine team. The experience of the Utah's women basketball team is far from isolated. In the same 2024 tournament, an *LA Times* column framed the matchup between LSU's largely Black team versus Iowa's team led by White superstar Caitlin Clark as, "Do you prefer America's sweetheart or its dirty debutantes? Milk and cookies or Louisiana hot sauce?"[93] (These atrocious lines were removed after the column was roundly and soundly criticized.) As championship-winning and Hall of Fame coach Dawn Staley advocated in the 2023 NCAA tournament, "We're not bar fighters. We're not thugs. We're not monkeys. We're not street fighters." The sentiment rings true for Black children in America's schools. Racism is still alive, and discipline disparities are revealing it.

In October 2024, Minneapolis Police Chief Brian O'Hara lamented that his department had failed Davis Moturi, a Black man who was allegedly shot by his White neighbor for pruning a tree in his own front yard.[94] Moturi had reported escalating harassment from his neighbors for months with the Minneapolis Police Department (MPD). After the shooting, his neighbor was charged but not arrested much to the dismay of several members of the Minneapolis City council. The reason for the delay in arrest was, as Chief O'Hara relayed, because he is "mentally ill" and has firearms. So, to summarize, in the United States, in 2024, a Black man was forced to live in fear and was ultimately shot because the MPD failed to protect him from a White male neighbor against whom harassment charges were filed.

Lest one think that being the victim of violence for being Black in American society is rare, sadly, there are myriad cases that reaffirm the vitriol of anti-Blackness in the United States. Consider the murder of Lo-Letha Hall, a Black woman, by William Brock, a White man, in South Charleston, Ohio, in March 2024.[95] The Uber driver showed up for a package and left without her life. Brock, who was the alleged victim of a scam call earlier in the day, felt emboldened to be judge, jury, and executioner. He pointed a gun at Hall, took her cellphone, physically prevented her from leaving, and for good measure fatally shot an unarmed Black woman three times before calling the police. Hall pleaded innocence and ignorance of the purported scam with her last breath. One wonders whether she would have met a similar fate if she had been a White woman.

The numerous examples of unprovoked killings of Black people in the United States make that less of a wonder and more of a cruel reaffirmation of the dangers of being Black in American society. The extrajudicial killings of Black people in the United States are slowly becoming a national pastime. Too many say their names—we'd rather see their smiles and hear their laughs. From George Floyd to Breonna Taylor to Sonya Massey (who was killed as I made my final edits), Black men, women, and children are all susceptible to and victimized by the pandemic of anti-Blackness in the United States. I maintain that parallel dangers of being Black exist in America's schools and exclusionary discipline has been weaponized to punish said Blackness.

Empirical Evidence of Anti-Blackness in School Discipline

There is ample empirical evidence that buttresses the notion that racial disparities in students' disciplinary outcomes are partly a result of ingrained anti-Black racism in American society and schools. School discipline studies have documented and examined different dimensions of anti-Blackness in the disciplinary experiences of Black students. Both quantitative and qualitative studies reveal the camouflage of anti-Black racism in the disciplinary process and have illustrated the central role that anti-Black racism plays in exclusionary discipline practices in schools. There is a crystallizing consensus that Black students do not feel welcomed, comfortable, or supported in public schools. Studies have highlighted that anti-Blackness in school discipline does not just point to the overpolicing of Black youth behavior and actions but reveals a more insidious reality where simply being Black is a crime in schools.[96] "Not all kids belong in the classroom anymore," Lubbock Republican Senator Charles Perry stated when promising to address school discipline in Texas.[97] This sentiment may be more pervasive than we would like to admit. Completing the vicious cycle, Black students realize that they are being disciplined because of their race rather than conduct, and this lends itself to further disengagement from schools.[98]

A survey item ("During your life, how often have you felt that you were treated badly or unfairly in school because of your race or ethnicity?") in the 2023 National Youth Risk Behavior Survey from the CDC assessed the experiences of racism of 9–12 graders.[99] The survey found that one in three high schoolers ever experienced racism in schools but 46 percent of Black students reported experiencing racism in schools. As noted by the CDC report, "Students might be experiencing racism in school because of discrimination and bias that are embedded within current school policies and practices (e.g., disciplinary practices) or as a result of interactions with students, teachers, or administrators and other staff members."[100] In the accompanying press release for a settlement agreement for "discriminatory treatment of Black students in the administration of discipline at multiple schools" in Wichita Public Schools in Kansas, Assistant Attorney General Kristen Clarke of the Justice Department's Civil Rights Division noted that "Black students inside our nation's public schools should not have to face discipline or a referral to law enforcement because of their race. And students with disabilities should not have to experience the trauma of seclusion or improper restraint. Schools in our communities should not be a place of fear or mistrust. This agreement upholds our core principles of ending the school to prison pipeline and protecting our most vulnerable students against all forms of discrimination and segregation."[101]

Building on the general tenets of BlackCrit and elements from Stacia Cedillo's synthesized framework for studying anti-Blackness in STEM education, I codeveloped the *Anti-Blackness in School Discipline* framework to better illustrate the potential ways anti-Blackness manifests in the disciplinary process.[102] The framework includes six theoretical constructs: (a) "Trading Away the Black," (b) "Whites as Propertied," (c) "Intersecting Blackness," (d) "Racial Neoliberalism," (e) "La Petite Misère," and (f) "Internalized Racism."[103] Using the *Anti-Blackness in School Discipline* framework with the help of my graduate research assistant Neha Sobti, I combed over one hundred journal articles published between 2000 and 2022 for empirical evidence of the manifestations of anti-Blackness in school discipline.

The majority of empirical studies focus on teachers' role in anti-Black disciplinary practices and outcomes and Black students' experiences with the disciplinary process.[104] Fewer studies have focused on the parent voice or perspective regarding disciplinary experiences or the role and voice of Black school leaders.[105] Most school discipline research on anti-Blackness falls into two theoretical tenets: (a) "Trading Away the Black," or studies that illuminate the criminalization, adultification, and differential treatment of Black students; and (b) "La Petite Misère," or studies that provide a deeper understanding of how Black students and caretakers experience anti-Blackness in school discipline. Within "Trading Away the Black," studies largely focus on whole-school trends using quantitative measures and the role of teachers using both quantitative and qualitative measures.[106] Almost all of the studies in "La Petite Misère" focus on student experience/perspective.[107] There are only a few studies analyzing how racial neoliberal policy may manifest as anti-Black racism, focusing on teachers' deficit beliefs about Black students and families that lead to the use of exclusion over support as their primary intervention.[108] Similarly, the internalization of anti-Blackness among Black school leaders and teachers is rarely discussed given the few studies focused on Black educators within school discipline.

Anti-Blackness manifests in subtle ways to create carceral-like environments for Black students in schools. Too often, disciplinary practices become a vehicle for educators' anti-Blackness. The prevalence of anti-Black beliefs, perceptions, and stereotypes among teachers and school leaders; low expectations for Black students; the protection of White educator comfort over Black student needs; and the silencing of Black students and families are some of the ways anti-Blackness surfaces within the school disciplinary process. The key mechanisms of anti-Blackness involve (a) compounding and layered ideologies of dehumanization including the criminalizing and adultifying of Black students, (b) the use of deficit frames about Black students and families to explain racial inequities, and (c) the universal insistence on White, middle-class behavioral standards for all students. Several scholars have pointed to the criminalization and adultification of Black boys and girls as a driving force of discipline disparities.[109] For instance, the disproportionality afflicting Black males, especially in elementary schools, has been linked to the adultification and criminalization of Black boys.[110] Black youth are seen as more adult-like and less innocent by the general population, parents, police officers, and college students in a process of adultification.[111] Cooke and Halberstadt conducted a study with 152 parents and found that when an adult perceived a Black child to be older, they also were more likely to perceive them as angrier than White children, suggesting that anti-Blackness leads to harsher punishment for Black youth due to a combination of adultification and anger bias.[112] Several studies find that educators view Black children automatically as adult-like, angry, criminal, pathologically bad, and troublemakers more often and to a higher degree than their non-Black peers.[113] The experience of being dehumanized for Black students involves being treated differently compared to their non-Black counterparts. As discussed earlier, a growing number of recent studies have provided empirical evidence of Black students' experiences with differential treatment from teachers and school leaders who punish Black students more often, more harshly, and for longer periods of time than White students for similar behaviors (both subjective and nonsubjective disciplinary infractions) or the same incident.[114] Colorblind and deficit beliefs about students and families are often used to explain discipline disparities.[115]

The empirical evidence paints a picture that, as Angela Davis writes, "when children attend schools that place a greater value on discipline and security than on knowledge and intellectual development, they are attending prep schools for prison."[116]

Race Neutrality and Cultural Responsiveness in School Discipline Reforms

Related to anti-Blackness, another reason why school discipline reforms have largely failed to reduce racial inequality in disciplinary outcomes is the lack of cultural responsiveness in the alternative approaches to exclusionary discipline.[117] School discipline reforms that emphasize cultural responsiveness are more effective at reducing ODRs and suspensions and offer an opportunity to disrupt racial disparities.[118] Cultural responsiveness encapsulates the awareness and acknowledgement of students' background and integrating students' values throughout the facets of learning. The CARES domains consisting of connection to the curriculum, authentic relationships, reflective thinking, effective communication, and sensitivity to students' culture are the crucial dimensions of culturally responsive practices.[119] Cultural congruence and connection—responsive to the cultural values, beliefs, practices, and ways of being of students and families in the classroom—are important parts of developing a positive experience for Black youth in schools.[120]

The efficacy of school discipline reforms in reducing racial inequality in suspensions in the past decade justifies scrutiny of race neutrality and colorblindness in school discipline interventions. Scholars have highlighted the failure of "race-neutral" or colorblind policies to address racial disparities in school discipline.[121] As school discipline expert Anne Gregory and colleagues highlighted, "Too often school discipline reforms are implemented without (a) considering the sociohistorical and structural conditions of oppression; (b) increasing cultural relevancy/responsiveness, competence, and bias awareness; (c) complementary approaches to developing socioemotional and behavioral competencies; and (d) instructional reforms that address opportunity gaps."[122] As I expound upon further in the concluding chapter, stubborn inequities in exclusionary discipline compel policy makers and practitioners to posit racially conscious solutions to address anti-Blackness in the disciplinary process.[123]

Misalignment of Contributors and Solutions

Are school discipline reforms focused on rectifying the issue driving racial inequality in exclusionary discipline? In addition to the lack of attention to anti-Blackness in school discipline, there is also a misalignment of the contributors and solutions to inequities in school discipline. Simply put, we have mainly tried to fix student behavior and have overlooked the behavior of adults in schools. As such, the overwhelming majority of school discipline reforms are student focused. Rather than focusing on how a largely White, middle-class, female educator workforce (teachers, assistant principals, and principals) is responding differently to the perceived misbehavior of students of color and their White peers, too many school discipline reformers fixate on the boogeyman of cultural deficits—Black students can't behave properly, Latinx families don't value education, or Black families can't teach their children how to comport themselves in schools. I maintain that one of the reasons why school discipline reforms have not reduced racial inequities in suspensions is a misalignment with the contributors. Prior school discipline reform efforts did not directly confront or challenge the underlying social and organizational processes in schools that produce discipline disparities. Student-focused interventions are necessary but not sufficient to reduce racial inequality in exclusionary discipline. *Suspended Futures* aims to disrupt this cultural deficit theorizing in school discipline with a simple notion: it's the adults, stupid.

In a 2018 literature review, my coauthor and I raised the prospect of the questionable theory of action underlying alternative approaches to exclusionary discipline.[124] As such, this book advances an educator-focused, rather than a student-focused, approach to solving the school discipline crisis. An educator-focused approach addresses the structure of schooling that drives disparities in disciplinary process rather than student-related factors as the main contributor to racial inequality in school discipline. Instead of focusing on what we can do to help the behavior of students, the Transforming School Discipline Strategic Framework discussed in the next chapter asks what we can do to help educators so that the adults in schools can better help students.

Implementation Challenges

Finally, the effectiveness of school discipline reforms has also been constrained by implementation fidelity ("the degree of compliance with which the core elements of program or intervention practices are used as intended").[125] Implementation fidelity shapes the outcomes of school discipline reforms across policy- and program-based approaches and varies across states, districts, and schools. The training and professional development of school personnel and a commitment to continuous improvement, hallmarks of the Transforming School Discipline Strategic Framework discussed in the next chapter, are key to the implementation fidelity of school discipline reforms.

School discipline researcher Kaitlin Anderson highlighted the incomplete implementation and significant compliance concerns accompanying a policy prohibiting OSS for truancy and posited that the impact of school discipline policy reforms is dependent on (a) effectively communicating changes to schools, (b) accountability to ensure compliance, and (c) schools' capacity to address behavior.[126] Education policy researchers Matthew Steinberg and Johanna Lacoe found that the effect on nonsuspended students of a policy change varied by the extent of implementation.[127] Challenges in the implementation of programs have received the most attention, and scholars have found that the programs' outcomes are dependent on the quality or fidelity of the implementation.[128] Programs are multifaceted and can be overwhelming for educators.[129] Factors such as the tiers and length of implementation (reforms may need sufficient time to take root) shape the overall effectiveness of programs such as PBIS on students' disciplinary outcomes.

States such as Missouri, Wisconsin, and Florida have used validated fidelity tools to monitor and assess "the extent to which the core features and practices of PBIS are in place and being implemented with integrity."[130] In Florida, a high fidelity of implementation was associated with lower ODRs and OSSs.[131] Similar results were found in Massachusetts underscoring the importance of implementation fidelity in effectiveness of school discipline reforms. Flannery and colleagues found that the frequency of ODRs declined as the fidelity of PBIS implementation improved.[132]

In many ways, studies examining the implementation of PBIS have found similar results to studies examining RJ. Implementation of RJ varies across schools and centers on relationship building and connections to the community.[133] School discipline researcher Anne Gregory and colleagues found that higher implementers of RJ were lower users of ODRs.[134] More recently, in their analysis of if and how RP improved school climate, Gregory and colleagues concluded that "initiatives may need to focus on fidelity of implementation and consistent implementation across more years for substantive school climate gains."[135] Additionally, schools struggling with disparities may also struggle with implementation of reforms. In Chicago, implementation of school discipline reforms was most difficult in the schools with the highest suspension rates, and similar trends were found in Philadelphia.[136]

THE ARC OF RACIAL EQUITY IN SCHOOL DISCIPLINE

Discipline disparities are durable and have endured decades of reform. Schools are grappling with the criminalization of the behavior of students of color, however benign, childlike, or age appropriate. How teachers judge students' perceived misbehavior is often the starting point of discipline disparities. There is mounting evidence that discrimination against marginalized groups in public schools is manifested through discipline disparities. Adult behavior in schools is amplifying student harm rather than catalyzing child development. If every behavior communicates a need, then the transformation of discipline disparities involves meeting both student and educator needs. Teachers who repeatedly refer students to the office are communicating needs. If every behavior communicates a need, then the guiding mantra of school discipline strategy ought to be support, not suspend.

If the discourse on school discipline resembles how we talk about criminals and the prison system, then the fundamental purpose of school to teach and develop has been hijacked. Schools are fundamentally places of learning and sites of development. Student behavior and mind-sets are not fully formed, yet the prevailing discourse centers on consequences rather than learning and development. When the language of school discipline mirrors that of the criminal justice system, we can argue that the criminalization of students has become disturbingly normalized. In this carceral climate, suspensions are a slap on the hand and the priority is to get tougher on students—to teach them lessons that society surely will. The fact of the matter is that in America's public schools, a student's race largely determines their disciplinary experiences and outcomes. And students' disciplinary outcomes are linked to their opportunities to learn and flourish, not only in K–12 schools but also as adults. In school discipline, the evidence points to rampant anti-Blackness in how educators are interacting with and molding Black students in public schools. This is a hard truth to accept and a tough pill to swallow, especially in the corners and corridors that still contest the pervasiveness and pernicious impact of racism. But the disruption of discipline disparities hinges on these truths becoming self-evident.

A positive interpretation of the state of school discipline is that transformation won't be overnight and the reduction in prevalence can be viewed as a checkpoint on the road to reducing racial inequality in school discipline. Thus, reduction in the prevalence can be characterized as inspiration to double our investment in intentionality and rejecting a colorblind approach to school discipline reform.

Another interpretation of the prevailing disciplinary landscape is less amenable to arc and more directed to disruption (or the lack thereof). We must take aim at the complex root causes of disparities in school disciplinary outcomes. This undoubtedly requires bold leaders willing to make disruptive decisions that will transform the disciplinary systems in schools and districts.

I posit that one of the reasons that school discipline reforms seemingly miss the target of disparities and fail to address the contributors is the invisible elephant of American society—the reluctance and inability to discuss and confront the roots and tentacles of racism in facets of work, play, pray, and learning.

Factors such as policies, practices, and personnel under the control of schools and districts play a preeminent role in contributing to and reducing racial inequities in suspensions. Indeed, the drivers of racial discipline disparities are related to the structural conditions of learning, namely issues of race, racism, and anti-Blackness compounded by a representation gap between school personnel and students, as well as structural issues in the teacher and school leader labor market such as inadequate teacher and school administrator preparation programs. In the next chapter, I outline a strategic approach to transform inequities in school discipline that better aligns the evidence on the contributors to disparities with what we know about the effectiveness of school discipline reforms.

[illegible] and [illegible] in [illegible]. But the disruption of these [illegible] on these [illegible] becomes self-evident.

[illegible] interpretation [illegible] of school discipline [illegible] transformation [illegible] can be viewed as [illegible] contributing [illegible] racial inequality in school discipline. [illegible] characterized as [illegible] in [illegible] and rejecting a colorblind approach to school discipline reform.

Another interpretation of the prevailing discipline [illegible] (or the lack thereof). We must take into account the complex root causes of disparities in school discipline [illegible] teachers with [illegible] schools and districts.

[illegible] one of the reasons that school discipline [illegible] resources [illegible] and [illegible] and [illegible].

Factors such as [illegible] policies, practices, and personnel [illegible] in the context of schools [illegible] play a paramount role in [illegible] contributing to and reducing racial [illegible] such as an adequate teacher and school [illegible]. In the next chapter, [illegible] strategies [illegible] school discipline [illegible] what [illegible] school discipline reform.

CHAPTER 2

The Transforming School Discipline Strategic Framework

Refashioning school discipline policies and practices has become the bane of policy makers' and educators' existence, especially with the uptick in students' needs and misbehavior in the post–COVID-19 era.[1] There is a sense of urgency to disrupt longstanding educational inequality in districts and schools nationwide. Indeed, equity is one of districts' strategic priorities, and school discipline is one of the central challenges in education equity. For instance, in Gwinnett County Public Schools (GCPS) (the largest district in Georgia), discipline disproportionality (the number of all student groups overrepresented in suspensions) is one of the key performance indicators for the opportunity and access goal of the equity dimensions of GCPS's strategic priorities.

Like GCPS, numerous schools and districts find themselves at a crossroads between punitive and restorative approaches to school discipline, a common predicament when attempting to pivot away from exclusionary discipline in hopes of reducing discipline disparities.[2] What are the investments to make and sustain to reduce discipline disproportionalities? How do we reduce office discipline referrals (ODRs) and suspension rates for Black students and students with disabilities (SWDs)? How does the district central office support schools with the highest rates and disparities?

School discipline is a highly racialized topic and there is no shortage of studies on what's driving discipline disproportionalities.[3] And the knowledge base for what school discipline reforms are working is rapidly expanding.[4] Yet there seems to be a disconnect between the wealth of research evidence, the prevailing discourse around school discipline reforms, and the decisions that will disrupt discipline disparities in schools and districts. There is little guidance for district and school leaders on school discipline strategy that incorporates what we know about the contributors to discipline disparities and what we know about the effectiveness of school discipline reforms.

Given the salience of school discipline for educational policy and equity, there is a need for a framework that links research evidence to the ways that decision makers and practitioners may reduce the prevalence of and disparities in students' disciplinary outcomes. It takes two hands to clap, and without a synthesis linking contributors to solutions as well as research connecting with experiential knowledge, school discipline strategy will lack the scope and voracity to disrupt discipline disparities.

In this chapter, I draw on the robust research evidence on policies and programs that have successfully reduced discipline disparities (not only the rates at which students are sent to the office, suspended, or expelled) and present the Transforming School Discipline Strategic Framework (TSDSF). The TSDSF is an approach to school discipline reform and a collection of evidence-based strategies to disrupt organizational routines that produce discipline disparities.[5] This chapter describes the underlying tenets and components of the framework.

SCHOOL DISCIPLINE REFORM NEEDS A STRATEGIC FRAMEWORK

Although schools and districts are doing their darndest to reduce discipline disparities, tinkering with a multitude of policy and programmatic changes and the mixed results of these efforts is likely due in part to ad hoc strategy (or lack thereof) underlying school discipline reforms. Districts and schools are rarely doing one thing to address school discipline. Typically, there is some combination of code-of-conduct changes as well as other possible investments in programs and personnel. There is little targeting and differentiated support based on school discipline metrics in the strategic approach of most districts. There is also little alignment between the severity of discipline disparities and the intensity of support offered by the district to schools (and schools to teachers). I argue that the prevailing national school discipline landscape in New York City Public Schools (NYCPS) and other urban districts empirically demonstrate the need for an integrative strategic framework to address racial disparities in school discipline.

The importance of limited resources and the need for targeting in school discipline reforms also contributes to the need for a strategic framework. The disruption of inequities in students' disciplinary outcomes requires resources. Consider the case of the Los Angeles Unified School District (LAUSD). The nonpunitive approach catalyzed by banning suspensions in 2013 and the hiring of school climate advocates, restorative justice teachers, and support advocates has cost a pretty penny (roughly $300 million in 2022–2023).[6] Most districts may not have a fraction of these resources.

Plus, even in LAUSD, these personnel were not in all schools. The inherent resource constraints compel targeting to disrupt discipline disparities. The TSDSF acknowledges this resource challenge and provides an approach to direct scarce resources to the schools most in need.

THE BENEFITS OF THE TSDSF

The TSDSF is both a call to action and a toolkit. It is an evidence-based strategic framework to disrupt discipline disparities and deepen the ways in which educational practitioners, policy makers, and researchers reflect and strategize to confront the school discipline crisis. The TSDSF leverages existing interdisciplinary research to connect contributors and mechanisms of racial inequality in school discipline to the evidence base on the effectiveness of school discipline reforms in a multifaceted framework to transform school discipline. The framework is the product of a synthesis of the robust school discipline literature and intended to improve the use of research evidence in school discipline policy and practice. However, the TSDSF is not intended to be another practical guide but a catalysis for the instrumental and conceptual use of research evidence on school discipline. The framework orients practitioners, researchers, and policy makers to the salient issues in school discipline reform, providing a coherent system that has both heuristic and explanatory power. The TSDSF facilitates and fosters the use of research evidence for targeted and differentiated support to educators and students. The TSDSF bolsters the conceptual use of research on school discipline by influencing the thinking on problems and solutions in school discipline. The framework also enhances the instrumental use of research evidence with specific programs for educational practitioners to improve the disciplinary process in schools.

The TSDSF entails a sequence of practical steps for districts and schools to disrupt discipline disparities and includes evidence-based strategies that enable practitioners to craft a multitiered school discipline reform strategy. The framework fosters alignment in the language and actions of district central office with schools via a systematic approach to interventions in school discipline. The framework is applicable at the school and district levels and is intended to support principals and superintendents as they craft an effective school discipline strategy. Simply put, the TSDSF will enable district leaders to better support schools and school leaders to better support teachers, students, and support staff. Specifically, the framework assists educational leaders in (a) taking stock of the nature of discipline disparities and the efficacy of current reform efforts and (b) linking interventions and solutions to salient mechanisms that contribute to racial inequities in exclusionary discipline. As such, the TSDSF is an invaluable tool to reduce inequality in school discipline in districts and schools across the United States.

The TSDSF adds to the lineage of frameworks that challenges the deficit narrative that permeates the schooling of Black children and offers concrete strategies and steps to disrupt disparities in students' disciplinary outcomes.[7] For instance, school discipline scholars such as Russell Skiba and Anne Gregory have offered a research-based framework to address disparities in school discipline.[8] The ten principles spanned prevention and intervention-oriented action and underlined the importance of "culturally conscious implementation" of school discipline reforms. One of the launching points of the TSDSF is the tenth principle that embodies both prevention and intervention. The dynamic framework is not intended to be prescriptive but solution generative with actionable insights that can be applied to the range of local contexts.

THE GUIDING TENETS OF THE TSDSF

The three core tenets of the TSDSF are grounded in insights from the extant school discipline literature. The pillars underlying TSDSF are as follows: (a) centering race and intersectionality to identify the victims of exclusionary discipline; (b) scrutinizing structures, not students, to better align the causes and solutions of discipline disparities; and (c) supporting educators, not just students, to reduce discipline disproportionalities. These tenets guide the understanding and transformation of racial inequities in school discipline. The reset in school discipline starts with change in thinking and disposition toward responding to misbehavior based on the foregoing evidence. Overall, the TSDSF is intended to *expose and target*—to identify the tentacles of anti-Blackness in the disciplinary process and attack the structural roots of discipline disparities.

Centering Race and Intersectionality

Rejecting race-neutral school discipline reforms is a central plank of transforming school discipline.[9] The depth of the prejudice in the disciplinary systems in schools demands a commensurate response. The color of a student's skin should not dictate whether they are sent to the office or suspended, but it does. And it has in America's schools for decades. A central objective of the TSDSF is to catalyze instructive talk about issues in school discipline. Often, educational stakeholders and practitioners may talk around racial inequality in school discipline and avoid the thorny issues of race and racism that accompany such discussions. The framework helps to surface the scope of discipline disparities to facilitate open and honest conversations and lay the foundation for school discipline reforms that combat the anti-Blackness that fuels differences in students' disciplinary outcomes.

Scrutinizing Structures, Not Students

The TSDSF centers schools as the primary agent of change in reducing racial inequality in school discipline and focuses on two key within-school factors—school personnel and school climate. The framework places the onus on adults in school to improve their behavior, interpretation, and responses to students' perceived misbehavior to reduce racial inequities in school discipline. The framework encourages education leaders to tackle structural problems in schools that engender racial inequality in students' disciplinary outcomes rather than a hyperfocus on students' behavior. Reducing racial inequality in school discipline is not a quick-fix, set-it-and-forget-it affair. To solve the school discipline crisis, there is a need for broader systemic change of how learning occurs in school. As such, the framework extends the focus beyond a singular program or policy and instead centers the alignment between mechanisms driving discipline disparities and educator-focused interventions.

Supporting Educators, Not Just Students

The theory of change underlying the TSDSF is to identify schools, school administrators, teachers, and students in need of support to improve disciplinary experiences and outcomes and create a system of cascading supports starting with the district supporting schools, school leaders supporting teachers, and teachers supporting students. There is a need for a two-pronged strategic approach to transforming inequities in school discipline that includes: (1) supporting students through student-focused interventions, such as social emotional learning and affirmations, and (2) supporting educators through educator-focused interventions, such as providing professional development and coaching.[10] The overarching goal is to give students and educators the support they need. Educator-focused programs are intended to bolster the professional capacity and empathy of teachers and school leaders whereas student-focused programs are intended the bolster the identity, genius, and joy of SWDs and Black, male, and low-income children in schools. The TSDSF provides a structured way of thinking about a continuum of support and multitiered interventions in school discipline.

Emphasizing educator-focused interventions as much as student-focused interventions is an important strategic direction in school discipline reforms. To be clear, the framework is not advocating for districts and schools to not pursue student-focused interventions. Focusing on educator-focused interventions does not subtract from the importance of supporting students in schools. If anything, it amplifies such an approach by improving educators' capabilities to meet student needs.

THE DISRUPTION SEQUENCE

There are three key steps in the disruption of discipline disparities: (a) determining the state of school discipline, (b) taking stock and mapping current reform efforts, and (c) developing and implementing a multitiered school discipline reform strategy.

Determining the State of School Discipline in Schools and Districts

The first step in disrupting discipline disparities is a comprehensive empirical portrait of the school discipline landscape in districts and schools. Reducing inequities in school discipline starts with the data and fostering an understanding of school discipline through an equity lens.[11] Getting a lay of the disciplinary landscape entails measuring and understanding the prevalence of and disparities in a range of disciplinary outcomes from ODRs to multiple suspension types. Centering and interrogating data allow district and school leaders to be strategic and proactive in their response to student behavior issues. Indeed, data highlight the need for and urgency of school discipline reform as well as inform the direction of school discipline strategy. Data identify the areas and actors in need of support to pivot from a punitive to a nonpunitive approach to school discipline. This understanding is foundational and shapes potential solutions by identifying schools (and classrooms) in need of support as well as schools that are inclusive disciplinary environments (more on this in chapter 5). For example, determining the state of school discipline may inform code of conduct revisions (and a complementary resource manual for school leaders) as districts target the most frequently occurring disciplinary infractions and consequences. Data will also allow schools to identify vulnerable decision points (VDPs) ("specific situations in which increased disproportionality tends to occur. VDPs are contextual events or elements, such as those that increase the likelihood of implicit bias affecting discipline decision making, including a teacher's decision to issue an ODR or an administrator's decision to suspend the student") to better target the generation of ODRs within the schooling environment.[12]

Recent studies have underscored the importance of data in school discipline and highlighted the need to reveal disparities as well as for school leaders to share discipline data with teachers.[13] School discipline expert Kent McIntosh and colleagues illustrated the importance of using discipline data to analyze the extent of disparities and identify vulnerable decision points and reported that this strategy slightly reduced racial disparities.[14] Yet, in a more recent study, McIntosh and colleagues revealed that awareness is not enough. In a randomized controlled trial, school administrators were provided with monthly discipline equity reports that resulted in "no meaningful change in disciplinary equity or equity goal setting."[15] Additionally, in order to foster coordination across the key educational governance levels (districts, schools, classrooms) in disrupting discipline disparities, district leaders need to share and discuss discipline data with school leaders. In my work with districts, a Discipline Data Dashboard has been useful in establishing data as part of the culture and providing a platform for teachers and school leaders as well as district leaders to review and interpret school discipline data. Equity-centered research–practice partnerships (discussed in greater detail in chapter 6) can also help with digesting data and plotting school discipline reform strategy as researchers and practitioners review data together and put discipline trends in conversation with evidence-based strategies from the research.

Districts typically have a host of data on ODRs and suspensions but may need to make tweaks to link discipline to personnel data for actionable insights. For instance, the identification of "top referrers" (the top 5 percent of referrers based on ODRs) is a central part of the strategy to support educators, yet this information may not be readily available to school leaders (anecdotally, most principals and assistant principals have a good idea of who their top referrers are).[16] Examining the various dimensions of school discipline—prevalence, disparities, differential selection, and differential processing—is critical to understanding the several possible crevices in the disciplinary process in which inequality may fester.[17] It may also be helpful for districts to situate themselves within the state, regional, and national context. This can be done using data from the Civil Rights Data Collection.

Taking Stock and Mapping Current School Discipline Reforms

The second step in the TSDSF is taking stock of existing school discipline reforms. School discipline reforms can be categorized into three main groups—the 3Ps—policies, programs, and personnel.[18] Mapping what the district and school is currently doing to disrupt discipline disparities is necessary before advancing to develop a multitiered school discipline reform strategy.

School discipline policy includes the content of the code of conduct as well as any accompanying guidance or manuals for school administrators and teachers. Policy-based approaches focus on changing the policies that guide school and district responses to behaviors.[19] Revising the code of conduct provides an opportunity to rethink the approach to school discipline and signals to educational stakeholders and educators the necessity to move away from exclusionary discipline.

Program-based approaches may target students or school personnel and mostly focus on initiatives that (a) improve school culture for the entire school, (b) bolster the professional capacity of educators and provide school personnel with skills and changes in perspectives (e.g., classroom management and empathy), and (c) enhance students' social and emotional learning (SEL). Positive Behavioral Interventions and Supports (PBIS) and restorative practices (RPs) are popular school-level program-based initiatives.[20] These approaches are not mutually exclusive and can be used collectively.

Personnel-based approaches entail the addition of support staff such as behavior specialists, social workers and guidance counselors to assist in the disciplinary process in schools whether through supporting educators (e.g., coaching) or supporting students (e.g., counseling). Abigail Gray and colleagues identified "the shortage of staffing, space, and supportive services as the biggest impediment to reducing the use of suspension."[21] Although, as discussed in the next chapter, the empirical evidence on the effectiveness on personnel-based approaches in reducing discipline disparities is not as robust as the evidence on policy and programmatic changes.

It is important for district and school leaders to remember that they are not starting from scratch. As such, commendations are an important part of mapping school discipline reforms. Commendations are the things that the district or school is doing well in school discipline or ways in which the groundwork has been laid for future progress. District and school leaders deserve a pat on the back for things they are doing well to reduce inequities in school discipline. This may include, but is not limited to, (a) the formation of a support office that becomes the engine of the multitiered school discipline reform strategy described below, (b) existing training in key areas such as cultural responsiveness and classroom management, and (c) a growing emphasis on norm setting given evidence on the timing of discipline disparities throughout the school year.[22]

There is a wealth of resources (e.g., guides and worksheets) to help district and school leaders take the first two steps of the disruption sequence of the TSDSF.[23] Regional Educational Laboratories (RELs), Office of Special

Education Programs (OSEP), Discipline and Behavior Blog Series, Center on PBIS, the Equity Assistance Center-South, and the School Discipline Lab are a few places where district and school leaders can access technical assistance resources to help implement the TSDSF.[24] For instance, RELs (see, for example, the "Using Data to Promote Equity in School Discipline" series) have provided several materials on the use of data as well as steps to revising discipline policy and practices that districts and schools can leverage to take the first two steps of the disruption sequence.[25] The Dimensions of School Discipline Framework also provides an overview of metrics to measure the prevalence of and disparities in exclusionary discipline.[26] The Center on PBIS also provides validated tools for measuring the fidelity of implementation.[27] The United States Departments of Justice and Education also provide resources for school discipline reforms.[28]

Crafting and Implementing a Multitiered School Discipline Reform Strategy

The third and final step of the disruption sequence of the TSDSF is perhaps the step with which most schools and districts struggle. And that is developing and implementing a multitiered school discipline reform strategy (MTSDRS). Crafting and implementing an MTSDRS will allow district and school leaders to (a) target intensive interventions to schools and classrooms in most need to better address discipline disparities, (b) coordinate the ecosystem of support and map the lines of collaboration between district and school personnel involved in the disciplinary process, and (c) monitor and respond to the variation in disciplinary outcomes across schools within a district and classrooms within a school.

How the MTSDRS Differs from MTSS

The ethos and approach of the multitiered system of supports (MTSS) is coupled with a robust understanding of trends in ODRs and suspensions as well as evidence-based nonpunitive interventions to arrive at an MTSDRS. The MTSS for behavior (MTSS-B) is student focused and aims to "change the school learning environment by consistently teaching and reinforcing good behavior for all students and then identifying and providing supplement support to students who need it."[29] Even though the MTSDRS adopts a parallel approach of support, there are two instructive differences. First, the MTSDRS is both student *and* educator focused. The goal is not to fix student behavior. The MTSDRS also recognizes the central role of educators in contributing to discipline disparities. Second, the MTSDRS is applicable to multiple educational governance levels. MTSDRS can be applied at both the district and school levels. It can be used to identify and support schools and classrooms in need of most support with regard to school discipline. Within these schools and classrooms, further support can be targeted to educators and students who need it. At the school level, principals and assistant principals may target high-referring grades and teachers similar to how districts target high-referring schools. Similarly, the use of data to identify Tier 2 and Tier 3 schools that district leaders can support is parallel to Tier 2 and Tier 3 classrooms that school leaders can support. MTSDRS also considers how principals may support teachers, especially novice teachers, in developing nonpunitive disciplinary practices.

The Components of an MTSDRS

Similar to MTSS, the MTSDRS is designed for three tiers of schools (and classrooms). School-level (and classroom-level) discipline metrics on the prevalence of and disparities in students' disciplinary outcomes (ODRs, in-school suspension [ISS], and out-of-school suspension [OSS]) are used to classify schools (and classrooms) into three tiers. Next, a menu of evidence-based practices for the three tiers of schools (and classrooms) is available for district and school leaders. The MTSDRS has three tiers of support that respond to the needs of students, educators, and schools. MTSDRS places the most emphasis on Tier 2 and Tier 3, with Tier 3 necessitating a hard reset of the disciplinary process. Developing an MTSDRS includes the following two steps:

1. *Identifying and targeting* schools (and classrooms) with largest prevalence and disparities in ODRs, ISS, and OSS (Tier 2 and Tier 3 schools) using school-level (and classroom-level) metrics.
2. *Supporting educators and students* with intensive interventions and support plans for Tier 2 and Tier 3 schools (and classrooms) grounded in evidence-based policy-, program-, and personnel-based approaches to reducing discipline disparities.

Identifying Tier 1, Tier 2, and Tier 3 Schools (and Classrooms)

Tier 1 encompasses universal support for nonpunitive disciplinary practices in all schools. Roughly 75 percent of schools within a district typically fall in Tier 1 given the extent of ODRs, ISS, and OSS. These are mostly elementary schools in addition to a few middle and high schools with low prevalence and disparities. *Tier 2* entails intensive support for schools generating a significant proportion of ODRs. Roughly 15 percent of schools within a district fall in Tier 2. Typically, these are mostly middle and high schools with high prevalence of ODRs but not so high disparities in suspensions. *Tier 3* includes "kitchen sink" support for schools with the largest disparities in both suspensions and ODRs. About 10 percent of schools in a district fall in Tier 3. These generally are middle and high schools with high prevalence *and* disparities.

Aligning Discipline Interventions with Tiers

After arraying schools (and classrooms) by tiers based on their discipline trends, interventions are then matched to each tier aligned with the severity of the prevalence of and disparities in exclusionary discipline. For Tier 1, there are universal practices and support, as well as support for schools demonstrating the early signs of disciplinary problems. For Tiers 2 and 3, there are targeted interventions for schools in the upper quartile of the school discipline distribution. Tier 2 and Tier 3 schools are the highest priorities with the most intensive monitoring of school discipline trends (e.g., regular reviews on discipline trends and goal setting to address disparities with school leadership) and a raft of interventions.

SUPPORTING EDUCATORS

The professional capacity of teachers, assistant principals, and principals is an often-overlooked lever to disrupt discipline disparities. Most states do not require schools to provide training to personnel on school discipline (about twelve of the fifty states do).[30] Investing in the professional development of both school leaders and teachers is central to the MTSDRS. Targeted training and support for teachers and school administrators is the centerpiece of educator-focused interventions to address inequality in school discipline. Training and on-the-job support will enhance professional capacity and catalyze adult learning and empathy, which in turn will likely result in nonpunitive and restorative disciplinary practices. The reality of the situation is that district leadership should be focused not only on the social and emotional needs of children but also on educators' and support staffs' emotional needs. Developing an empathic mind-set, coaching, and professional development in classroom management and culturally responsive practices for educators are evidence-based reforms that show promise of disrupting discipline disparities via the reduction of ODRs.[31]

The nation's educators have been given the proverbial basket to carry water. Upgrading teachers' capacity to better manage classrooms is a central plank of reducing discipline disproportionality, based largely on the documented deficiencies in teacher-preparation programs. Better teacher preparation was one of the needs highlighted by principals in a nationally representative survey.[32] About one thousand public school principals were surveyed in November 2021 using RAND's nationally representative American School Leader Panel and most principals disagree or strongly disagree with the statement "Teachers at my school are for the most part adequately trained by their teacher-training program to handle problems of misbehavior and discipline."[33] The emerging consensus is that most teachers are ill-equipped and have not been properly trained to deal with the behaviors of children in their classrooms. Sending students to the principal's office—the starting point of disparities in students who are disciplined—has become a crutch for educators who struggle with classroom management or building relationships with the increasingly diverse student population in public schools. This is not to blame the teachers and school leaders who are doing the day-to-day work of educating our children. The scarcity of resources and tools to prepare teachers for complex and challenging contexts and the lack of sustained on-the-job support are no fault of individual teachers themselves. These are structural issues in the teacher labor market that feed into discipline disparities. This motivates the need for professional development for teachers. It is sad and unfortunate that teachers are seeking comfort through exclusionary discipline because their classroom management, relationship-building skills, and connections to diverse students are struggling. Unfortunately, too many teachers enter the classrooms unprepared for school discipline challenges.

Many teachers will reference the lack of tools outside of exclusionary discipline. Yet ODRs and suspensions cannot be the first resort and should be viewed as the last resort for perceived student misbehavior. The question of what comes before a suspension is an operative one and partly motivates the emphasis on educator-focused school discipline reforms. Teachers need better skills to manage student behavior without quickly resorting to exclusion. It is paramount that teachers are supported in order to create inclusive disciplinary environments. There remains a strong demand to support our teachers to better handle perceived misbehavior and proactively create classroom environments that prevent infractions.

Supporting School Leaders

School leaders also need training based on the theory of action that school leaders will become the teachers of teachers (a train-the-trainer model of sorts). There is also a need for a shared understanding of school discipline among school leaders in a district that can foster a common vision and consistency in disciplinary practices. School leaders need to collaborate and have conversations on disciplinary philosophy and beliefs. School leaders need time to reflect on discipline data. Creating time and space for school leaders to discuss school discipline challenges and innovations is a key responsibility of districts. Connecting school leaders and giving them time to reflect on their disciplinary practices as well as the opportunity to share ideas and strategies will bode well for disrupting discipline disparities. In addition, in some cases, there are also new school administrators in need of additional support to develop inclusive disciplinary environments.

Data-driven workshops for school administrators (especially new principals and assistant principals) may provide them with time to reflect on and share challenges and strategies on the essential dimensions of transforming school discipline including but not limited to (a) conducting a hard reset in their school, (b) reporting disciplinary infractions and responding to misbehavior (e.g., Code of Conduct and the Hearing Process; flow chart distinguishing office versus classroom managed infractions), (c) building a positive school climate and a culture of empathy, (d) modeling effective classroom management, and (e) connecting with the community and fostering school–community relationships. In addition to school leaders, the training of support personnel (e.g., behavior specialists) is another key plank of addressing inequities in school discipline, especially given the growing role of support personnel in the disciplinary process in schools.

District leaders should also remain cognizant of the demands of training and reform fatigue. Training takes time for educators when there is not a lot of built-in time for professional development. The structure of professional learning should also be reviewed to include fewer presentations and more workshops to provide educators with examples, role-play, modeling, and active strategies and tools they can bring back to their school buildings and classrooms. The scheduling and timing of these professional development sessions should also be thoughtfully considered to ensure adequate coverage of school leadership at schools. There is a demand for school leaders and teachers to share strategies that may be used across the district. As such, professional development should also create time and space for educators to share strategies and best practices.

The Core-Four Topics for School Discipline Professional Development

Arming educators with nonpunitive tools requires intentional and sustained training on four core school discipline–specific topics including (a) classroom management, (b) cultural responsiveness, (c) the disciplining of SWDs, and (d) building relationships and setting norms and expectations. There is a need to embed school discipline training in the district's and school's professional learning plan. These four core topics constitute the content and focus of universal professional development for all teachers and school leaders in efforts to bolster capacity in school discipline–specific areas such as classroom management and relationship building. These professional development topics are critical to manifesting the five prevention principles in Gregory and colleagues' framework.[34] Other areas worthy of additional training include but are not limited to (a) child development, particularly identifying age-appropriate behavior; (b) instructional engagement; and (c) building students' SEL skills.

Classroom Management

Inadequate classroom management skills contribute to ODRs that are the genesis of discipline disparities.[35] Training in classroom management has been consistently linked to school discipline disparities.[36] As such, training and support in classroom management and how to alternatively respond to student behavior without exclusion is one of the starting points of reducing inequality in school discipline. Classroom management is a skill that teachers (particularly novices) underdevelop in their preparation.[37] Teacher preparation programs do not sufficiently arm teachers with the know-how to develop relationships and detect and respond to students' behavioral cues to reduce ODRs. Too often, sending students to the office acts as a band-aid for the deep wounds of lack of classroom management skills. Bolstering teachers' classroom management skills is pivotal to disrupting discipline disparities. A student intervention flowchart that distinguishes between administrator-managed and teacher-managed behaviors is a useful tool for training teachers. An intervention plan that spells out the sequence from nonpunitive steps, such as student and parent conferences, to suspensions is another key training document for teachers.

Cultural Responsiveness

Cultural responsiveness is another important ingredient of transforming inequities in school discipline. One of the key principles for prevention of discipline disparities in Gregory and colleagues Framework for Increasing Equity in School Discipline is culturally relevant and responsive teaching.[38] This is especially important given the demographic mismatch between educators and students in public schools (I discuss this further in chapter 3). Cultural responsiveness allows teachers to better understand the behavior of Black students via a better understanding of their culture as well as developing relationships.[39] Proficiency in programs such as Check In–Check Out can also help bridge the gap between students and adults in school buildings.

Disciplining of SWDs

The prevalence of and disparities in the disciplinary outcomes of SWDs is especially concerning given recent federal guidance on the dubious connection between special education and school discipline.[40] SWDs have some of the highest referral and suspension rates. It is a timely moment to review and revisit the professional development offered to teachers (and school leaders) on the process and protocol of how SWDs are disciplined. Addressing the disciplinary experiences of SWDs may require increased training and on-the-job support for personnel involved in special education. Providing more training on how to update and enact students' individualized education programs (IEPs) and behavior intervention plans (BIPs) is a starting point to reduce inequities afflicting SWDs. A priority area for school discipline reform is how to support school administrators and teachers who may be struggling to update and implement BIPs to students in real time. There is a need to review the adherence to the manifestation guidelines to ensure students' civil rights are not violated. Additionally, district and school leaders may also consider the assignment of more experienced teachers to classes populated with SWDs.

Relationship Building

Authentic engagement with students is necessary to prevent disruptions in classrooms. Relationship-building skills are a key component of students knowing that you care for them. This flows from the belief that support, rather than exclusion, is a better response to the needs that student behavior communicates. Professional development should prioritize building relationships with students given its importance for both instructional quality and school discipline while reinforcing classroom management strategies.[41] Relatedly, teachers need help with setting expectations and norms so there is structure and order in classrooms to facilitate academic engagement.

Additionally, training in child development bolsters the ability of educators to perceive student misbehavior through an empathetic lens. This is especially important for Black students who have been subjected to adultification.[42] Training in child development will also enable educators to better identify the underlying reasons of misbehavior (diagnosis of behavior). High-engagement teaching strategies are a vaccine to students disrupting and defying authority in classrooms. Modeling and teaching skills such as self-awareness and self-management are essential to reduce the incidences of disruption and defiance that account for the bulk of disciplinary infractions.

Target and Support Top Referrers and New Teachers

Professional learning should be targeted to the personnel most in need. Research has revealed that a significant proportion of disparities in disciplinary outcomes are driven by a select group of teachers who generate multiple ODRs.[43] These "top referrers"—the small number of educators who send the most students to the office for discipline—contribute significantly to discipline disparities. Thus, there is a need for schools to identify and support these teachers as part of the MTSDRS. One of the main interventions for Tier 2 and Tier 3 schools is identifying and supporting top referrers. As discussed below, the intensive support provided to these teachers may entail training and professional development (e.g., empathy intervention), coaching, mentorship, and modeling of nonpunitive techniques by school leaders.

In addition to top referrers, another personnel group in need of further support is novice teachers. Unsurprisingly, novice teachers struggle the most with referring students to the office—the genesis of exclusionary discipline. Results from the 2024 State of the American Survey highlighted that "teachers with five or fewer years of experience were especially likely to report that managing student behavior was among their top three sources of stress."[44] There should be an explicit focus on helping new teachers with school discipline. In this regard, a district-wide induction coupled with community-building and professional development activities specifically targeted to new teachers may be beneficial. These two groups of personnel ought to be a high priority at the start of the school year in anticipation of some of the challenges they may encounter during the school year.

EVIDENCE-BASED EDUCATOR-FOCUSED STRATEGIES BY TIERS

Table 2.1 presents the starting point of aligning support to the tiers of schools (and classrooms) in the MTSDRS. These evidence-based school discipline reforms are a work in progress and will evolve with research evidence. Indeed, the school discipline literature is robust; thus as the conditions for causal inferences for new innovations are strengthened, the toolkit available to district and school leaders will invariably expand. I use the Every Student Succeeds Act (ESSA) tiers of evidence to organize studies on the effectiveness of school discipline reforms.[45] In developing the MTSDRS, I emphasize school discipline reforms with empirical evidence spanning Tier 1 through Tier 3 of the ESSA tiers of evidence.

TABLE 2.1 Tiers of support in the MTSDRS

School discipline reforms	*Tier 1: Universal supports across all schools*	*Tier 2: Specialized support for schools with highest prevalence of and disparities in ODRs*	*Tier 3: Specialized support for schools with highest prevalence of and disparities in ODRs* and *suspensions*
Educator focused	**School Discipline Policy Changes:** *Tier 2 ESSA tiers of evidence* (Anderson 2020; Anderson et al. 2019; Craigie 2022; Fisher & Devlin 2024; Hashim et al. 2018; Lacoe & Steinberg 2018; Steinberg & Lacoe 2018; Wang 2022)[46] **PBIS:** *Tier 1 ESSA tiers of evidence* (Bradshaw et al. 2009, 2010, 2012, 2015; McIntosh et al. 2021);[47] *Tier 2 ESSA tiers of evidence* (Caldarella et al. 2011; Gage et al. 2018, 2019, 2020; Grasley-Boy et al. 2019; Lee et al. 2021)[48] **RP:** *Tier 1 of ESSA tiers of evidence* (Acosta et al. 2019; Augustine et al. 2018; Gregory et al. 2022);[49] RP with SEL and racial equity efforts (Huang et al. 2023);[50] *Tier 2 of ESSA tiers of evidence* (Davison et al. 2022; Joseph et al. 2021)[51] **The Core-Four School Discipline–Specific Professional Development:** Classroom management; cultural responsiveness; disciplining of SWDs; relationship-building	***What:*** *Professional development for teachers* ***Who:*** *Target (a) top referrers, (b) new teachers, (c) teachers in focus grades (8–10)* **Empathy Interventions (Empathic Mind-Set):** *Tier 1 ESSA tiers of evidence* (Goyer et al. 2019; Okonofua et al. 2016, 2022)[52] **Project ReACT (Equity-Focused PBIS Professional Learning):** *Tier 2 ESSA tiers of evidence* (McIntosh et al. 2021)[53] **GREET-STOP-PROMPT:** *Tier 3 ESSA tiers of evidence* (Cook et al. 2018)[54] **Culturally Responsive Teaching:** *Tier 3 ESSA tiers of evidence* (Larson et al. 2018)[55] **Double Check Model:** *Tier 3 ESSA tiers of evidence* (Bradshaw et al. 2018)[56] **Addition of Support Personnel (e.g., guidance counselors, social workers, school psychologists):** See chapter 3	***What:*** *Professional development for teachers AND school leaders (principals and assistant principals)* ***Who:*** *School leaders and teachers* **Tier 2 supports** **Coaching and Professional Development for Teachers:** *Tier 1 ESSA tiers of evidence* (Gion et al. 2022 [modified version of Classroom Check-Up]; Gregory et al. 2014, 2015, 2019; Havighurst et al. 2024; Okonofua et al. 2020);[57] My Teacher Partner: *Tier 1 ESSA tiers of evidence* (Gregory et al. 2016, 2019)[58] **Interconnected Systems Framework (ISF):** *Tier 1 ESSA tiers of evidence* (Weist et al. 2022)[59]

(*Continued*)

TABLE 2.1 Tiers of support in the MTSDRS (*Continued*)

School discipline reforms	*Tier 1: Universal supports across all schools*	*Tier 2: Specialized support for schools with highest prevalence of and disparities in ODRs*	*Tier 3: Specialized support for schools with highest prevalence of and disparities in ODRs and suspensions*
Student focused	**Social and Emotional Learning (e.g., Leader in Me):** *Tier 2 of ESSA tiers of evidence* (Bergin et al. 2024)[60] **A Positive School Climate:** See chapter 4	**Student Self-Affirmation:** *Tier 1 of ESSA tiers of evidence* (Binning et al. 2019; Borman et al. 2021; Caldarella et al. 2023; Goyer et al. 2019);[61] *Tier 2 of ESSA tiers of evidence* (Bal et al. 2018)[62] **Student Threat Assessment:** *Tier 1 of ESSA tiers of evidence* (Cornell et al. 2012);[63] *Tier 2 of ESSA tiers of evidence* (Cornell et al. 2011)[64]	**Tier 2 supports**

The four most prevalent types of school discipline reform—PBIS, coaching and professional development, RP, and policy change—are represented in all four tiers of the ESSA tiers of evidence, with the exception of no Tier 1 evidence for policy change. There is experimental evidence (Tier 1) for a handful of programs such as PBIS, RP, and the Interconnected Systems Framework (ISF).[65] Several Tier 1 studies are related to coaching and professional development, accounting for a third of Tier 1 evidence.[66] There is limited quasi-experimental evidence (Tier 2) for PBIS and even less for RP.[67] Studies on the impact of school discipline policy changes typically fall in Tier 2 given the use of a quasi-experimental analytic strategy (difference in differences), an approach common in analyzing natural experiments.[68] Tier 3 of the MTSDRS also includes innovative school discipline interventions that are endorsed by district and school leaders such as additional personnel, yet the empirical base of these interventions is still nascent.

Tier 1: PBIS and RP, Policy Changes and School Discipline-Specific Professional Development

Revisions in the code of conduct are typically the first act districts consider when embarking on the journey to transform inequities in school discipline.

Indeed, almost always the resolution agreements between districts and the Office of Civil Right for discrimination in disciplinary practices will include code of conduct revisions.[69] There is ESSA Tier 2 and Tier 3 evidence in support of school discipline policy changes.[70] Yet, as detailed in chapter 1, at both the state and district level, changes in school discipline policy have led to a reduction of suspensions or the general use of exclusionary discipline, but racial disparities remained persistent. The tiers of MTSDRS are predominantly focused on programs to support educators and students.

The bulk of the research on the effectiveness of school discipline reforms has focused on PBIS and RP. Districts and schools are increasingly implementing these two programs concurrently. These approaches provide rigorous behavior supports and target school culture via school personnel. School personnel receive training for (a) identifying the circumstances surrounding behaviors, (b) establishing and communicating clear behavior expectations, (c) tailoring consequences with infractions, and (d) reinforcing positive behaviors.[71] RPs also employ personnel training to improve school culture.[72] RJ programs focus on establishing safer school environments via responsive, reintegrative, and restorative approaches.[73] The approach consists of fostering community, establishing and mending relationships, and adopting a schoolwide culture.[74] RJ is not tied to punitive consequences.[75] Instead, the philosophical framework (a) repairs misconduct through dialogue and accountability, uniting "persons harmed with persons responsible"; and (b) prioritizes mediation and conflict resolution.[76]

There is ample research evidence on the effectiveness of both programs across the four ESSA tiers of evidence. At Tier 1 of the ESSA evidence tiers, there is experimental evidence for both programs.[77] Across ESSA Tier 2 to Tier 4, there is further empirical support to provide justification for the investment in these programs universally across all schools, thus forming the foundation of Tier 1 in MTSDRS.[78] Complementing popular school-level programs such as PBIS with school mental health help also shows promise of reducing racial inequality in ODRs and suspensions. PBIS in tandem with school mental health may reduce the overall use of exclusionary discipline and, importantly, the rates at which Black students are referred to the office and suspended.[79]

PBIS and RP also contribute to a positive school climate, which, in turn, also reduces the likelihood of receiving exclusionary discipline (as discussed in further detail in chapter 4). Indeed, PBIS has been associated with improving school climate perceptions, whereas prior research has found mixed results on the relationship between RJ and school climate (results are mostly positive with the exception of a randomized controlled trial of RJ in middle schools in Maine that found no differences in student-reported measures of school climate between schools implementing RJ and a control group of schools).[80] Several studies have found a positive relationship between the implementation of schoolwide RP and school climate.[81] For example, using interviews with students and administrators in a high school in the southeastern United States, Ortega and colleagues found that the implementation of RJ led to increases in SEL and improved relationships.[82] In Oakland, the majority of school staff believed RJ improved school climate.[83] In Pittsburgh, teachers in schools implementing RJ reported improved teacher–student relationships and enhanced working conditions.[84]

Critiques of PBIS have highlighted the fixation on fixing student behavior. Indeed, in a prior literature review, my coauthor Shafiqua Little and I argued that "the vast majority of the alternative approaches (e.g. RTI, PBIS and restorative justice) are most concerned with assisting students with assimilating to school culture rather than crafting the school culture to fit the social, emotional and cultural needs of students."[85] Said differently, schools focus more on achieving behavior management through conformity and less on addressing the biases and cultural clashes driving discipline disparities. The fear is that PBIS will emphasize changing student behavior at the expense of building trust, developing student–teacher relationships, and addressing implicit biases that are necessary to reduce racial disparities.[86]

I still maintain that there is a need to pivot to educator-focused strategies, as exemplified by the MTSDRS. Yet over time and through multiple conversations with school and district leaders as well as countless school walk-throughs, I realize that it is the orientation of PBIS that truly shapes whether it promotes a superficial reward system for good student behavior or fosters strong classroom management practices and a community within schools. District and school leaders should use PBIS to spur intrinsic motivation by teaching skills, values, and community-building (e.g., classroom celebrations for good behavior rather than individual rewards) rather than focus on gifts and creating a token economy. Moreover, an equity-centered approach to PBIS shows promise of not only reducing the prevalence of exclusionary discipline but also disrupting inequities in school discipline.[87]

Tier 2: Teacher-Focused Professional Development

Tier 2 of the MTSDRS focuses on the generation of ODRs. As such, teachers are the main target of Tier 2 of the MTSDRS. More specifically, the primary targets of Tier 2 educator-focused professional development are novice teachers, top referrers, and teachers in focus grades (these are grades with the highest prevalence of and disparities in ODRs, typically grades 8–10). Tier 2 is largely focused on increasing the capacity of teachers to reduce ODRs. Tier 2 interventions address differential selection or racial inequality in how students are sent to the office. These interventions target classroom management, cultural responsiveness, and relationship-building skills through professional development programs with demonstrated impacts. Employing programs such as PBIS in tandem with teacher professional development to bolster classroom management skills may reduce racial disparities.[88] Tier 2 also focuses on brief, low-cost interventions that are not time intensive (as opposed to the more time- and resource-intensive interventions in Tier 3) to reduce overall ODRs and ODRs for Black students.

Investment in Teachers' Empathic Mind-Set

Developing teacher empathy is a central part of bolstering teachers' professional capacity to build relationships and better manage perceived misbehavior in classrooms. An empathic mind-set matters for discipline disparities. Empathy interventions are "a 45- to 70-min online exercise to refocus middle school teachers on understanding and valuing the perspectives of students and on sustaining positive relationships even when students misbehave."[89] Empathic mind-set interventions target both classroom management and school climate. This intervention also addresses teachers' mind-set and closes pathways through which racial bias may manifest in teachers' responses to perceived student misbehavior. There is evidence from experimental study designs (Tier 1 according to the ESSA tiers of evidence) in support of empathic mind-set interventions.[90] These interventions have resulted in a host of disciplinary benefits including reducing suspension rates and improving teacher–student relationships. Suspension rates were reduced by half over just one year, and there were reductions across all racial categories; however, White, Asian, and female students had the most gains. In a follow-up study in 2022, the empathic mind-set intervention resulted in a 45 percent reduction in racial disparities through the reduction of suspension rates for Black and Hispanic students.[91]

Investment in ReACT and Culturally Responsive Teaching

ReACT (Racial equity through Assessing data for vulnerable decision points, Culturally responsive behavior strategies, and Teaching about implicit bias and strategies to neutralize it) includes four intensive professional development sessions focused on diving into discipline data, learning about implicit bias, and designing and implementing a plan encompassing culturally responsive behavioral support and antibias training, with an emphasis on vulnerable decision points. There is empirical evidence demonstrating that this intervention is associated with improvements in school discipline and school climate.[92] Though largely classified as Tier 3 according to the ESSA tier of evidence, programs with a culturally responsive emphasis show promise of reducing discipline disparities. For example, an evaluation of GREET-STOP-PROMPT found that the relative risk ratios for receiving an ODR declined for African American students in elementary schools.[93]

Tier 3: Teacher- and School Leader–Focused Professional Development and Coaching

Tier 3 of the MTSDRS focuses on both the generation of and inequities in both ODRs and suspensions. As such, teachers and school leaders are the main targets of school discipline reforms in Tier 3 in MTSDRS. Tier 3 interventions address both differential selection (generation of ODRs) as well as differential processing (conversion of ODRs into suspensions). In addition to the low-cost interventions of Tier 2, districts and schools should also invest in more costly and time-intensive interventions given the limited number of Tier 3 schools (and classrooms). These resource-intensive interventions should focus on the schools, school leaders, and teachers with the greatest needs. Coaching is a major difference in the educator-focused interventions between Tier 2 and Tier 3 of the MTSDRS. There are several studies with experimental study design providing empirical justification for investing in coaching and professional development.[94] Indeed, individual coaching is emerging as a critical factor in the efficacy of professional development to reduce racial inequality in school discipline. Policy makers may consider providing coaching in tandem with professional development that places emphasis on school discipline–relevant skills and strategies to proactively address struggles encountered in the disciplinary process.

Investment in My Teaching Partner

MTP is another intervention with strong evidence according to the ESSA tiers of evidence.[95] A randomized controlled trial of the MTP program, a two-year coaching program, found that teachers in the treatment group had lower use of referrals than teachers in the control group (especially with Black students), and the racial discipline gap was eradicated in classrooms with teachers receiving MTP.[96] Teacher training programs like MTP assist teachers with creating more proactive climates via clear routines, consistent rules, and behavior monitoring, as well as redefining the interactions between students and teachers in order to yield positive outcomes.[97]

Investment in One-on-One Coaching

Training on cultural responsiveness coupled with classroom coaching for teachers resulted in lower ODRs overall and for Black students. Programs such as Double Check Self-Assessment that foster culturally responsive practices (e.g., reflective thinking, authentic relationships, connection to curriculum) have resulted in improvement in classroom management strategy and resulted in lower ODRs for Black students. In a randomized controlled trial of elementary and middle school teachers in Maryland, school discipline expert Catherine Bradshaw and colleagues found that classrooms with teachers who received one-on-one coaching in addition to professional development focused on culturally responsive practices had improvements in classroom management practices and reductions in ODRs among Black students.[98]

In addition to evidence-based strategies, Tier 3 schools may implement innovative approaches to school discipline that currently lack the evidentiary base (this may change with time and emerging research evidence) including but not limited to (a) assigning behavioral coaches and behavioral specialists at the school level, (b) assigning behavioral coaches for top referrers (individual coaching for top 5 percent of referrers in each school), (c) scheduling quarterly school discipline–focused school walk-throughs and observations with district and school leadership, (d) proactive group and individual counseling sessions for Tier 4 students, and (e) providing targeted support for SWDs including mentoring, reviewing the implementation of IEPs and BIPs, and conducting manifestation determination audits.

SUPPORTING STUDENTS

Although I maintain that supporting educators can often be overlooked, it is not the only part of the equation for disrupting discipline disparities. Students need support, too. Student-focused interventions prioritize student support to reduce not only the prevalence of but also the disparities in exclusionary discipline. Student-focused school discipline reforms aim to provide students with skills, such as time management and study skills, to help with their personal success. Student-focused programs can also bolster the attention to the identity, genius, and joy of SWDs and Black, male, and low-income children in schools.

Students need skills to help them manage their emotions and develop their identities. Here is where an SEL framework provides useful guidance on the skills students need, especially when returning from the isolation catalyzed by the COVID-19 pandemic. Self-awareness, self-management, social awareness, relationship skills, and responsible decision-making are the five core SEL competences according the CASEL Wheel.[99] It is important to note that although SEL is seen as a remedy for discipline disparities among many of the school and district leaders, there is little evidence for SEL as an effective program for discipline.[100] Nonetheless, recent research provides evidence that investing in SEL may contribute to the reduction of discipline disparities. Education researcher Christi Bergin and colleagues studied the effects of SEL program Leader in Me (LiM) and found that LiM resulted in improvements in school climate, SEL competencies for teachers and students, and fewer discipline incidents.[101] In their evaluation of SEL implementation in ten urban districts, CASEL found that educator-facing SEL also contributed to reducing the use of suspensions and teachers were supported in evaluating their decision-making.[102] The importance of SEL for adults is supported by broader research on VDPs.[103] Importantly, scholars emphasize that SEL can be a vehicle through which to disrupt or reinforce whiteness supremacy.[104] Quasi-experimental research on SEL interventions have found that racially marginalized students demonstrate heightened social emotional competencies growth relative to White students and this provides further support for SEL as a mechanism to reduce discipline rates and disparities.[105]

Fostering belonging in schools is another key plank of a student-focused approach to school discipline reform. Indeed, the lack of a sense of belonging contributes to discipline disparities.[106] Scholars such as Gholdy Muhammad have highlighted the need for belonging and created frameworks to help educators make schools a place where Black students feel welcomed, cared for, and supported.[107]

Student self-affirmation has evidence from both studies with experimental study design as well as quasi-experimental studies that justify its investment as a student-focused intervention to disrupt discipline disparities.[108] For instance, in randomized field trials, Borman and colleagues found that brief self-affirmation exercises to assist students in accessing positive aspects of their identities led to a reduction in Black–White disparities in ODRs and suspensions with greater effects for Black students with prior disciplinary history.[109] In a multiyear experiment, periodic student affirmation interventions lowered overall discipline incidents (i.e., cumulative ODRs and suspensions) 69 percent relative to the control condition. The treatment involved a writing assignment on personal value(s), while the control was a writing assignment that did not invoke personal value.[110] Moreover, other multiyear experiments testing identity affirmation interventions found that these programs narrowed the high school discipline disparity between White and Black boys by 75 percent when implemented in sixth and seventh grades.[111] In addition to disciplinary outcomes, similar interventions also narrowed racial achievement and graduation rate disparities during high school.[112]

What happens after a student receives an ISS or OSS is a critical yet overlooked dimension of the disciplinary process in schools. Often, districts and schools do not devote attention or resources to the reentry of disciplined students or do not have a consistent or formalized process to reintegrate punished students into the learning environment. I contend that RPs may play an instrumental role in the reintegration process. Peer–peer and peer–teacher relationships are typically fractured and in need of RPs to stave off recidivism. Empathy and relationship building are fostered though RPs, and these are key ingredients of effectively reintegrating disciplined students back into schools and classrooms. This reflective conversation sparked by RPs is key to bridging differences in the aftermath of conflict. Incorporating RP into the reintegration of suspended students may also help staunch suspension recidivism. Indeed, Gregory and colleagues highlighted that "RP may help reduce cycles of re-suspension and prevent incidents from arising in the first place."[113] It is important to have consistency in the process through which suspended students are reintroduced into classrooms and this consistency can be fostered by districtwide commitment to incorporating RPs into the reintegration after disciplinary consequences.

Tier 4? Addressing Persistently Disciplined Students

Similar to the notion of top referrers, district and school leaders will readily relay that there is a small group of students who account for frequent (and often the most severe) disciplinary infractions.[114] As such, these persistently disciplined students warrant specialized support.[115] What are effective strategies to support persistently disciplined students?

Often, these students require additional specialized support such as one-on-one instruction or outside counseling. Districts and schools need to have a comprehensive plan to support these persistently disciplined students beyond simple exclusion from regular classrooms. A comprehensive support program for these students prevents further disruption of the overall classroom and school climate while providing intensive wraparound services to get closer to the root cause of these students' disruptive behavior. The intensive nature of this support will require district- and school-level coordination. This is not a "put these repeat offenders in a box approach," but a more thoughtful approach to reintegrating these students into their regular schools. Social workers, counselors, and behavior specialists should play a significant role in the case consultation model and reintegration of persistently disciplined students. A comprehensive program may include but is not limited to (a) identification of persistently disciplined students based by the disciplinary data from the current school year and consultations with school leaders; (b) one-on-one tutoring; (c) counseling services to students; (d) proactive restorative circles, mediation, and harm circles; (e) case consultation model (assign a social worker to the student and pilot the case consultation model to facilitate the reintroduction into in-person learning inclusive of parent conference and family engagement); (f) established feedback loop to listen to these students, identify root causes to behavior, and hear their needs; and (g) one-on-one mentoring.

TOWARD THE DISRUPTION OF DISCIPLINE DISPARITIES: INTENTION, INVESTMENT, IMPLEMENTATION, AND ITERATION

Intention: Bold Leadership and Disruptive Decisions

The path to disrupt discipline disparities is an intentional and strategic approach to dismantling structures and organizational routines that produce and sustain inequities in disciplinary outcomes. Tinkering or experimenting with scattershot policies and programs will not substantively move the school discipline needle. We need disruptive decisions.

The TSDSF is intended to guide decision-making and provide direction on school discipline interventions by local, state, and federal policy makers. It is important to highlight that the framework is akin to a raisin in the sun without courageous and creative leadership at both the district and school levels. The TSDSF is a framework for frontline leaders, and we need frontline leaders in school discipline to disrupt discipline disparities.[116] A key question that district and school leaders must ask is whether school discipline reforms are educator focused or student focused. Each tier of investment in the MTSDRS targets various mechanisms such as teacher discretion, teacher–student interactions, and school climate. Each approach to school discipline reform (whether policy-, program- or personnel-based) also has short- and long-term options. For instance, adding support personnel may be employed in the short term, whereas diversifying the teacher workforce may be a longer-term strategic goal. Given the multiple contributors to discipline disparities, there is likely no silver bullet or panacea. The TSDSF provides a solid understanding of how to create a strategic plan for reducing discipline disparities that is grounded in the foregoing knowledge base of what works.

Coordination Between the District and Schools Is Pivotal

Coordination between district and school leadership in deploying resources to support schools and students is critical to the implementation and success of the TSDSF. This is especially important for schools with the highest prevalence of and disparities in exclusionary discipline. The TSDSF catalyzes coordination in school discipline strategy among district and school leaders—the disruptive decision-makers in school discipline. The framework is applicable to school discipline strategy at both the district and school levels with evidence-based interventions linked to the mechanisms driving racial inequality in school discipline. The framework also helps district and school leaders get on the same page regarding school discipline reforms and provides a pathway to consensus and action in transforming inequities in school discipline.

Investing in the Disruption of Discipline Disparities

A key component of courageous and creative leadership is making (and sustaining) the investments to disrupt discipline disparities. The TSDSF posits that in order to reduce racial inequality in school discipline, practitioners and policy makers should consider a series of evidence-based investments in programs that bolster the professional capacity of school personnel, improve school climate, and support students most affected by discipline disparities. I contend that the disruption of discipline disparities starts with the adults in schools and investing in school personnel (the diversity and experience of school leaders, teachers, and support staff plus school discipline–specific professional development and programs as outlined in the MTSDRS). The solution to discipline disparities is not through investment in fixing student behavior, which is the current fixation of school discipline reforms. Instead, disrupting discipline disparities necessitates a more intentional approach and investment in supporting teachers, principals, assistant principals, and school support staff (e.g., guidance counselors, school psychologists). I maintain that school-level programs such as RP and PBIS are necessary but not sufficient to improve school climate and will not disrupt discipline disparities without concurrent investments in the diversity and capacity of educators.

Implementation Matters

The success and sustainability of school discipline reform depend on the quality of implementation.[117] As such, district and school leaders ought to prioritize the fidelity of the implementation of school-based programs such as RP and PBIS. Sudden changes are unsettling and typically fuel some of the backlash to school discipline reforms. As such, sequencing capacity building and policy changes is a key component of the efficacy and sustainability of school discipline reforms. Implementing policy changes without the prerequisite training is akin to putting the cart before the horse.

Iteration

Finally, the disruption of disparities should not be expected to be instantaneous. The disruption of disparities in students' disciplinary outcomes will not occur overnight. It will require bold and sustained action to rectify the structural issues that contribute to how student behavior is perceived and addressed in schools. It will also require patience as well as honest conversations about what success in disrupting discipline disparities looks like. It will require courageous and creative leadership. It will require staying the course, monitoring progress, and charting new disruptive directions. The TSDSF encourages the use of a range of metrics in the prevalence of and disparities in school discipline for districts and schools to track their progress in school discipline. School discipline reforms require fidelity as well as patience to realize returns on investments.

Learning from exemplars (as discussed in chapter 5) and establishing a culture of innovation and improvement in school discipline are key ingredients of continuous learning and innovation in school discipline. Research–practice partnerships dedicated to advancing racial equity in school discipline (as discussed in chapter 6) will help districts and schools stay the course and monitor progress in the quest to disrupt discipline disparities. In addition to a reorientation of the approach to school discipline reform and a research-based framework, this book focuses on two key elements: school climate and school personnel. Structural features such as the personnel and the climate within schools are key levers of change. In the next two chapters, drawing on data from NYCPS, I discuss why practitioners and policy makers should start with investments in school personnel and school climate to reduce racial inequities in school discipline. Chapter 3 makes the case for investment in diversifying and supporting school leaders, teachers, and support staff in order to reduce racial inequality in school discipline. Chapter 4 illustrates the importance of a positive school climate for students' disciplinary outcomes. Setting the right climate matters, and school climate is pivotal to disrupting racial inequality in school discipline.

It's the Adults, Stupid

The importance of school personnel in the disciplinary process harks back to the landmark *Brown v. Board of Education* court ruling in 1954. Preeminent education policy and leadership scholars such as Leslie Fenwick and Linda Tillman have documented and extolled the deleterious effects of the ruling on Black educators.[1] Prior to *Brown*, nearly one hundred thousand Black teachers in schools increased the likelihood of racial congruence with the two million Black students. After *Brown*, the existence of less than forty thousand Black educators increased the likelihood that many Black students would not benefit from a class led by Black teachers. Leslie Fenwick has highlighted that the operative unfulfilled promise of *Brown* was the lack of integration in school personnel. Even though educators of color were more credentialed and professionally superior, numerous Black principals and teachers were displaced.[2] The effects of this mass displacement on students' disciplinary outcomes reverberate throughout history and are evident in today's state of school discipline. The demographic mismatch between educators and students in public schools and its accompanying implications for the disciplinary experiences and outcomes of Black students show that the legacy of *Brown v. Board of Education* is alive and well.

We tend to forget that in many classrooms and schools, school personnel are the only adults in the room. And it is not farfetched to hold these adults responsible for their response to perceived misbehavior and the use of discretion in their disciplinary decisions. Racial disparities in students' disciplinary outcomes are largely due to subjective offenses (e.g., student incivility, disorderly conduct) and disciplinary decisions that are at the discretion of educators in response to perceived misbehavior.[3] Scholars have argued that inequities in exclusionary discipline arising from teachers and school administrators subjective decision-making are tied to structural inequities and racism within schools.[4] I contend that there is little to no accountability for the discretion in disciplinary decision-making in America's schools. Behavioral expectations and responses are being filtered through beliefs such as deficit mind-sets and racial stereotypes. In many ways, some students are expected to be perfect beings, whereas others are afforded the space, warmth, and support to make childlike mistakes on their path to developing as productive citizens. Black students are excluded if they do not assimilate and meet the bar of White behavioral expectations in schools.[5]

It seems that educators are forgetting that they are working with teenagers and even younger children. But the adultification of some students (read, largely Black students) will do that, ultimately normalizing exclusion.[6] Are teachers aware of and judicious in assessing developmentally appropriate behaviors? Or are behaviors being filtered through the color of a student's skin? There is a need to shift the gaze from student behavior and place the microscope on the structures that allow discipline disparities to fester in schools and districts. Although discipline disparities are explained by multiple factors, recent evidence underlines the importance of classroom- and school-level variables.[7] Discipline disparities are a function of school-based disciplinary decisions and discretion among school personnel.

This chapter uses administrative data from New York City Public Schools (NYCPS) to illustrate the central role that school personnel—school leaders, teachers, and school support staff—play in the likelihood of being referred to the office and being suspended. I illustrate the contribution of school personnel to discipline disparities and contend that starting with the adults in schools is the key to solving the school discipline crisis. In what follows, I describe how the adults in schools contribute to the interrelated disciplinary outcomes of office discipline referrals (ODRs) and suspensions and argue that addressing how adults react to perceived student misbehavior and the use of discretion in disciplinary decisions are paramount considerations in the disruption of racial inequality in school discipline. This chapter illustrates why an educator-focused approach is foundational to the reduction of discipline disproportionalities.

EDUCATORS IN THE DISCIPLINARY PROCESS

The Demographic Mismatch and Discipline Disparities

The bureaucratic representation and human capital of school personnel have important implications for the disciplinary process.[8] The racial divide between educators and students, coupled with pervasive and persistent racial disparities in exclusionary discipline in schools, underlies important concerns about anti-Black racism in public education. The race of teachers and school administrators interacts with students' race and cultural backgrounds in nuanced ways to shape disciplinary outcomes. The diversity of school personnel may directly influence the interpersonal relationships between students and adults within schools, which, in turn, have implications for how perceived misbehavior is addressed.[9] Scholars have underlined the significance of teachers being culturally congruent with their students in the disciplinary process.[10] Cultural congruence, which pertains to a teacher's responsiveness to the cultural values, beliefs, practices, and ways of being of students and families in the classroom, is linked to racial congruence. Capers noted that "teachers that share the race of their students are more likely to align culturally with the students, though other identities (i.e., gender, nationality) may also foster cultural congruence."[11]

There is a demographic mismatch in America's schools that is foundational to understanding discipline disparities. Indeed, several scholars have highlighted the demographic mismatch between teachers and students and how it may affect school discipline.[12] In short, teachers in public schools are mostly White women, whereas the students in their classrooms are increasingly diverse, with growing proportions of Hispanic, Asian, and multirace students.[13] Of the nearly four million public school teachers in the 2020–2021 school year, 77 percent were female and 80 percent were White.[14] Conversely, of the roughly fifty million students enrolled in public elementary and secondary schools in fall 2022, 5 percent were Asian, 15 percent were Black, 29 percent were Hispanic, and 44 percent were White.[15] Students of color—American Indian/Alaska Native, Asian, Black, Hispanic, Pacific Islander, and multirace (two or more races)—account for the majority of students in public schools in the United States. Similarly, most of the school leaders in public schools do not resemble their students. Data from the 2020–2021 school year from the National Center for Education Statistics (NCES) illustrate the magnitude of the demographic mismatch in K–12 schools in the United States. Most principals are White (77 percent) and female (56 percent). Only 9 percent of principals are Latinx, and 10 percent are African American.[16]

In essence, the diversification of the student population has not been matched by school leadership or teachers. Students in public schools are not seeing themselves represented in the adults in the school buildings, and this shapes cultural congruence, relationship building, empathy, and ultimately disciplinary outcomes. Race at the individual and school level plays an important role in whether students are referred to the office and suspended, and teacher–student racial mismatch has been highlighted as a pertinent consideration in discipline disparities.[17] School leader–student racial congruence is also instructive for students' disciplinary experiences and outcomes.[18]

Social control is linked to the racial demography of schools. Social processes and social ties in schools produce social control.[19] As defined by scholar David Kirk, social control "is a general process by which youth behavior and behavioral outcomes are regulated, but multiple pathways (i.e., mechanisms) exist by which social control may be achieved across contexts and even within the same context."[20] Several scholars have highlighted the manifestation of social control in schools through school discipline policies and practices.[21] School discipline scholars Rebecca Cruz and Allison Firestone characterized "schools as sites of surveillance and social control."[22] Possible mechanisms of social control manifesting in school discipline include monitoring, surveillance, and punishment of perceived misbehavior of students of color.[23] Education policy and equity scholar Decoteau Irby characterized school discipline systems as nets of social control, or "a space and web of relationships where the enforcement machinery of school discipline coalesces to give values symbolic and material meaning."[24] School personnel are key cogs in this enforcement machinery. Social control is imposed by adults in schools.[25] Within the disciplinary process in schools, teachers and school administrators have been characterized as street-level bureaucrats or moral entrepreneurs, with significant discretion on the distribution of punishment.[26] Teachers fall into the upper net of Irby's school discipline nets framework because "teachers are the most plentiful and arguably the most important in-school personnel that students encounter."[27]

The Role of Teachers in Discipline Disparities

Most studies on the role of educators in the disciplinary process in schools have largely focused on teacher-related factors including teacher–student racial mismatch and teachers' perceptions, beliefs, expectations, and bias.[28] Teachers' classroom management skills, teacher–student racial mismatch and the lack of racial diversity within the educator workforce, and teachers' negative perceptions, beliefs, expectations, and bias regarding students can significantly shape the prevalence of and disparities in exclusionary discipline.[29] Simply put, teachers play an important role in the production (and disruption) of racial inequities in school discipline. Teachers often initiate the process for students by reporting instances of student misbehavior through an ODR to identify a student for behavioral intervention.[30] Teachers interact with students, parents, and school leadership throughout the disciplinary process, and as such, teachers are an important figure among many educational stakeholders who contribute to a student's (and parent's) experience with discipline in schools.[31] Teachers also play a pivotal role in the implementation of school discipline policy changes made in the name of "protecting" teachers (as discussed in the introduction and chapter 6).[32]

The bulk of prior research on the role of teachers in school discipline has focused on race and gender congruence with students.[33] These studies have emphasized the importance of teacher race to school discipline but have rarely examined the influence of other observable teacher characteristics.[34] Black students tend to be suspended less when exposed to more Black teachers.[35] There is also evidence that teachers may also implicitly believe that Black students specifically are innately less stable, more likely to misbehave and create trouble, and more likely to be a potential risk or threat.[36] Recently, sociologist Jayanti Owens investigated possible reasons for Black and Latinx boys' higher likelihood of receiving exclusionary discipline by analyzing data from a video experiment involving a nationally representative sample of teachers across 295 schools, combined with school-level data on racial composition.[37] The author found that Black and Latinx boys were perceived by teachers as more blameworthy for identical behavior compared to White boys. In addition, boys of all races were perceived by teachers as being more blameworthy for identical misbehavior in schools with large proportions of Black and Latinx students compared to schools with predominantly White students.

School Leaders and Student Disciplinary Outcomes

A growing number of studies have investigated the disciplinary practices of principals and assistant principals and highlighted the importance of school leaders in how perceived student misbehavior is addressed.[38] Notwithstanding, most studies have examined principals' perspectives, and little attention has been paid to principals' characteristics outside of disciplinary perspectives.[39] Similarly, relatively few studies have examined the role of assistant principals in school discipline in K–12 schools.[40] Principals' perspectives are one of the most significant school-level predictors of the rates of and disparities in disciplinary outcomes (students' race was statistically insignificant in predicting OSSs when percentage of Black enrollment, average achievement, and principals' disciplinary perspectives were considered).[41] Principals' discretion is guided and constrained by norms, professional standards, and social and organizational rules, regardless of the autonomy they expressed having.[42] School administrators' decisions were also influenced by their upbringing, parental experiences, job requirements, parent expectations, and fear of reprisal.[43] Numerous administrators were uneasy about the rigidity of discipline codes and made compromises based on multiple factors.[44]

Differential processing or receiving harsher punishment for similar infractions encompasses school administrators' discretion in adjudicating ODRs for further disciplinary consequences. And there is mounting evidence of differential processing in school discipline.[45] For example, education researchers Ying Shi and Maria Zhu used statewide infraction-level data from North Carolina and found evidence of differential processing, especially for Black students. Black students have a higher likelihood of suspensions (and longer suspensions) than White students, and racial differences are largely driven by subjective infractions.[46] Research has highlighted that the growing concerns about race and bias in school discipline are not just limited to teachers but also extend to school leaders. School discipline researchers Shoshana Jarvis and Jason Okonofua examined racial stereotyping processes in school leaders' disciplinary decisions using a sample of ninety-one middle and high school assistant principals from a large school district in a southeastern state. They found that school leaders were more likely to label students with typically Black names as troublemakers and endorse more severe discipline for these students, compared to students with typically White names with the same misbehavior.[47] School discipline expert Kathryn Wiley found that principals understood discipline through a punitive framework and used different logics when disciplining Black as opposed to White students—Black students were criminalized by the principal, which led to harsher punitive responses to their behavior.[48]

School discipline is also linked to the turnover in school leadership. Using data from the Charlotte-Mecklenburg district in North Carolina, scholar Andrew Bacher-Hicks and colleagues found that suspension rates changed significantly with a new principal.[49] Additionally, school leaders may also shape student–teacher racial congruence and promote positive student–teacher relationships that have disciplinary implications.[50] For instance, education researchers Brendan Bartanen and Jason Grissom found that having a same-race principal is associated with an increase in teacher–student racial matching at a school and that having a Black principal is associated with significantly improved math achievement for Black students.[51]

It is important to note that school discipline is an important source of disagreement between teachers and principals.[52] Most principals believed that teacher effectiveness influenced student behavior and that misbehavior should be handled by teachers in the classroom.[53] A recent survey suggested that there are important differences in how teachers and school leaders view classroom disruptions as well as a lack of clear and consistent guidelines for behavior management.[54] In prior work, I highlighted the importance of navigating the disciplinary tensions that characterize the interactions between school leaders and teachers.[55]

The Overlooked Role of School Support Staff in School Discipline

Different types of support staff (e.g., guidance counselors, social workers, school psychologists) can potentially enhance educator and administrator capacity to address student behavioral issues and improve school climate, and support students one-on-one outside of the classroom.[56] Initially entering schools as noninstructional personnel, support staff in each specialty area have designated tasks to address specific needs and problem areas in schools. Scholar Eric Madfis and colleagues refer to guidance counselors, social workers, and school psychologists as "school helping professionals," emphasizing that this corps of school support staff create both physical and psychological safety in schools.[57] Likewise, school psychologist Charles Bartholomew presented integrated suggestions for how these three types of school staff can deliver preventative and responsive interventions to disrupt racial disparities and the school-to-prison pipeline.[58]

The role of school support staff in the disciplinary process has been relatively overlooked.[59] There is little prior research on the role and impact of guidance counselors, school psychologists, and social workers in the disciplinary process, particularly the ways in which the presence of such support staff may reduce the prevalence and disproportionality of exclusionary discipline experienced by students, particularly Black students, who are the most referred and suspended student group.[60] Few studies have considered how the experience and diversity of school support staff may be related to school discipline.

Guidance Counselors

Guidance counseling roles vary considerably, particularly across elementary, middle, and high schools. At the elementary and middle school levels, guidance counseling activities may involve general and academic advisement as well as behavioral, socioemotional, and disciplinary counseling.[61] Guidance counselors may also engage in nonguidance and noncounseling activities, such as lunchroom and clerical duties.[62] Guidance counselors at the elementary and middle school levels often function as a resource for teachers, working through a team-oriented approach to address student needs via group and classroom counseling.[63] Additionally, guidance counselors may consult with other staff members in planning school programs to meet the special needs of children as indicated in their Individualized Education Plans.[64] At the high school level, guidance counselors play a central role in advising students on the transition from high school to college.[65]

The research literature on the relationship between guidance counselors and school discipline is perhaps the most developed among all three types of support staff. There is mixed evidence on the relationship between guidance counselors and school discipline. Some studies have found that the presence of counselors is associated with a decrease in exclusionary discipline whereas others have found a positive relationship.[66] For example, contrary to their hypotheses, scholar Meghan Mitchell and colleagues found that the presence of counselors and mental health personnel was associated with significant increases in the use of either exclusionary and restorative discipline.[67] While increases in restorative discipline were expected, increases in exclusionary discipline were not. The authors made sense of these findings through other literature documenting the changing role(s) of school counselors, which sometimes includes acting as disciplinarians.[68] Other research have similarly found that counselors' presence is associated with punitive disciplinary outcomes (or at least null results regarding punitive outcomes).[69]

However, multiple studies have found positive relationships between counselor presence, improvements in desired student behaviors, and decreases in exclusion. Importantly, education researcher Caitlin Kearney and colleagues' meta-analysis found that increased student–counselor ratios were associated with decreased disciplinary incidents (even without finding a similar relationship for academics).[70] In Missouri high schools, lower student-to-school counselor ratios were associated with fewer disciplinary incidents.[71] In Florida's Alachua County School District, lower student-to-counselor ratios contributed to a decrease in the recurrence of student disciplinary problems and a reduction in the number of students involved in disciplinary incidents.[72] Notably, these effects were more pronounced for minority and low-income students. The addition of one counselor resulted in a decrease in student misbehavior, particularly among boys, and corresponded to an estimated decline in disciplinary infractions of 15 to 29 percent.[73] Education policy researcher Randall Reback found that additional state subsidies for counselors reduced the frequency of disciplinary incidents and that increased counselor presence moderated severe behaviors, but not more mild systemic behaviors.[74]

School counselors hold a wide range of perspectives not only on racial disparities in school discipline, but on their role as potential disruptors of discipline disparities.[75] School counselors are tasked with multiple and sometimes conflicting roles with regards to school discipline (i.e., tracking, monitoring, or enforcing exclusion while also implementing restorative or community-building approaches).[76] The association between counselors and lower suspension rates are also mediated by the positive relationships these support staff help facilitate between teachers, students, and families.[77] Taken together, the capacity, role, and responsibilities of counselors in the disciplinary process—not simply their presence in schools—matters for students' disciplinary outcomes.

School Psychologists

Traditionally, school psychologists facilitate the psychoeducational assessment of children to determine their eligibility for special education services.[78] However, in recent decades, the role of school psychologists has expanded beyond psychological assessment to include the provision of a broad variety of mental health services in schools, with an emphasis on group and individual counseling as well as suicide or crisis intervention.[79] Similar to guidance counselors and social workers, school psychologists are equipped to disrupt school discipline disparities through work with classroom teachers on their classroom management and interpretation of and response to student behavior.[80]

There are numerous conceptual articles outlining the possibilities of how school psychologists may reduce the use of exclusionary discipline but relatively few empirical studies. Schools that have school psychologists have lower rates of student suspension, especially for Black students.[81] School psychologists may also play a role in supporting teachers in the disciplinary process. For instance, in an experimental study of an intervention in which school psychologists collaborated with other school support staff to deliver classroom management coaching and professional development to early career teachers, intervention teachers more effectively managed classrooms.[82] Similarly, case study research found that when school psychologists collaborated with other specialized support staff such as speech-language pathologists to implement MTSS districtwide, teachers referred fewer students (both for special education evaluation and discipline) and engaged more deeply in consultative/coaching relationships with specialized staff.[83]

Social Workers

School social workers have diverse responsibilities within the school community. Traditionally serving as facilitators of communication and linkage between school, home, and community, they act as counselors, mediators, and advocates, bridging resources to meet the needs of students, families, and school staff.[84] More specifically, common duties of school social workers involve case management, supportive counseling, and crisis intervention.[85] Typically, school social workers work closely with students who have been identified as "at risk" or in need of special education services.[86] Given their professional training on how structural and experiential factors intersect to impact child development and outcomes, social workers are uniquely positioned to contribute to the disruption of inequities in school discipline.

Similar to school psychologists, few studies have considered the relationship between social workers and school discipline. Schools that have social workers have lower rates of student suspension, especially for Black students.[87] School social workers can facilitate courageous conversations and professional development for teachers and staff on power, privilege, structural inequities, and implicit bias.[88] A partnership between a school of social work and a school district implemented a program termed the "Just Discipline Model," produced a 28 percent decrease in the number of students suspended, a 30 percent decrease in ODRs, and a 19 percent increase in students' perceptions of safety at school. Furthermore, 85 percent of the reductions in referrals and suspensions benefited African American students.[89]

EDUCATORS MATTER FOR DISCIPLINE DISPARITIES: EVIDENCE FROM NYCPS

In recent years, the hiring of social workers and other school support staff was announced as a significant NYCPS initiative in response to the challenges posed to schools and youth socioemotional well-being by the pandemic. Mayor de Blasio proposed using federal stimulus funds to invest in hiring five hundred social workers across New York City (NYC) and ninety school psychologists in high-needs schools to help with the trauma associated with the COVID-19 pandemic.[90]

Using administrative data provided by the New York City Department of Education (NYCDOE) and maintained by the Research Alliance for New York City Schools (RANYCS) and a series of logistic regression analyses, I examine how school personnel characteristics predict the likelihood of students receiving an ODR or receiving a suspension during a particular year (while controlling for student and school characteristics) as well as examine how the number and characteristics of school support staff predict the likelihood of students receiving an ODR or suspension.[91]

As table 3.1 outlines, although the demographic composition of school leaders and support staff in NYC is more diverse compared to other contexts

TABLE 3.1 The demographic composition of school leaders and support staff in NYC

	Principals		*Assistant principals*		*Guidance counselors*		*Social workers*		*School psychologists*	
	Mean	*SD*	*Mean*	*SD*	*Mean*	*SD*	*Mean*	*SD*	*Mean*	*SD*
Average years of experience	19.52	5.67	16.53	4.93	12.43	5.99	10.47	6.87	12.19	8.09
Education attainment, %										
BA	0.00	0.00	0.07	1.89	0.04	0.98	0.00	0.00	0.00	0.00
MA	5.99	23.43	42.94	38.35	4.60	17.28	1.11	9.05	1.30	10.95
Other degree	94.01	23.43	56.96	38.33	95.36	17.30	98.44	11.19	98.70	10.95
Male, %	47.37	50.29	36.50	63.03	19.25	69.24	18.32	63.68	17.83	62.66
Race/ethnicity, %										
Black	16.93	37.34	15.78	29.46	28.22	37.88	22.31	37.66	21.92	40.42
Latinx	28.25	44.93	28.90	38.79	25.55	38.01	18.87	36.06	7.78	25.34
Asian	3.65	18.57	4.76	15.38	3.58	14.47	1.44	10.10	3.83	18.73
White	50.73	49.85	48.27	40.79	29.22	37.91	31.69	42.43	45.46	48.33
Other race	0.29	5.40	1.84	10.70	1.15	8.42	3.18	15.54	3.18	16.79
Average no. per school	1.02	0.15	2.45	2.05	2.26	2.18	1.44	0.74	1.16	0.42
Total no.	701		1,716		1,482		431		298	

Notes: Based on authors' calculation of school administrative data (2018–2019 school year) provided by the Research Alliance for New York City Schools. BA = bachelor of arts; MA = master of arts; SD = standard deviation.

nationally, the diversity of school personnel is still not representative of the student population being served. For instance, while a sizable proportion of principals and assistant principals are Black (15–17 percent) and Latinx (27–28 percent), the demographic makeup of school leaders is notably less diverse than the population of students served in NYC, 31 and 43 percent of whom are Black and Latinx, respectively.[92]

Teacher Diversity Matters

In NYCPS middle and high schools between 2012–2019, 66 percent of teachers were female, 52 percent were White, 23 percent were Black, 14 percent were Latinx, and 7 percent were Asian. The overwhelming majority of teachers are master's degree (92 percent) and the average years of teaching is ten years. Schools with higher suspension rates are staffed by teachers with lower years of teaching experience as well as a larger share of Black teachers. On average, these schools serve a higher share of students who are Black and Latinx, low socioeconomic status, living in temporary housing, and receiving special education services with discernibly lower proficiency in math and ELA at the middle school level and rates of graduation at the high school level.

In NYC, similar to previous studies, teacher racial/ethnic diversity is associated with lower rates of exclusionary discipline.[93] A larger percentage of Black teachers is associated with lower rates of suspension, overall and specifically for Black and Latinx students. A one percentage point increase in the percent of Black teachers is associated with about a .05 percentage point decrease in ODR rates and .04 percentage point decrease in suspension rates.

The benefits of Black teaching staff may also extend to the disciplining of Latinx students. Latinx student suspension rates were not associated with the percentage of teachers who identify as Latinx; however, a greater percentage of Black teachers was associated with lower suspension rates for Latinx students, suggesting that the presence of a greater share of Black teachers may translate to better outcomes for other marginalized racial/ethnic student groups. This could also be reflective of a level of heterogeneity among Latinx students not captured by available racial/ethnic indicators, namely congruence among students identifying as Afro-Latinx.

Teacher Experience Matters

Teacher experience also matters in school discipline. In NYC, schools with teachers who had more years of experience had significantly lower rates of office referrals and suspensions, overall and especially for Black and Latinx students.[94] Schools staffed by teachers that, on average, have one more year of teaching experience are predicted to have lower ODR and suspension rates by 0.37 and 0.16 percentage points, respectively, which translates to about a 9 to 10 percent reduction off baseline ODR and suspension rates for one SD increase in the average years of teaching experience within a school. Evidence from NYC is congruent with recent studies that found that schools with more experienced teachers have lower rates of suspension (though there is mixed evidence on whether more experienced teaching staff is associated with lower disproportionate discipline among Black students).[95]

The significance of teacher experience highlights the differences in the approach to school discipline between novice and veteran teachers.[96] For instance, school discipline scholar Daniel Losen and colleagues found that novice teachers were more likely to suspend African American students.[97] Teacher experience may hint at the significance of increasing proficiency in classroom management to disrupt discipline disparities. Classroom management is a major challenge for novice teachers, which may also partly explain the significance of teacher experience.[98] Prior research has emphasized classroom management as an area of growth for novice teachers, with some qualitative evidence to suggest that teachers of varying experience levels employ different approaches to classroom management.[99]

The Allocation of School Support Staff

Figure 3.1 illustrates the percentage of schools with support staff over time in NYCPS. In NYCPS, the majority of schools have at least one guidance counselor, but social workers and school psychologists are less common. Virtually all schools in the available sample are staffed by one principal and two assistant principals. There is greater variation in the presence of support staff across schools, on average, schools have more guidance counselors than social workers and school psychologists.[100] Overall, there was an upward trend in the number of schools with support staff between 2011 and 2022.

Prior to the pandemic (between 2011 and 2019), it was most common for schools to have guidance counselors only (between 20 and 35 percent of schools across all years, with an upward trend in these years). But from 2020 onwards it was most common for schools to have all three types of support staff present (rising to almost 30 percent of all schools in 2022, while less than 10 percent of schools then had only guidance counselors). The next most common is for schools to have guidance counselors and social workers only (between 5 percent and 10 percent of schools up until 2021, but with

FIGURE 3.1 Percentage of schools with support staff over time in New York City Public Schools

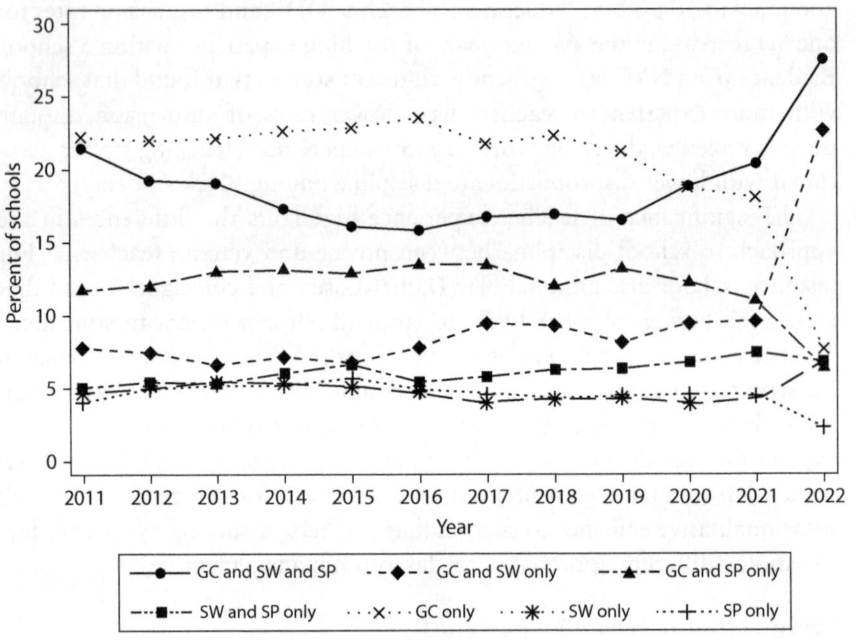

Note: GC = guidance counselor; SP = school psychologist; SW = social worker.

a large increase in 2022 with a percentage above 20 percent). It is relatively rare for schools to have social workers and/or school psychologists without having guidance counselors. Guidance counselors and social workers are more likely to be racially diverse compared to psychologists (or teachers, principals, or assistant principals).

Student enrollment and the racial composition of students is related to the allocation of support staff. Schools with higher proportions of Black students tend to have more guidance counselors but fewer overall support staff and school psychologists. Schools with more Latinx students also tend to have more guidance counselors, social workers, and school psychologists.

A higher percentage of teachers who are Black or Latinx is related to more social workers, guidance counselors, and psychologists. A higher average teacher experience and the percent of new teachers at a school are related to more overall support staff and more of each type (except the percent of new teachers is not significantly related to school psychologist placement).

Schools with Black or Latinx principals are more likely to have psychologists, while schools with male principals are more likely to have support staff, guidance counselors, and social workers. Greater principal experience is associated with more support staff both overall and for each type, while schools having new principals is not significantly associated with any support staff placement. Schools with more assistant principal racial diversity are more likely to have guidance counselors, psychologists, and support staff.

The Presence of School Support Staff

Schools having support staff is associated with lower risk of students receiving exclusionary discipline and student infractions leading to suspensions. In NYCPS, the presence of guidance counselors and social workers is related to a significantly lower likelihood of ODR and suspension, whereas the presence of school psychologists is associated with a higher likelihood of ODR.

The presence of guidance counselors matters for school discipline. Consistent with prior studies, there is a significant negative relationship between guidance counselors and student risk of ODR and suspension. Relative to schools with no guidance counselors, the presence of one guidance counselor is associated with approximately a 10 percent decrease in the odds of student ODR and an 18 percent decrease in the odds of student suspension, whereas the presence of two or more guidance counselors is associated with a 10 percent decline in odds of ODR and a 15 percent decline in odds of suspension. There is a significant negative relationship between the number of guidance counselors at a school and the risk of student infraction leading to suspension. The presence of one guidance counselor is associated with a 19 percent decrease in the odds of a student infraction leading to suspension. Having two or more guidance counselors is related to a 11 percent decline in the odds of infractions becoming suspensions.

Similar to guidance counselors, there is also a negative association between the number of social workers at a school and exclusionary discipline. Relative to schools with no social workers, the presence of one social worker is associated with approximately a 4 percent decrease in the odds of a student receiving an ODR and a 6 percent decrease in suspension, whereas having two or more social workers is related to a 9 percent decline in ODR and a 10 percent decline in suspension. The number of social workers at a school is negatively related to the risk of student infraction leading to suspension, but this relationship is not statistically significant.

Regarding the number of school psychologists at a school, there is a significant positive association with student risk of ODR but no significant relationship with suspension. The presence of one school psychologist is related to approximately a 3 percent increase in the odds of a student receiving an ODR, whereas the presence of two or more psychologists is related to a 16 percent increase in odds of ODR, relative to schools with no psychologists. There is a significant negative relationship between the number of psychologists and the risk of student infraction leading to suspension. The presence of a single school psychologist is associated with approximately a 6 percent decrease in the odds of student infractions leading to suspensions, whereas the presence of two or more psychologists is related to a 25 percent decline in the odds of infractions becoming suspensions. These odds are relative to schools with no psychologists.

The presence of support staff is especially associated with better disciplinary outcomes for students in middle schools. In middle schools, there is a stronger negative relationship between the presence of guidance counselors and social workers and disciplinary outcomes, while the positive relationship between the presence of school psychologists and student likelihood of ODR disappears. The relationship between the number of social workers and lower likelihood of students receiving exclusionary discipline also disappears in combined schools.

Experience, Diversity, and Education of School Support Staff

There is much variation in how the characteristics of guidance counselors, social workers, and school psychologists are related to the likelihood of receiving ODRs and suspensions. Notwithstanding, guidance counselors, social workers, and school psychologists play a lesser (positive) role in the generation of ODRs and a greater role in the disciplinary process outside the classroom. As such, the experience, education, and diversity of guidance counselors and social workers are more related to suspensions and infractions leading to suspensions than to ODRs. The percentage of support staff who are new to a school is not significantly related to students' disciplinary outcomes, except for school psychologists.

An increase in the number of years of experience of guidance counselors is associated with a higher likelihood of ODR but not suspension or infractions leading to suspensions. Similarly, an increase in the education levels of guidance counselors is related to higher likelihood of ODR but lower likelihood of suspension and infractions leading to suspensions. An increase in the diversity of guidance counselors (the percentage of guidance counselors who are Black) is related to lower likelihood of suspension and infractions leading to suspension, but not to ODR. An increase in the racial diversity of guidance counselors (the percentage of guidance counselors who are Black) is related to lower likelihood of ODR or suspension for Black students, but a slightly higher risk of ODR and suspension for students who are not Black.

For school social workers, both experience and education levels are related to higher risk of ODR but lower risk of suspension and infractions leading to suspensions. The percentage of social workers who are Black is related to a higher likelihood of ODR and suspension but lower likelihood of infractions becoming suspensions. Similarly, the diversity of social workers (the percentage of social workers who are Black) is related to lower likelihood of suspension for Black students, but not for non-Black students and not for ODR.

School psychologist experience is associated with lower risk of suspension, not significantly related to risk of ODR, and associated with higher risk of infractions leading to suspensions. Psychologist education levels are related to higher student risk of both ODR and suspension but not risk of infractions becoming suspensions. A higher percentage of school psychologists who are Black is related to a higher risk of ODR (but not suspension) and lower risk of infractions leading to suspensions. Similarly, a higher percentage of psychologists who are new to the school is related to higher risk of suspension and infractions leading to suspensions but not related to risk of ODR.

The presence of Black support staff has a differential relationship with the disciplinary outcomes of Black students. In particular, the presence of Black guidance counselors and Black social workers is associated with a larger reduction in exclusionary discipline for Black students than for non-Black students. This provides further support for the growing efforts to recruit and retain more Black and Latinx school personnel.

THE CASE FOR DIVERSIFYING AND SUPPORTING EDUCATORS TO DISRUPT DISCIPLINE DISPARITIES

Discipline Disparities Are Not a Student Problem but an Adult Problem

School discipline is not a student problem but an adult problem. The blame for disparities in school discipline has traditionally been placed at students' feet: Their mental health. Their threatening teachers. Their disrupting orderly students. Their homes. However, students have been wrongly blamed for driving disparities in disciplinary outcomes. The onus to reduce racial disparities in disciplinary outcomes is not on Black students or students with disabilities behaving better.

School discipline disparities are an adult problem. The disparities in student disciplinary outcomes have less to do with the behavior of students in school buildings and more to do with the actions, discretion, perceptions, and decision-making of adults in schools. Racial disparities in exclusionary discipline are attributable more to the diversity, mind-set, experience, and training of adults in schools than to raucous and dangerous behavior of students of color.[101]

If inequality in school discipline is an adult problem rather than a student deficiency, then teachers, principals, assistant principals, and school support staff are central to improving students' disciplinary experiences and outcomes. Thus, the transformation of inequities in school discipline will be propelled by increased bureaucratic representation, adult learning, and on-the-job support. The path to disrupting discipline disparities runs through adult learning even more so than student learning. This book offers a radical notion that the path to solving the school discipline crisis starts with the adults in schools—principals, assistant principals, teachers, and school support staff—not the students. Yeah, I said it—it's the adults, stupid.

Blame Structures, Not Individuals

The adult problem does not reflect the deficiencies of individuals in schools but rather the structural deficiencies within educational systems. School personnel is a singular yet critical component of the structure of schooling. The diversity and qualification of teachers, assistant principals, principals, and school support staff contribute to the likelihood of students receiving exclusionary discipline (ODRs and suspensions). The structures of schools that lack diversity, capacity, and skills of educators are driving Black students to be disproportionately excluded from classrooms. Consequently, racial inequities in exclusionary discipline can be characterized as manifestations of structural deficiencies in the K–12 schooling system. Teachers and school administrators are markedly less racially diverse than the students in their classrooms and schools. In addition to the lack of diversity of school personnel, there are preparation shortfalls that leave teachers ill-equipped for today's classrooms. Critics of nonpunitive policies and programs are quick to highlight the chaos in classrooms and school discipline challenges as the reasons why teachers leave the profession, without giving ode to the thought that the teachers may not have been prepared to adequately perform in that setting. School personnel need to build skills to manage the behavior of an increasingly diverse population.

Teachers show up every day fighting through their own personal struggles to give their best to their students. Sometimes they fall short, but they are undeserving of blame. Structurally, they have been set up to fail in school discipline. Very little in their segregated upbringing and life experiences will prepare them for their diverse, boundary-pushing students. Limits will be tested. There is a reason why teacher experience matters in school discipline—experienced teachers have learned techniques and strategies on the job that they did not have when they entered the classrooms. Teachers have been failed, and in turn, some teachers are failing the students they choose to serve. In essence, the burden of deficiencies in teacher education and shying away from race and racism in schools and society falls squarely on the instructional time and ultimately educational outcomes of Black children through school discipline.

Teachers have a hard time relating and connecting with students. We should not blame teachers for this lack of connection because it is not personal; it is systemic. Teachers, too, are crying for help and begging for strategies and support when they refer students to the office. We can acknowledge bias in disciplinary practices without blaming and shaming. We should acknowledge the demographic mismatch in classrooms without labeling all teachers as racists. To be clear, this book does not attribute discipline disparities to teachers. It is a structural failure.

Diversify the Adults in Schools

The diversity of school personnel is important for not only academic achievement but also school discipline, as evidenced by the growing body of work documenting the benefits accrued to minoritized students from having race-congruent teachers and school administrators.[102] Indeed, no one should doubt the importance of the racial/ethnic composition of teachers in suspension patterns in light of mounting empirical evidence. In the racialized organization of schools and the racialized process of perceiving and responding to student misbehavior, Black and Latinx teachers may discipline differently in several ways that benefit students of color.[103] Substantial investments in diversifying the educator pipeline are essential to rectify the historical trauma and harm that followed displacement of educators of color in response to *Brown v. Board of Education.*

States and districts should invest in initiatives that diversify school leaders, teachers, and school support staff. Policy makers should bolster the diversity of teachers and teacher educators through several programs including recruitment to teacher education programs. The current efforts of the NYCDOE and other schooling systems to diversify the teaching workforce and retain educators of color are a promising way to reduce discipline disparities. Yet, given the immediate supply constraints of teacher candidates of color, diversifying teachers should not be the single lever through which districts aim to do so.[104] Moreover, the salience of teacher diversity for school discipline also compels a reexamination of teacher educators as well as the candidates entering into teacher education programs and provides a boost for "grow-your-own" programs that develop teachers from local contexts and that develop teachers who are familiar with the cultures and communities of the students within their schools.[105]

Likewise, the importance of retaining teachers, so they can accumulate valuable classroom experience, cannot be understated. More than half of all NYC middle school teachers left their school within three years of entering.[106] Many of these teachers exited the system altogether. Initiatives that focus on supporting and holding onto teachers may have a role to play in decreasing the use of suspensions and improving overall school culture.

Diversification of school personnel is a medium-/long-term solution to discipline disparities. Even with the most generous and effective investment, the teachers and principals in classrooms and schools won't suddenly become blacker and browner. It won't happen overnight, but these are worthy and necessary seeds to plant to transform disciplinary systems from punitive to nonpunitive. In the present, the strategy ought to be supporting the current crop of educators and filling the deficiencies in the training of the next batch of teachers, principals, and assistant principals. It is also imperative not to overlook the other adults in schools who are also actors in the disciplinary process. The guidance counselors, social workers, and school psychologists also need to be on the radar in the journey to disrupt discipline disproportionalities.

Not Simply More, but the Right Personnel

The presence of school support staff is related to lower exclusionary discipline, but this relationship varies depending on the type and characteristics of support personnel. Overall, there is an empirical basis for investing in expanding the presence of school support staff and the growing efforts to recruit more Black school personnel. Giving more schools access to support staff may help reduce exclusionary discipline, but having more support staff by itself may not necessarily be effective in reducing racial or socioeconomic discipline disparities. The diversity, professional capacity, onboarding and training, and coordination of roles among support personnel are arguably more important than simply more bodies in buildings. The racial diversity of school support staff also has disciplinary implications. There is also a need to invest in personnel for the effective implementation of restorative justice and the transformation of ISSs.

Teacher Preparation and On-the-Job Support

There is an urgent need to improve teacher preparation and training. There is also a need to support school administrators and provide guidance to school leaders about how to develop and sustain learning environments that are conducive to equitable disciplinary practices. Indeed, the seeming permanence of discipline disparities ought to inspire and inform revisions and upgrades to the preparation of teachers to meet contemporary school discipline challenges by situating school discipline not only as a matter of classroom management but, more broadly, as a matter of school climate affecting teachers. There is a need to target teacher education and professional development focused on discipline-related topics such as relationship building, classroom management, and cultural competency to bolster novice teachers' capacities to address student behavioral issues.

Education scholar Dorinda Carter Andrews and colleagues similarly argue that "just as teacher education programs depend upon practicing teachers for the quality and integrity of their programs, they have a responsibility for playing a role in ongoing support for these educators."[107] The significance of teacher experience on school discipline hints that preservice experiential learning and in-service professional development may be an integral part of reducing racial inequality in suspensions. Experiential learning and professional development may function as crucial channels through which preservice and novice teachers can develop well-needed experience in managing classrooms and addressing disciplinary issues. Despite national standards requiring clinical and field experience in diverse environments, this experience is often neglected by teacher education programs.[108] It is a fitting moment to resurvey the role and prominence of classroom discipline and management in teacher education curriculum, especially as there is relatively limited empirical research addressing the efficacy of specific strategies for classroom management.[109]

The significance of teacher experience also behooves educational policy makers and administrators to consider more robust on-the-job support for novice teachers to enhance their capacity to address disciplinary issues (as suggested in the MTSDRS in chapter 2). In the wake of the COVID-19 pandemic, teacher support has acquired even greater significance as both novice and experienced teachers navigate unprecedented challenges.[110] This places a microscope on interventions that aim to enhance teacher self-efficacy and address emotional exhaustion.[111] This may include establishing school norms and practices that promote teachers' socioemotional well-being and putting teachers in a better position to respond to and deescalate situations involving student misbehavior.[112] Efforts to reduce the use of exclusionary discipline may benefit from an explicit focus on creating more positive school climates for teachers and students. The hope is that diverse and well-trained school personnel will help address the scourge of anti-Blackness in schools and reduce discipline disparities. As I discuss in the next chapter, school personnel also matter for school climate and who benefits from a positive school climate.

Setting the Right School Climate

The opportunity to visit schools is one of my favorite parts of being a researcher involved in an equity-centered research–practice partnership. Each semester, my district partner (typically the director of behavior and support services) and I venture into school buildings to check in with school leaders regarding school discipline challenges and updates. One can immediately detect the state of school discipline from the feeling and the vibe as we walk through the hallways. It is in the interactions among students and the interactions between students and adults. It is in how students are transitioning between classes. It is in the school leaders knowing students by name; redirecting in a compassionate, relatable manner (e.g., "Charles, your hoodie"); and high-fiving students as we make our way through the compound. This feeling, this sense of belonging and community—this is school climate. It is palpable. And it matters for students' disciplinary outcomes.

School climate is widely viewed as an important intervention for school improvement.[1] Prior studies have established that school climate is associated with a range of academic, socioemotional, and school improvement outcomes.[2] For instance, school climate expert Ruth Berkowitz and colleagues conducted a comprehensive review of studies on the relationship between school climate and academic achievement and found that more positive school climate is related to better academic achievement for all students and especially for low-socioeconomic status (SES) students.[3] Scholars and the federal government have posited that improving school climate can reduce racial inequality in school discipline.[4] Popular school-based programs such as restorative justice (RJ) are intended to disrupt racial disparities in suspensions through improvements in school climate.[5]

Notwithstanding, the relationship between school climate and school discipline is important yet understudied. Most prior studies linking school climate to students' disciplinary outcomes have relied on students' perception using cross-sectional data. Few studies have linked how teachers perceive their school climate or how parents perceive schools to students' disciplinary outcomes.[6] Various studies have investigated how student perceptions vary across student characteristics such as race, ethnicity, and gender, but less attention has been paid to how school contextual factors, such the composition of school personnel, may affect students' perceptions of school climate.[7] The relationship between school discipline and school climate is a complex one and may partly answer the bigger question: Why have school discipline reforms reduced rates of but not narrowed disparities in students' disciplinary outcomes? A key element of the answer to this question is the possibility of differential relationships between school climate and students' disciplinary outcomes. Yet few studies have explored whether the association between a positive school climate and a student's likelihood of an office discipline referral (ODR) or suspension vary across different students and different schools.[8]

In this chapter, I leverage student, teacher, and parent surveys from New York City Public Schools (NYCPS) to examine whether the disciplinary experiences of students of color benefit from a positive school climate. This chapter provides empirical support for investments in school climate and draws attention to important factors that moderate which students' disciplinary outcomes benefit from more positive school climates. Regardless of how school climate is measured, whether using students', teachers', and parents' perceptions, school climate matters for school discipline. A positive school climate reduces the likelihood of receiving an ODR or suspension. Moreover, the diversity of teachers and school leaders is significant in shaping school climate as well as how students benefit from a positive school climate.

BUT WHAT IS SCHOOL CLIMATE?

Formally defined, school climate represents the "the quality and character of school life," which is determined by the "patterns of students', parents', and school personnels' experiences of school life."[9] School climate has multiple dimensions; is measured according to the personal experiences of students, parents, and teachers; and reflects the norms, goals, values, relationships, instruction, and organizational structures within schools.[10] The US Department of Education Center on Safe and Supportive Learning Environments defines school climate as "a broad, multifaceted concept that involves many aspects of the student's educational experience. A positive school climate is the product of a school's attention to fostering safety; promoting a supportive academic, disciplinary, and physical environment; and encouraging and maintaining respectful, trusting, and caring relationships throughout the school community no matter the setting—from Pre-K/Elementary School to higher education."[11] The center measures thirteen subtopics in three main domains (engagement, safety, and environment) in surveys. School climate expert Jonathan Cohen and colleagues defined school climate as "the quality and character of school life . . . based on patterns of people's experiences of school life and reflects norms, goals, values, interpersonal relationships, teaching and learning practices, and organizational structures."[12] There are four essential dimensions of school climate according to Cohen et al.: safety (physical and social-emotional), teaching and learning (e.g., quality of instruction, professional development, leadership), relationships (diversity, community, and connectedness), and environmental-structural (e.g., cleanliness, resources). In a seminal review of research on school climate, scholar Amrit Thapa and colleagues identified five essential dimensions of school climate: (a) safety, (b) relationships, (c) teaching and learning, (d) institutional environment, and (e) the school improvement process.[13]

School climate is a complex construct because it can be defined and measured in different ways, and there is a lack of consensus on a universal approach to conceptualizing and measuring school climate.[14] Studies examining school climate have employed varying frameworks to organize the dimensions of school climate.[15] In sum, school climate is a perceptual construct. School climate captures how the key actors—students, school personnel, and families—feel about their schooling environment. It entails students' belonging, teachers' job satisfaction and on-the-job support, and school–family ties. Although conceptually school climate is multidimensional with vast domains and varying definitions, empirically, a substantial proportion of research has relied on students' perceptions culled from student surveys as a measure of school climate.[16]

A SYSTEMS VIEW OF SCHOOL CLIMATE

Drawing on the tenets of the Systems View of School Climate (SVSC), students and educators contribute to, function within, and are affected by school climate and school disciplinary process.[17] SVSC provides a useful lens to specify school climate and understand how the components within schools may shape students' perceptions and students' disciplinary outcomes. Under SVSC, school climate is defined as "the affective and cognitive perceptions regarding social interactions, relationships, values, and beliefs held by students, teachers, administrators, and staff within a school."[18] Scholar Kathleen Rudasill and colleagues further distinguish between school climate, which reflects group-level perceptions of a school, and other aspects of a school such as its structure (e.g., enrollment or class size), other contextual characteristics (e.g., student and staff composition or the prevalence of bullying, absenteeism, or teacher turnover), and processes that govern school norms and rules (e.g., school discipline practices).[19] The disciplinary process or the sequence from perceived student misbehavior to a disciplinary consequence is an example of decision-making processes in schools that "may form a base from which perceptions are formed, but they are conceptually and empirically different than school climate."[20]

I use SVSC to situate the role of both student and school characteristics in shaping disciplinary outcomes. Along with school climate, the compositional characteristics of teachers (e.g., race/ethnicity, gender, years of experience) serve as school contextual characteristics that can independently and interactively predict the prevalence of exclusionary discipline. Given that SVSC offers a clear distinction between school climate and related concepts like school context, structures, and processes that inform and reflect school climate, this framework serves as a valuable perspective for analyzing the connection among key school stakeholders, such as teachers, the way they perceive school climate, and the results of school processes, including the prevalence of exclusionary discipline stemming from school disciplinary practices.

Rudasill et al. incorporate Bronfenbrenner's Ecological Systems Theory that posits that students learn in various nested systems—microsystem, mesosystem, exosystem, and macrosystem—that interact with each other.[21] Rudasill and colleagues extend this framework to include nanosystems, which are situated within the microsystem and consist of structures within schools such as classrooms. SVSC highlights how teachers, students, and other school stakeholders interact in their immediate contexts or microsystems as well as within nanosystems nested within microsystems such as classrooms. The likelihood of being referred to the office or being suspended may be influenced by students' family backgrounds or schools (microsystems) or their teachers or peers in the classroom (nanosystems).

Classrooms are nested in schools; thus, the interactions and relationships in the classroom are an important component of the disciplinary process in schools, as well as school climate.[22] Classrooms are the sites of many disciplinary infractions at the core of disparities.[23] The majority of ODRs stem from minor behavior issues in the classroom, not violent offenses.[24] Prior studies (and chapter 3) have highlighted the importance of teachers in the disciplinary process and the centrality of classroom management.[25] The characteristics of teachers shape school discipline and school climate in complex ways.[26] SVSC captures the complexity of the interactions of students and school personnel within classrooms and acknowledges the presence of disciplinary moments and tensions that may shape students' perceptions.[27]

Rudasill et al. argue that conceptual clarity is necessary for school climate construct validity. As such, school climate constructs should focus on any or all of the three components of school climate: (a) perceptions of social interactions and relationships within the school, (b) shared beliefs and values in the school, and (c) the sense of safety within the school. Although SVSC categorizes relationships and social interactions as one of three key components of school climate, most research on school climate has focused on the teaching and learning or safety dimensions of school climate.[28] A positive and inclusive school climate, characterized by a sense of trust, safety, respect, and a sense of belonging, is often fostered by educators who prioritize students' social and emotional development alongside academics.[29]

Don't Forget About Racial Climate

Education researcher Charity Brown Griffin and colleagues artfully articulated the distinctions between school climate and school racial climate, noting, "Studies have consistently demonstrated that students of different races experienced school climate differently."[30] Both school climate and racial climate examine students' perception of their schooling environments, yet racial school climate studies prioritize "the identification of unique dimensions of the school environment that negatively impact racially-minoritized students' experiences of the school environment."[31] This entails attention to racism in interpersonal interactions, race relations and stereotypes, and racial diversity within schools. Racial school climate acknowledges the within-school differences in school climate experiences across student race/ethnicity.[32] Griffin and colleagues highlighted four key themes of racial climate: (a) interpersonal interactions, (b) fair treatment and racial equity, (c) stereotypes and race relations, and (d) support.

Prior studies have documented this variation in how students perceive their schooling environment. Black students tend to report more negative perceptions of school climate than White students.[33] Black students had more negative perceptions of school equity and school belonging in schools with substantial racial discipline disparities.[34] Black and Latinx students reported lower perceptions of safety and school connectedness than White students, and the magnitude of these differences varied significantly by school characteristics.[35] Education researcher Jessika Bottiani and colleagues assessed school climate by students' perceptions of support from teachers and found that Black students reported significantly lower levels of perceived support from teachers, even after controlling for SES.[36]

EMPIRICAL EVIDENCE ON THE RELATIONSHIP BETWEEN SCHOOL CLIMATE AND SCHOOL DISCIPLINE

The bulk of studies linking school climate to exclusionary discipline have relied on students' perception of school climate and have largely found that higher rates of out-of-school suspensions and expulsions are associated with more negative perceptions of school climate.[37] Research has tested hypotheses related to the authoritative school climate theory, which emphasizes disciplinary structure and student support as the salient dimensions of school climate, and found that middle and high schools with structure (i.e., students perceive the rules as fair and strict) and support tend to have lower suspension rates.[38] For instance, school discipline expert Anne Gregory and colleagues examined the relationship between high school climate and suspensions using student surveys measuring school characteristics and found that less structured and supportive schools were associated with higher racial discipline gaps.[39] Positive teacher perceptions of school climate are also associated with lower rates of exclusionary discipline.[40] In sum, when students feel safe, supported, and nurtured, the prevalence of exclusionary discipline declines.[41] Conversely, a negative or more authoritative school climate can exacerbate discipline problems.[42]

The literature has largely established that school climate influences school discipline, but there is a growing notion that school discipline may also contribute to school climate.[43] For example, the US Department of Education National Center on Safe and Supportive Learning Environments includes discipline as an aspect of the school environment component of school climate.[44] And in Denver, Colorado, discipline permissibility, or whether disciplinary consequences are commensurate with infractions, is an indicator of school climate.[45] Students who are suspended tend to have worse perceptions of school climate than their nonsuspended peers, which is consistent with a bidirectional relationship between discipline and climate.[46]

SCHOOL CLIMATE MATTERS FOR SCHOOL DISCIPLINE: EVIDENCE FROM NYCPS

In a series of papers, Dr. Luis Rodriguez, doctoral candidate Blaise Joseph, and myself examined the relationship between school climate and school discipline in New York City Public Schools.[47] This strand of research emphasized measuring school climate using different stakeholder perceptions (i.e., students, parents, and teachers), as well as measuring school discipline using different student-level outcomes such as the likelihood of receiving ODRs and suspensions.

It is important to highlight at the outset that regardless of how school climate is measured, it matters for school discipline. Better school climate (regardless of which climate construct used) is associated with reduced likelihood of both student ODRs and suspensions, across all student groups, even after controlling for student and school characteristics and prior disciplinary history. This further buttresses the importance of improving school climate as a way to reduce exclusionary discipline.

The Perceptions of Students

Let's start with the students in schools. Student surveys provide one of the few feedback loops for students to systematically share insights on their experiences in schools. Subjective assessment methods can capture the psychological experience of students that cannot necessarily be directly observed.[48] As such, students' perceptions provide crucial insights regarding how students' view their experiences in classrooms and schools including their peers' behavior, treatment by the school personnel, instruction and engagement, and the overall schooling environment. Students' perceptions of school climate are important because their perceptions are associated with a range of academic, socioemotional, and school improvement outcomes, including more positive child socioemotional development and higher student academic achievement.[49]

We use student surveys to construct two measures of school climate. The student behavior factor was based on students' responses to four items about the prevalence of other students' behaviors (i.e., harassment, bullying, and intimidation; physical fights; use of alcohol, illegal drugs, and prescription drug abuse; and gang activity) using a four-point scale ranging from one (*none of the time*) to four (*most of the time*). The school environment factor was based on students' responses to seven questions about the school environment (i.e., inclusion of students with disabilities; variety of programs and classes to keep students interested; students treat each other with respect; students feel safe in class; students feel safe in halls, bathrooms, etc.; students feel safe around the school; and school cleanliness) using a four-point scale ranging from one (*strongly*) to four (*strongly agree*). The two school climate constructs are consistent with the SVSC framework discussed earlier. The peer student behavior construct measured students' perceptions of social interactions and relationships between students. The overall school environment construct measured students' perceptions of safety and inclusive relationships between school staff and students.[50]

School climate, as measured by students' perceptions of student behavior and overall school environment, influences the likelihood of a student receiving exclusionary discipline (disciplinary outcomes at the student-level). Both the peer student behavior and school environment climate constructs have significant negative associations with the likelihood of receiving both an ODR or suspension. Students with a more positive perception of their school climate have a significantly reduced risk of being referred to the office or suspended.

Importantly, school climate is related with better disciplinary outcomes at the student level, after controlling for student and school characteristics, prior student disciplinary history, and school and year fixed effects.[51] This corroborates and extends the existing literature by showing a significant link between school climate and students' disciplinary outcomes with a longitudinal dataset, whereas prior research on the relationship has been limited by cross-sectional data. Furthermore, controlling for students' prior disciplinary outcomes provides some evidence that school climate actually influences disciplinary outcomes, above and beyond a mere association between students' perceptions of school climate and student disciplinary outcomes.

The Perceptions of Teachers

Next, let's consider how teachers perceive schools. Teachers and their perceptions of school climate provide an invaluable window into the disciplinary process for a few reasons. Teachers play a central role in shaping the school climate through their interactions with students, colleagues, and the overall learning environment they cultivate. Teachers interact with students, parents, and school leadership throughout the disciplinary process; thus, teachers are a central figure among many stakeholders who contribute to a student's and family's experience with discipline in schools.[52] Teachers have a unique vantage point of school climate that may be particularly informative given their range of interactions with other key contributors to school climate as well as their centrality in the disciplinary process in schools. Teachers' perspectives shed light on several of the essential dimensions of school climate not captured through a student lens. Drawing on the tenets of SVSC, teachers contribute to, function within, and are affected by school climate and school disciplinary processes affecting students. Indeed, in NYCPS, teachers' perceptions of school climate and teacher characteristics are independently and noninteractively related to school ODR and suspension patterns.

Drawing on teachers' responses to the annual New York City School Survey, a measure of the "overall school environment" in each school was constructed.[53] This measure of school climate captured broad organizational features, including the behavioral climate ("Order and discipline are maintained at my school"), teacher job satisfaction ("I usually look forward to coming to work"), teacher collaboration ("Teachers in the school trust each other"), and school leadership.[54]

A more positive overall school climate, as perceived by teachers, is associated with lower overall, Black, and Latinx ODR suspensions rates. A one standard deviation increase in the "overall school climate" measure was associated with a roughly 0.65 percentage point decline in ODR rates and 0.36 percentage point decline in suspension rates when controlling for other observable school characteristics. This shift represents about a 5 percent decline in the baseline average of ODRs observed among middle and high schools across the studied period and a 7 percent decline in the baseline average rate of suspensions.

For Black and Latinx students, an increase in teachers' perception of "overall school climate" is associated with a decline in ODR and suspension rates. However, the magnitudes are well over 50 percent larger when predicting Black student ODR and suspension rates, which suggests that teacher perceptions of school climate are a substantially stronger predictor of disciplinary outcomes of Black students.

The Perceptions of Parents

Finally, let's consider the views of parents. Parent's perceptions capture a key component of school climate not measured by student and teacher surveys. Parents' perceptions are a window into school–family relationships.[55] Parent perceptions capture interactions and relationships with school personnel and may also influence students' outcomes in nuanced ways.[56] In essence, parents and families have a unique vantage point of the disciplinary process, and parents' perspectives are particularly informative given their centrality in school discipline practices and myriad relationships and interactions with students, teachers, and school leaders.

We draw on parent surveys in middle schools to measure school climate. In any given year, the survey comprises responses to approximately forty items coded on a Likert scale. After disregarding items that were not consistently available across the five-year panel, a set of thirteen items measuring four distinct aspects of school–family relations was determined: (a) parent–principal trust, (b) parent–teacher trust, (c) parent involvement, and (d) school outreach and communication.[57]

Parental trust in school staff was a significant predictor of the likelihood that students would receive an ODR or suspension throughout the school year. The variation in parental trust in school staff is predictive of lower likelihood of their child experiencing exclusionary discipline, irrespective of whether their child received an ODR or suspension in the year prior and parents' general perceptions of school safety and leadership beyond their level of interpersonal trust in principals. Parent involvement was particularly important for students most affected by exclusionary discipline—Black students and students with special needs. Black students were less likely to receive an ODR when parents reported more involvement and less likely to be suspended when parents reported stronger trust with principals. Students with special needs whose parents reported more involvement were less likely to receive an ODR.

Stronger parent trust toward teachers is associated with a reduced probability that their child will receive an ODR. A one standard deviation increase in parent trust in teachers is associated with 3.2 percent lower odds of that parent's child receiving an ODR. Higher trust of teachers is also associated with lower odds of a student receiving more than one ODR in a year (i.e., being "persistently referred"). Stronger trust between parents and principals is related to a lower likelihood that students will receive a suspension. Higher levels of parent trust of the principal are associated with 11.9 percent lower odds of their child being suspended. It is telling (and aligns with the use of discretion in disciplinary decision-making discussed in chapter 1) that parental trust toward teachers shape ODRs whereas greater trust in principals shape suspensions.

In sum, positive school climate, whether measured using students', teachers', or parents' perception, is associated with lower use of exclusionary discipline. There are similar overall results for racial climate—student perceptions of both racial climate and emotional safety are related to a lower likelihood of ODRs and suspensions, albeit with less strong relationships compared to our peer student behavior and school environment constructs. However, there are possible variations in who benefits most from a positive climate and under what conditions that we know relatively little about. The next section provides insights on how the benefits of a positive school climate for school discipline may vary with student and school characteristics.

THE DISCIPLINARY BENEFITS OF SCHOOL CLIMATE USING STUDENTS' PERCEPTION OF SCHOOL CLIMATE

It is established that a positive school climate bodes well for school discipline. A growing number of studies have demonstrated the potential of school climate to reduce racial inequality in exclusionary discipline.[58] In

NYCPS, better school climate (regardless of which climate construct) is associated with reduced likelihood of both student ODR and suspension, across all student groups, even after controlling for student and school characteristics and prior student discipline outcomes. This highlights the importance of improving school climate to reduce the use of exclusionary discipline.

However, there are unresolved questions on whether students' disciplinary outcomes benefit differentially from positive school climates. School climate scholars Ming-Te Wang and Jessica Degol highlighted that "most studies to date have relied upon variable-centered approaches instead of person-centered approaches to study school climate. . . . Given the lack of person-centered approaches in school climate research, the examination of heterogeneity and varying configurations among domains of school climate has been vastly overlooked."[59]

The benefits of school climate depend on a student's context. This may run counter to the widespread view that a positive school climate benefits everyone equally in every school. The differential relationships between school climate and students' disciplinary outcomes raise questions about the theory of action for how improvements in school climate will reduce racial disparities in exclusionary discipline.

The limited empirical evidence on whether Black, Latinx, and low-income students benefit differentially from school climate improvements has found mixed results. Using a cross-sectional sample of middle school students in Virginia, education researchers Francis Huang and Dewey Cornell found that even though positive school climate was associated with a decrease in the likelihood of suspensions, the benefits of school climate did not vary differentially by student race/ethnicity.[60] Scholar Anna Heilbrun and colleagues used student and teacher reported measures of school climate in a cross-sectional sample of middle schools in Virginia and found that only student-reported measures predicted lower suspensions rates, and higher disciplinary structure (i.e., student perceptions of fairer and stricter school discipline policies) was significant for Black but not White students.[61] School discipline expert Anne Gregory and colleagues used a cross-sectional student-level dataset for students who received an ODR from Denver public schools and found that restorative interventions significantly reduced the likelihood of student suspension, but the reduction was only slightly larger for Black students compared to White students.[62]

My coauthors and I focused on a range of student characteristics beyond student race/ethnicity to examine whether school climate improvements benefit certain students more than others in NYCPS. Evidence from NYCPS illustrates that the association between school climate and disciplinary outcomes varies significantly by student and school characteristics.

Who Benefits the Most from a Positive School Climate?

As I mentioned above, to be clear, students across all racial/ethnic backgrounds (Asian, Black, Latinx, and White) are less likely to receive ODRs and suspensions when enrolled in schools with a more positive climate for both measures of school climate (using student perceptions). However, the reduction in the likelihood of ODRs and suspensions is smaller for Black and Latinx students compared to White students.[63] Being in a more positive school climate is also associated with a smaller reduction in likelihood of exclusionary discipline for male and special education students as well as students who are economically disadvantaged (low socioeconomic status or in temporary housing)compared to other students.[64] The relationship between climate and discipline is stronger for Black female students than it is for Black male students, and Black–White racial disparities become worse for males and better for females in better school climates. In other words, female students appear to have a significantly larger reduced risk of receiving exclusionary discipline associated with more positive school climates than male students, and this is the case for both school climate measures and both ODRs and suspensions.

I am becoming more convinced that changes in school climate are associated with subsequent changes in school discipline outcomes. School climate is a tide that lifts all boats, but the boats in need of most relief do not benefit most from the school climate tide. School climate reduces the risk of being referred to the office or suspended, but the students who are most frequently referred and suspended—Black, male, special education status students—have a smaller reduced risk of exclusionary discipline with more positive climates. In other words, the students with the highest ODR rates have the weakest relationship between school climate and disciplinary outcomes, even though school climate (using both student factors for both ODR and suspension) is related to lower likelihood of exclusionary discipline for all student groups. Additionally, student perceptions of both racial climate and physical safety are related to lower likelihood of ODRs and suspensions. Similar to school climate, there are differential relationships with the exception that for school racial climate there is a less strong differential relationship between climate and discipline outcomes for Black and White students (i.e., White students still seem to benefit most from better racial school climates, but to a lesser degree compared to peer student behavior or school environment).

School Attributes Matter for Who Benefits from School Climate

The next operative question is whether school attributes moderate the association between school climate and disciplinary outcomes. The answer is yes, they do. School racial composition, school achievement, and the diversity of teachers and school leaders moderate the association between school climate and disciplinary outcomes for Black and Latinx students.

School racial composition significantly moderates the relationship between school climate and the disciplinary outcomes of Black and Latinx students. More positive perceived peer behavior is associated with a lower probability a student receives a suspension; however, the strength of the relationship is moderated by the race of the individual student as well as the racial composition of students in that student's school. For example, even though Black students tend to have the highest probability of receiving a suspension, the predicted relationship between perceived peer behavior and the probability of receiving a suspension is significantly weaker for Black students compared to all other students, particularly for Black students who are in schools that are serving an above-median percentage of students who are Black or Latinx.

The patterns are similar for Black students in low-achieving schools and schools with greater teacher and school leader diversity. In other words, in better school climates, Black and Latinx students have a greater reduced likelihood of exclusionary discipline compared to White students if they are in schools with higher proportions of Black and Latinx students, low academic achievement, and more staff racial diversity (although some of these interactions are not significant depending on the school climate or exclusionary discipline measure). Additionally, male students have a significantly larger reduction in risk of suspension and ODR associated with a more positive school climate (using both school climate measures) in schools with more student and teacher racial diversity than female students. Similarly, in low-achieving schools, improvements in school climate are associated with reductions in likelihood of exclusionary discipline for male students, students from a low socioeconomic background, and students receiving special education, without increasing disparities.

A Positive School Climate but Widening Disparities?

A positive school climate does not automatically translate into differentially benefiting the disciplinary experiences of students in most need. As previously discussed, the students with the highest likelihood of receiving ODRs and suspensions are Black, male, low-income, and special education students.[65] Yet these students appear to benefit less from more positive school climates compared to their peers.[66] School leaders (both principals and assistant principals) and teacher diversity matters for who benefits most from a positive school climate. If the disciplinary experiences of Black, male, and low-income students do not differentially improve in more positive climates compared to their peers, then how investments in school climate will reduce racial inequities in ODRs and suspensions remains unclear. Ignorance of and lack of attention to the potential differential associations can contribute to the permanence of discipline disparities despite interventions to improve school climate.

Evidence from NYCPS challenges the notion that a positive school climate benefits all students equally and raises potential equity concerns, especially given that students of color have lower perceptions of school climate.[67] Perceptions of school climate vary across student groups—which may explain part of the differential associations found—but schoolwide climate constructs still help explain discipline outcomes.

DELVING DEEPER INTO STUDENTS' PERCEPTION AND SCHOOL PERSONNEL

Nationwide, Black students are perceiving that they are being treated and disciplined differently. This is being confirmed by district-level studies as well as national research referenced in the discussion on anti-Blackness in chapter 1. There are marked differences between how Black students perceive schools and how Latinx, Other Race, and Asian students perceive schools in NYCPS. Black students have more negative perceptions of schools relative to other students of color. Students of color are experiencing schools differently, thus lumping them into one category for analysis and policy making purposes erases important differences that should shape the direction of interventions. With regards to students' perceptions, exclusionary discipline is making a bad situation worse.

Black students do not perceive their schools similar to their counterparts. Similar to prior research, Black students had lower perceptions of both student behavior and school environment than White students. Approximately 40 percent of Black students were in the lowest tercile for perceptions of school climate on both measures, whereas only about 28 percent of Black students were in the highest terciles. There are also concerning similarities in the students with the worse perceptions and the students receiving the most exclusionary discipline. The intersectional lens introduced in chapter 1 is useful to illustrate the trends. Similar to students with the highest rates of ODRs and suspensions, for the student behavior school climate construct, of all the student groups, those with the worst perceptions of school climate were clearly Black male students and Black students receiving special education services (even more so than Black students, male students, or students receiving special education services in general). Forty-three percent of Black male students and 41 percent of Black students receiving special education services were in the lowest tercile of school climate, compared to 40 percent of all Black students, 35 percent of all male students, and 38 percent of all students receiving special education. Students in schools with higher percentages of Black students tended to have worse perceptions of student behavior and school environment—22 percent of students were Black in the highest climate tercile of schools, compared to 29 percent in the lowest climate tercile.

Asian and Latinx students had more positive perceptions of student behavior but more negative perceptions of school environment than White students. Latinx and other race students had similar proportions of students in the low and high terciles, suggesting they were evenly distributed across perceptions of school climate. Asian and White students were much more likely to have positive perceptions of school climate (there were substantially more than one-third of students in the highest tercile and substantially less in the lowest tercile). The proportion of Latinx students at a school did not have any clear relationship with students' perceptions of school climate, but higher proportions of Asian students were associated with slightly better student perceptions of school climate.

There were less definitive patterns by student gender. Female students had more positive perceptions of student behavior but more negative perceptions of school environment relative to male students. The intersectional lens reveals differences in students' perception among male students—low-income male students, black male students, and black male students with disabilities. For instance, male low socioeconomic status students had significantly worse perceptions of student behavior and school environment as compared to other students. Male students who were receiving special education services also had significantly worse perceptions of school climate based on both measures. Male Black students had significantly worse perceptions of school climate on both school climate constructs compared to other students.

Low socioeconomic status students had slightly more positive perceptions of the school environment, but not of student behavior. Students receiving special education services had more negative perceptions of student behavior. Students who were receiving special education services were much more likely to have had more negative perceptions of school climate (on both measures), with 37 to 38 percent of students with disabilities being in the lowest terciles and 31 to 32 percent of students with disabilities in the highest terciles.

Peers also matter. Interestingly, White student perceptions have a stronger association with student composition than Black and Latinx student perceptions, suggesting that peers mattered more for how White students perceived behavior and the schooling environment than for their Black and Latinx counterparts. For example, there was little variation in Black and Latinx students' perceptions of school climate across schools with varying proportions of Latinx students (in both the lowest and highest school climate terciles for both Black and Latinx student perceptions, approximately 39 to 40 percent of students were Latinx), but there was a negative relationship between White students' perceptions and the percentage of Latinx students (ranging from 41 percent Latinx students in the lowest school climate tercile to 37 percent Latinx students in the highest climate tercile). Conversely, White students' perceptions of school climate tended to increase with the proportion of Asian students in a school—for example, in the lowest climate tercile for White students there was 14 percent Asian students and in the highest tercile there was 19 percent Asian students, but for Black students there was 16 to 17 percent Asian students in both the lowest and highest climate terciles. There are similar trends for student socioeconomic composition where White students' perceptions of behavior were noticeably higher in schools with a low proportion of low socioeconomic status students: the highest tercile of White student perceptions had 83 percent low-SES students compared to only 75 percent in the lowest tercile, but for other students the range between the highest and lowest terciles was only 78 to 81 percent.

Predicting Students' Perceptions: The Role of School Characteristics

Black students have some of the worst perceptions of school climate.[68] Why? What shapes students' perceptions? The contextual and structural features of schools may provide a starting point to answer this critical question. School personnel can significantly influence students' perceptions of school climate regardless of student disciplinary history.

The two measures of students' perception of school climate (i.e., student behavior and school environment) had significant relationships with several of the school personnel variables.[69] Student perceptions of school climate were the product of both student characteristics and changes in teacher characteristics, in addition to changes in other school characteristics, such as school size and attendance rates. Overall, student perceptions of school climate were shaped by changes in teacher characteristics rather than changes in school leader characteristics. Changes in the diversity and qualifications of school personnel were significantly related to changes in students' perception of school climate in nuanced ways.

Increased teacher experience was associated with more positive student perceptions. In other words, students in schools where there was an increase in experienced teachers tended to have more positive perceptions of student behavior and school environment.

Conversely, changes in teacher diversity (i.e., the percentage of teachers who were Black or Latinx) had a negative association with students' perceptions of school climate. Students in schools with an increase in the diversity of teaching staff tended to have lower perceptions of student behavior and school environment.

Unlike teacher experience and diversity, there was no statistically significant association between changes in assistant principals' or principals' experience and diversity and student perception of school climate. Both teacher and school leader turnover were significantly negatively associated with students' perceptions of school climate for both measures of students' perception of school climate. School personnel diversity was negatively associated with students' perceptions of school climate.

Diverse school leaders and teachers were positively associated with students' perceptions of school climate for students of color. Although teacher diversity was negatively associated with students' perceptions of school climate, there is a differential association for Black and Latinx students' perceptions. Teacher diversity was associated with more positive perceptions of student behavior for both Black and Latinx students. The same pattern was found for Black and Latinx students in schools with either principals or assistant principals who were also Black or Latinx; that is, school personnel diversity was negatively associated with students' perceptions in general, but there is evidence of a positive association for Black and Latinx students. In sum, a higher percentage of teachers, principals, or assistant principals who were Black or Latinx was associated with more positive perceptions for both Black and Latinx students. The improvement in students' perceptions of school climate was associated with more teacher racial diversity and was larger for Black male students (compared to Black female students) and for

Black low socioeconomic status students (compared to Black high-income students). In other words, Black boys and Black low-income students may benefit the most from being in schools with more racially diverse staff in terms of school climate.

CREATING A POSITIVE SCHOOL CLIMATE THAT DIFFERENTIALLY BENEFITS BLACK STUDENTS

There is an urgent need to create welcoming and supportive environments for Black students in public schools. The negative perceptions of Black students, particularly Black male students and Black SWDs, raise concerns about whether classrooms and schools are providing spaces for Black children to thrive. Black students have a distinctly negative orientation of how they were treated and interacted with in schools that constitutes a pressing education equity and policy issue. Moreover, the focus of anti-Blackness and antiracism in public schools has been on supporting students. Yet a greater presence of Black and Latinx teachers in schools may result in more positive perceptions of the school climate among Black and Latinx students but not for White students. This motivates continued research and policy focus on the ways in which educators of color experience forms of racism and anti-Blackness as well as successful retention strategies for Black and Latinx educators.

School climate is important for school discipline. More importantly, improvements in school climate may widen discipline disparities if Black students do not differentially benefit. As such, system-wide improvements in school climate may reduce exclusionary discipline while widening discipline disparities. However, in schools where perhaps there are most concerns about exclusionary discipline (i.e., schools that are academically low achieving and schools that serve predominantly students of color), improvements in climate may still differentially benefit Black, Latinx, male, low-income, and special education students, thereby reducing (or at least not increasing) discipline disparities.

So, how does one build a positive school climate that differentially benefits Black students' disciplinary experiences and outcomes? Improving school climate is a multi-step, context-dependent process.[70] School leadership (e.g., principal vision, proactive and purposeful decision-making, and turnover) plays a critical role in shaping and changing school climate.[71] In addition to the centrality of school leaders, three focus areas come to mind from my research on school discipline and working knowledge of the school climate literature: (a) a focus on the diversity of school personnel, (b) a focus on academics and SEL, and (c) a focus on family engagement and building trust.

School climate expert Catherine Bradshaw and colleagues classified programs and practices to improve school climate in three buckets: (a) schoolwide approaches such as PBIS, (b) social-emotional learning or character education, and (c) environmental programming such as securitization. The authors emphasized the negative associations between environmental interventions and racial disparities.[72] In their systematic review of school climate improvement literature, education researchers Adam Voight and Maury Nation identified nine common elements which overlap with Bradshaw et al.'s buckets: (a) classroom SEL, (b) teacher-provided structure and support in the classroom, (c) "small group sessions for students with behavior problems," (d) "One-on-One Student-Staff Contact," (e) student voice, (f) "clean and Inviting School Building and Grounds," (g) community partnerships, (h) "Incorporating School Climate into School Policy and Mission," and (i) "social events and groups."[73] Scholar Cade Charlton and colleagues highlighted that interventions based in PBIS or SEL produce the largest effect sizes for positive changes in school climate.[74] Many of the Tier 1 interventions in the MTSDRS outlined in chapter 2, namely PBIS, RP, and SEL, are linked to improving school climate.

Policymakers should consider concurrent investments in school climate and the diversity of school personnel. The diversity and qualifications of school personnel is perhaps one of the most essential ingredients of a positive school climate. The insights from chapters 3 and 4 suggest that school climate and diversity of school personnel are complementary investments to reduce discipline disparities. The chapters illustrate the nuances and interrelation between two common school discipline interventions—improving school climate and diversifying school personnel. Diversifying the workforce may improve school climate and in turn reduce inequities in exclusionary discipline, particularly for students from marginalized backgrounds.[75] Additionally, as discussed in chapter 3, educational policymakers should consider investments not only in the diversity of the teaching staff, but also school leadership.

Chapters 3 and 4 also underline the connection between belonging in schools and the racial diversity of teachers and its importance for the disciplinary experiences and outcomes of Black boys and girls. The diversity of school personnel moderates the disciplinary benefits of school climate. In other words, the diversity of school personnel influences which students most benefit from a positive school climate and adds to the mounting evidence for the benefits of teacher diversity and investments in diversification of the teaching and school leader workforce.[76] Black and Latinx teachers, principals, and assistant principals shape students' perception in positive ways. The benefits of having school personnel who are racially diverse enhances the perceptions of students who typically have some of the worst perceptions of schools, including Black male students, Black low-income students, and Black students receiving special education services. In addition, the presence of diverse school personnel helps to differentially improve the disciplinary experiences and outcomes of Black students.

A positive and inclusive school climate, characterized by a sense of trust, safety, respect, and a sense of belonging, is often fostered by educators who prioritize students' social and emotional development alongside academics.[77] Improving academics also improves school climate. Scholar Rami Benbenishty and colleagues found that "a school's overall improvement in academic performance is a central causal factor in enhancing a school's climate."[78]

Trust is a crucial aspect of parent-school personnel relationships in predicting whether students are referred to the office or suspended. It is not only the teacher-student or teacher-parent relationships that matter for school discipline; the significance of parent-principal trust adds to a growing number of studies underscoring the role of school leadership and a host of relationships among students, teachers, school administrators, and families in school disciplinary processes.[79] Promoting trust between parents and teachers as well as parents and school leaders may be an integral strategy to improve school climate and reduce the prevalence and disparities in exclusionary discipline.

Inclusive Disciplinary Environments

Reverse Engineering Success in School Discipline

In the midst of despair, there are beacons of hope. This is the thinking underlying the identification and examination of inclusive disciplinary environments. Persistent disparities in exclusionary discipline emphasize the importance of identifying, understanding, highlighting, and replicating inclusionary disciplinary environments occurring in states, districts, and schools. Regardless of educational governance level, whether state, district, or school level, there are examples of disciplinary environments that are excluding Black students less than expected. And we can and should learn from these exemplars in our quest to disrupt discipline disparities.

Reverse engineering of positive outliers is an important yet underexplored approach in school discipline reform. I contend that an overlooked path to more impactful school discipline reforms is identifying and learning from success stories. States, districts, and schools that are outperforming disciplinary expectations have been largely ignored even though they have significant potential to improve the understanding of transformation of school discipline in education systems. Inclusive disciplinary environments provide an inspiration for the disruptive design of school discipline reform strategy. These inclusive disciplinary environments or states, districts, and schools beating the school discipline odds illustrate that school discipline does not need to be punitive. Misbehavior can be addressed in ways that don't result in disproportionalities in lost instructional time due to exclusionary discipline.

What states, districts, and schools across the nation are already doing well to address the "school discipline crisis"? The goal is to identify states, districts, and schools where the disciplinary experiences and outcomes of Black students are unlike similarly situated educational environments. Identifying these inclusive disciplinary environments is a complicated affair given the divergence of prevalence of and disparities in disciplinary outcomes as well as the variation in the demographic composition and context of states, districts, and schools. Indeed, different criteria will inevitably yield different sets of inclusive disciplinary environments. States such as North Carolina identify school districts that have "significant disproportionality" in order to better support these districts. Although some states mandate reviewing data for discipline disproportionalities, identifying districts that are "beating the school discipline odds" is an uncommon policy and research approach. Indeed, little attention has been paid to districts performing well in school discipline. There is much variation in the prevalence of and disparities in suspensions within states, which makes examining the variation at the district level even more important.[1]

There are few comparative or national studies on school discipline; thus, little is known about how disciplinary practices vary across districts in the United States.[2] Empirical studies documenting school discipline patterns have largely relied on state- or district-specific data, and there has been little empirical work using national data that are capable of making cross-district comparisons and examining variations in the prevalence of and disparities in suspensions across districts and geographic regions.[3] As such, there is limited knowledge on which districts are practicing nonpunitive disciplinary practices as evidenced by their rates of and disparities in exclusionary discipline. This positive outlier approach also acknowledges that there are states, districts, and schools already achieving the goal of being inclusive disciplinary environments. These jurisdictions represent an important source of actionable insights in the quest to disrupt discipline disparities.

This chapter identifies and examines the districts and schools that are beating the school discipline odds in hopes of gleaning actionable insights for policy makers and practitioners. This chapter starts with a conceptual discussion of inclusive disciplinary environments situated within a critique of the deficit approach to school discipline research and reform. Next, the chapter empirically explores the concept of inclusive disciplinary environments using data from the Civil Rights Data Collection (CRDC) and New York City Public Schools (NYCPS). Using nationwide district-level data from the CRDC, the chapter identifies and discusses districts that are beating the school discipline odds (inclusive disciplinary districts). Using administrative data from New York City (NYC), the chapter identifies and discusses inclusive disciplinary schools in NYC. Drawing on school visits and interviews with school personnel, I describe some of the strategies employed in inclusive disciplinary schools. This chapter helps to fill the need for school discipline research that accentuates the existing positive developments while extending the understanding of the contributors of disproportionalities through the identification and description of inclusive disciplinary environments.

BEATING THE SCHOOL DISCIPLINE ODDS

Beating the odds is a common analytical approach applied to student achievement but rarely to educational equity phenomena such as school discipline. An increasingly prominent way of supporting school improvement is identifying similar groups of schools with varying outcomes. This "beat the odds" approach has been limited to academic performance, with prior research considering how some schools in low-income areas have achieved academic success in terms of standardized assessments, attendance rates, and graduation rates.[4]

There is a need for an antideficit and positive outlier–based approach to understanding how schools disrupt and mitigate inequality in students' disciplinary experiences and outcomes.[5] School discipline, like urban districts, has been riddled by deficit lenses.[6] An asset-based approach puts the focus squarely on how Black students are punished in schools.

Inclusive disciplinary environments are an analytical tool as well as an approach to school discipline reform. They provide exemplars to learn more about the process of reforming school discipline and attempt to shift away from the predominant approach of understanding inequities in school discipline to the pivotal step of transforming discipline. The exploration of school discipline outliers contributes to a better understanding of the policies, programs, and practices that may disrupt racial disparities in office discipline referrals (ODRs) and suspensions for Black students. Scholars may find the results helpful for follow-up studies to delve deeper into the context and disciplinary approach of inclusive disciplinary environments that may reduce discipline disparities. State policy makers and district and school leaders may use the findings as an entry point into tailoring what works in other states, districts, and schools to fit their school discipline challenges. Simply put, inclusive disciplinary environments may inform the strategies that disrupt racial disparities in suspensions that would be of interest to education policy makers. The shift in approach to disrupting discipline disparities is a clarion call for educational researchers and policy makers to identify and deconstruct inclusive disciplinary environments as a strategic approach to transforming school discipline.

DEFINING INCLUSIVE DISCIPLINARY ENVIRONMENTS

So, what are inclusive disciplinary environments? In sum, inclusive disciplinary environments are educational settings that have low rates of and disparities in exclusionary discipline for Black students. The identification of these schooling environments is grounded in the prevalence of and disparities in student disciplinary outcomes and captures schools that have desirable disciplinary outcomes for Black students. This is a pressing priority in the strategic approach to school discipline reform given that Black students have received the lion's share of the attention and carry the heaviest burden of exclusion. Conceptually, inclusive disciplinary environments include schools that have counteracted racial threat in school discipline—a high proportion of African American students but limited use of exclusionary discipline.[7] The conceptualization of states, districts, and schools that beat the school discipline odds builds on school discipline scholar Anne Gregory and colleagues' Framework for Increasing Equity in School Discipline and applies an asset-based approach to the analysis of discipline disparities guided by insights from the robust school discipline literature.[8]

First, there is an explicit focus on Black students given the prevalence and virulence of anti-Blackness in school discipline. The reduction of the use of exclusionary discipline, particularly for Black students, is a key crux of the school discipline reforms.[9] As detailed in chapter 1, although Latinx and Native American students disproportionately experience exclusionary discipline in certain schooling contexts across elementary, middle, and high schools, disparities between Black and White students are by far the largest.[10]

Second, there is a focus on both the prevalence of and disparities in student disciplinary outcomes. Low prevalence *and* low disparities are defining features of inclusive disciplinary environments. The definition of inclusive disciplinary environments considers the tensions in prevalence and disparities. Low prevalence does not automatically mean low disparities. And high prevalence does not automatically mean high disparities. The divergence of the prevalence of and disparities in disciplinary outcomes is one of the challenges in defining and identifying inclusive disciplinary environments. A growing number of studies have illustrated this divergence. For example, scholar Lora Henderson Smith and colleagues found that students in majority Black schools had the highest rates of suspension, followed by students in majority White schools, with the lowest rates belonging to majority Latinx schools.[11] However, Black students in majority White schools had a higher risk of suspension than in majority Black or racially diverse schools, with racial discipline disparities being highest in White majority schools. Congruent with prior studies, I found evidence of a similar phenomenon in NYCPS: predominantly Black schools have the highest overall discipline rates, but predominantly White schools have the highest Black–White discipline disparities. Black students are especially disproportionately disciplined (relative to White students) in predominantly White schools.[12]

IDENTIFYING INCLUSIVE DISCIPLINARY ENVIRONMENTS

The conceptualization of inclusive disciplinary environments is operationalized by prioritizing both overall and Black rates of exclusionary discipline as well as Black–White disparities. The identification of inclusive disciplinary environments also spans multiple disciplinary outcomes, where data allows. There is a focus on trends in ODRs as well as both suspension types—in-school suspension (ISS) and out-of-school suspension (OSS).

Serving Different Students

There are several challenges to identifying inclusive disciplinary environments. First, states, districts, and schools serve different students. A robust body of evidence has illustrated that the overall (prevalence) and discriminate use (disparities) of exclusionary discipline is intricately linked to the demographic composition of students. Differences in student characteristics may partly account for differences between inclusive disciplinary environments and comparison educational environments, because inclusive disciplinary environments may serve a less diverse, more advantaged student population. In order to address the fact that inclusive disciplinary environments may serve different students, I use four different samples of districts and schools to identify outliers: (a) all districts/schools, (b) majority Black districts/schools, (c) majority Latinx districts/schools, and (d) majority low-income districts/schools.

Inclusive disciplinary environments may differ from high-suspension environments not only in student characteristics but also in the levels of social disorder and student misbehavior that may spur the use of exclusionary discipline.[13] For instance, students in inclusive disciplinary schools may behave differently or be punished differently (or a combination of both) compared to students in other schools. Additionally, the surrounding social, economic, and historical context is another key consideration in identifying inclusive disciplinary environments. Several factors outside of schools such as the neighborhoods students live in and where schools are located, as well as family circumstances, may influence student behavior and how this behavior is addressed by adults in schools.[14] Although these external factors may shape students' overall development and how they navigate challenges and behave in the school environment, the disciplinary process that produces racial inequality in students' disciplinary outcomes is largely situated within schools.[15]

In addition to inclusive disciplinary environments, I also identify a comparison group of high-discipline settings that is on the other end of the spectrum of these dimensions of school discipline. For example, for inclusive discipline schools (IDSs) (within each of the four groups of schools), I identify a contrasting group of high disciplinary schools (HDSs) that is on the other end of the spectrum of these dimensions of school discipline. Specifically, I define HDSs using the seven criteria analogous to the aforementioned to include schools that have both (a) a high prevalence of exclusionary discipline (i.e., overall and Black student suspension and ODR rates and the overall chronic suspension rate in the top quartile of all schools) and (b) extreme disparities in exclusionary discipline by race (i.e., difference between Black–White suspension and ODR rates in the top quartile of all schools). I then include a comparison group consisting of all other schools (i.e., schools that are neither IDS nor HDS) within each group, which I call median disciplinary schools (MDSs). MDSs are schools that do not meet all of the seven criteria for being an IDS or HDS. I compare IDSs to schools with varying school discipline outcomes across a robust set of school and neighborhood characteristics. I also examine the association between schools categorized as IDSs and school and neighborhood characteristics using multinomial logistic regression analyses. I adopt a similar approach at the district level.

INCLUSIVE DISCIPLINARY DISTRICTS

Why Districts Matter for School Discipline

The district level is a pivotal educational governance level for the reduction in disparities in student disciplinary outcomes. Although the federal and state levels may play an important part in setting school discipline policy and financing school discipline reforms, school discipline is administered at the district and school levels.[16] Districts play a central role in school discipline and whether a punitive or nonpunitive approach is adopted in schools.[17] School discipline policy (codes of conduct) varies across districts.[18] Districts also play a key role in the hiring and determining the extent of support staff (e.g., social workers, counselors, behavior support specialists) involved in the disciplinary process.

Identifying Inclusive Disciplinary Districts

To identify inclusive disciplinary districts (IDDs), I use district-level data from the CRDC for the years 2011–2012, 2013–2014, 2015–2016, and 2017–2018. The CRDC data includes student enrollment and the number of suspensions by district, disaggregated by student race. The identification of IDDs is limited to suspensions—both ISSs and OSSs—due to lack of data on ODRs. An IDD is a district with both (a) low prevalence of exclusionary discipline, in the bottom quartiles of all districts for each of ISS and OSS, and (b) low to no disparities in exclusionary discipline by race (measured by the Absolute Risk Difference [ARD]), in the bottom quartile of all districts for each of difference between Black and White student ISS rates and difference between Black and White student OSS rates.[19]

Additionally, I conduct analyses separately within four groups of districts: all districts, predominantly Black districts, predominantly Latinx districts, and predominantly free or reduced-price lunch (FRPL)–eligible student districts. In regression analyses (with all districts and limited to majority Black districts only), I examine the likelihood of a district being an IDD or high disciplinary district (HDD), compared to a median disciplinary district (MDD) as the base category.[20]

Characteristics of IDDs, MDDs, and HDDs (All Districts)

Of the 12,053 districts for which there are discipline observations across the 2012–2018 period, 185 are IDDs (2 percent), 369 are HDDs (3 percent), and 11,499 are MDDs (95 percent). IDDs and HDDs have vastly different average discipline outcomes. IDDs have an average ISS rate of 1.28 percent, with a Black–White ISS ARD of –1.72 percent, and an OSS rate of 1.36 percent with a Black–White OSS ARD of –1.84 percent. In stark contrast, HDDs have an average ISS rate of 16.41 percent, with a Black–White ISS ARD of 17.92 percent, and an OSS rate of 14.19 percent, with a Black–White OSS ARD of 17.67 percent. These are compared to the national averages of 5.42 percent for ISS, 5.03 percent for Black–White ISS ARD, 5.08 percent for OSS, and 5.27 percent for Black–White OSS ARD (the average MDD discipline rates are very similar to these national averages). Thus, IDDs and HDDs represent positive and negative outliers, respectively, of district-level exclusionary discipline outcomes in the United States.

Among the 12,053 districts, 793 are majority Black districts (i.e., the student population comprises at least 50 percent Black students), of which 0 are IDDs and 60 are HDDs. By contrast, among the 5,031 majority White districts, 79 are IDDs and 129 are HDDs.

Regional Differences

The South has a disproportionately lower share of IDDs and higher share of HDDs. Both the Northeast and the West have slightly more IDDs than HDDs, the Midwest has slightly more HDDs than IDDs, and the South has much more HDDs than IDDs. In other words, IDDs are more likely to be in the Northeast or West, followed by the Midwest, then the South. HDDs are clearly most likely to be in the South.[21]

Regional and state differences may influence district disciplinary outcomes above and beyond socioeconomic characteristics. Districts are much more likely to be HDDs in the South and Northeast regions, even after controlling for district and neighborhood characteristics. Districts in the West are significantly more likely to be IDDs and less likely to be HDDs, whereas districts in the South and Northeast are significantly more likely to be HDDs, relative to the Midwest. Districts in the Northeast region become more likely to be HDDs once neighborhood variables are included in the analyses (whereas previously they appeared to have relatively more IDDs). This suggests that apparent region-level differences in district discipline outcomes may be partly explained by differences in average neighborhood characteristics such as income and unemployment between regions.

Neighborhood Differences

IDDs and HDDs are also located in different neighborhoods. IDDs serve relatively more economically advantaged areas. Income, racial income inequality, poverty and unemployment rates, crime rates, education levels, the proportion of single-mother households, and the proportion of Black residents vary significantly across the neighborhoods of IDDs, MDDs, and HDDs. IDDs have lower proportions of Black residents, higher proportions of White and Asian residents, less racial income inequality, and better economic outcomes, compared to MDDs and HDDs. IDDs and MDDs have similar average household income, whereas HDDs have much lower average income. Regarding household composition, IDDs serve areas with relatively fewer single-mother households compared to MDDs or HDDs. HDDs are serving underresourced communities with higher poverty and lower income, whereas IDDs are located in neighborhoods with lower crime and unemployment.

Districts with smaller Black–White income disparities, lower unemployment rates, lower crime rates, lower proportions of Black residents, higher proportions of Asian residents, and lower proportions of single-mother households are more likely to be IDDs. Districts with larger Black–White income gaps, lower average household income, higher poverty rates, higher proportions of Black, Latinx, and Asian residents, lower proportion of multirace residents, and higher proportion of single-mother households are more likely to be HDDs.

Interestingly, districts in more educated neighborhoods (higher proportion of residents with college degrees) are more likely to be HDDs. Why? Neighborhoods with higher-educated residents may be a proxy for gentrifying neighborhoods. Prior research has linked gentrification to school discipline; thus, it is reasonable that schools are more likely to discipline students in gentrifying neighborhoods.[22] There may be more active, vocal parents in more educated neighborhoods who are demanding punitive discipline and placing pressure on administrators to respond forcefully to infractions. This is consistent with prior nationwide cross-district research on racial disparities in academic achievement and school discipline, which has found that differences in average achievement and exclusionary discipline between Black and White students are larger in districts with higher adult educational attainment.[23]

IDDs are generally smaller in terms of student enrollment compared to MDDs and HDDs. District size is negatively related to IDD status and positively related to HDD status; that is, smaller districts are more likely to be IDDs and less likely to be HDDs. IDDs also have more revenue per student, smaller student–teacher ratios, and lower proportions of students attending charter schools. Revenue per student, student–teacher ratios, and the proportion of students in charter schools in a district were not significantly related to either IDD or HDD status. Urban, suburban, and town districts are all significantly less likely to be IDDs and more likely to be HDDs, relative to rural districts. Rural districts are also more likely to be IDDs and less likely to be HDDs. Indeed, there may be factors above and beyond differences in student behavior in rural districts that result in the lower use of exclusionary discipline worthy of further examination. Urban neighborhoods are the epicenters for discipline disparities.

District-level English language arts (ELA) and math achievement are not significantly related to IDD or HDD status, suggesting that IDDs are not necessarily the same as districts that are academically high performing.

Overall, district-level disciplinary outcomes in regions vary above and beyond demographic and socioeconomic composition, which suggests there may be distinctive policies and practices in IDDs that may help HDDs reduce the use of and disparities in exclusionary discipline.

Student Composition Differences

When the sample includes all districts in the United States, IDDs and HDDs serve different students and populations, which would explain in part why they have such vastly different discipline outcomes. More economically advantaged and a higher proportion of White residents are served by IDDs, whereas higher proportions of Latinx, multirace, and FRPL-eligible students are served by HDDs. This suggests the presence of racial threat at the district level—a higher proportion of Latinx and Black students spurs greater use of exclusionary discipline.[24] However, differences between IDDs and HDDs are similar even when the sample of districts is limited to predominantly Black districts, predominantly Latinx districts, or predominantly low-income districts.

Districts with a higher proportion of students who are Latinx, multirace, and FRPL-eligible are significantly more likely to be HDDs whereas the percentage of Asian students is significantly positively associated with a district being an IDD. The proportion of students who are English language learners is positively related to the likelihood of a district being an IDD and negatively related to the likelihood of a district being HDD.

Notably, the proportion of Black students is not significantly related to IDD or HDD status.

Predominantly Black IDDs across the Nation

There are some subtle differences that indicate predominantly Black IDDs may differ in minor ways from other IDDs. The percentage of Black students in a district significantly predicts IDD status (i.e., among predominantly Black districts, a higher proportion of Black students increases the likelihood of being an IDD), in contrast to the finding for all districts. There is also generally a weaker relationship between neighborhood indicators and IDD/HDD status when the sample is limited to predominantly Black districts. For example, average household income, poverty, and unemployment do not predict either IDD or HDD status among predominantly Black districts (although they do for all districts, as described earlier), although larger Black–White income gaps are still significantly related to HDD status.

IDD, MDD, and HDD majority Black districts serve broadly similar populations in terms of their economic characteristics. In other words, there is a weaker association between predominantly Black IDDs and economic advantage than there is for other IDDs. Regardless of income levels, predominantly Black districts have similar exclusionary discipline levels. The weaker relationship between the neighborhood economic indicators and IDD/HDD status for predominantly Black districts than is present for all districts suggests that improving the economic outcomes of majority Black communities may not necessarily translate into better discipline outcomes. Stated differently, a better economic environment is less helpful for predominantly Black districts in becoming IDDs compared to other districts.

IDDs in the South

The American South is a distinctive place, and scholars have posited that an understanding of the South is essential to understanding the United States.[25] In her book, *South to America: A Journey Below the Mason-Dixon to Understand the Soul of a Nation*, scholar Imani Perry highlighted that the South holds the answers to many of the questions posed by persistent inequality. As such, a granular understanding of the patterns of exclusionary discipline in the South can help unlock the path to disrupting discipline disparities. However, as I argued in chapter 1, the South as a region is largely understudied in school discipline literature.[26] The disciplinary experiences and outcomes of Black students in the American South are worthy of additional scrutiny.

Black students constitute a significant population in southern public schools.[27] The three states with the largest African American populations in the United States are in the South (Texas, Georgia, and Florida).[28] Black students make up the majority of the population in southern public schools, with these schools serving 4,392,811 of the nation's 7,381,565 Black students (approximately 59.5 percent).[29]

I reran the IDD analyses on a sample of districts in the South. Of the 3,225 southern districts for which there are discipline observations across the 2012–2018 period, 155 are IDDs (4.8 percent), 169 are HDDs (5.2 percent), and 2,901 are MDDs (90.0 percent). IDDs and HDDs have vastly different average discipline outcomes. IDDs have an average ISS rate of 2.8 percent, with a Black–White ISS ARD of –3.0 percent, and an OSS rate of 1.6 percent, with a Black–White OSS ARD of –1.9 percent. In stark contrast, HDDs have an average ISS rate of 24.1 percent, with a Black–White ISS ARD of 21.4 percent, and an OSS rate of 16.8 percent, with a Black–White OSS ARD of 17.3 percent. These are compared to the southern averages of 9.5 percent for ISS, 7.2 percent for Black–White ISS ARD, 6.3 percent for OSS, and 4.9 percent for Black–White OSS ARD (the average MDD discipline rates are very similar to these region averages). Among the 3,225 districts, 401 are majority Black districts (i.e., the student population comprises at least 50 percent Black students), of which 0 are IDDs and 70 are HDDs. By contrast, among the 2,318 majority White districts, 163 are IDDs and 98 are HDDs.

The vast majority of the 155 IDDs in the South are in just four states: Texas (60), Oklahoma (38), Arkansas (22), and Kentucky (15). Six states have no IDDs: Alabama, Delaware, Florida, Georgia, Louisiana, and South Carolina, in addition to the District of Columbia. With respect to the 169 HDDs, again, the vast majority are in just four states: Arkansas (31), Texas (30), Mississippi (23), and Georgia (20). Only the District of Columbia and Maryland do not have any HDDs.

IDDs are mostly in rural areas (129), with relatively fewer in towns (19), suburban areas (3), and urban areas (4). For HDDs, the majority are still in rural areas (79), but there are still 66 in towns, 11 in suburban areas, and 13 in urban areas. IDDs are relatively more likely to be in rural areas and less likely to be in urban cities compared to HDDs.

Most district and neighborhood characteristics do not significantly predict IDD or HDD status. Among all districts, a greater percentage of Black students in a district is related to higher likelihood of HDD whereas a greater percentage of multirace students is related to lower likelihood of IDD. A higher percentage of FRPL-eligible students predicts HDD status. Among neighborhood characteristics, the Black–White income gap is associated with lower likelihood of IDD and higher likelihood of HDD. A greater percentage of Black residents is related to lower likelihood of IDD. A greater percentage of the population with college degrees is associated with a lower likelihood of HDD.

Predominantly Black IDDs in the South

Overall, in operationalizing inclusive disciplinary environments, it is crucial to limit the sample of districts to those serving predominantly Black students to better isolate districts that may serve similar students but have vastly different disciplinary outcomes. I also restrict the sample to districts that serve predominantly Black students given that these districts may especially contribute to district-level discipline disparities across the South.

When the IDD/HDD/MDD classification process is performed as above but limited to only these districts, there are 14 IDDs, 388 MDDs, and 15 HDDs. Among predominantly Black districts, IDDs have, on average, an ISS rate of 2.9 percent, an ISS Black–White ARD of –1.0 percent, an OSS rate of 4.4 percent, and an OSS Black–White ARD of –1.2 percent. These are similar rates to IDDs for all districts, but with considerably higher OSS prevalence in predominantly Black IDDs. In HDDs among predominantly Black districts, on average, there is an ISS rate of 32.9 percent, an ISS ARD of 22.8 percent, an OSS rate of 27.5 percent, and an OSS ARD of 19.0 percent. ISS and OSS rates in predominantly Black HDDs are much higher than in HDDs across all districts, but the disparities are only marginally higher.

When the sample is limited to predominantly Black districts only, the 14 IDDs are spread out across eight states (2 in Arkansas, 1 in Georgia, 1 in Kentucky, 2 in Louisiana, 1 in Maryland, 4 in Mississippi, 2 in South Carolina, and 1 in Texas), while the 25 HDDs are in six states (1 in Alabama, 5 in Arkansas, 4 in Georgia, 8 in Mississippi, 3 in South Carolina, and 4 in Virginia). When the sample is limited to predominantly Black districts, IDDs are most commonly in rural areas (6) and relatively less common in towns (3), suburban areas (2), and urban locations (3). But predominantly Black HDDs are most likely to be in towns (11), followed by rural communities (10), then suburban (1) and urban (3) areas.

It is worth noting, however, that there is a weaker relationship between the neighborhood economic indicators and IDD/HDD status for predominantly Black districts than there is for all districts; in other words, improving the neighborhood conditions of schools serving predominantly Black student populations may not necessarily translate into better discipline outcomes.

INCLUSIVE DISCIPLINARY SCHOOLS

Why Schools Matter for School Discipline

Studies on the contributors to racial inequality in exclusionary discipline have highlighted the importance of school-level variables in predicting suspension disparities.[30] However, far less attention has been paid to the ways in which schools disrupt racial inequality in suspensions.[31]

Schools that are outperforming disciplinary expectations are largely overlooked; only a handful of studies have examined the differences between high- and low-suspending schools.[32] Another set of studies have contrasted low- and high-suspending schools across school characteristics.[33]

Identifying Inclusive Disciplinary Schools

Using NYCPS as an empirical case, my coauthors and I identified and analyzed IDSs, or schools that have "beat the school discipline odds."[34]

In sum, IDSs and HDSs have vastly different average exclusionary discipline rates for Black and Latinx students, which drives differences in overall suspension rates. The pattern is very similar for ODRs, with large differences in the Black and Latinx ODR rates appearing to drive the average difference in overall ODRs between HDSs and IDSs, rather than differences in White ODR rates. IDSs, MDSs, and HDSs have vastly different exclusionary discipline rates for Black and Latinx students (both suspensions and ODRs). HDSs suspend significantly more students overall; the suspension rate in HDSs is 16 percent compared to less than 1 percent in IDSs. IDS suspension rates hover around 1 percent for all students, regardless of race/ethnicity, whereas MDSs and HDSs have higher suspension rates for all students. There are particularly large differences in the overall exclusionary discipline rate and both the Black and Latinx discipline rates between HDSs and IDSs, for both suspension and ODR. In HDSs, on average, Black students are suspended more than any other racial group; 23 percent of Black students are suspended in HDSs, nearly double the Latinx rate of 13 percent and significantly higher than the 3 percent rate for White students. However, the difference in the average White suspension rates between IDSs and HDSs is considerably smaller compared to the differences in the overall, Black, and Latinx suspension rates. Interestingly, in IDSs, the ODR rate of Black students is lower than the ODR rate for all other student groups, suggesting that Black students are referred to the office less, and this may be the starting point of disrupting the high prevalence of and disparities in exclusionary discipline. In both MDSs and HDSs, the Black student rate of ODRs is higher than the overall rate and the rate of any other student group.

Black–White disparities in exclusionary discipline are highest in HDSs. Latinx–White disparities largely exist only in HDSs. The White and Latinx suspension rates are relatively similar in both IDSs and MDSs, whereas in HDSs, the Latinx suspension rate (13 percent) is roughly four times the White suspension rate (3 percent). The racial disparities in ODRs are noticeably higher in HDSs relative to MDSs and IDSs. The chronic suspension rate (proportion of students receiving more than one suspension in a given school year) of HDSs (6 percent) is nearly three times that of MDSs (2 percent) and six times that of IDSs (less than 1 percent). HDSs also have a significantly higher proportion of students suspended at each infraction level (levels 1–5) compared to IDSs, indicating that differences in discipline outcomes are not due solely to differences in the severity of infractions.

Overall, there are more HDSs than IDSs in NYC. There are 155 unique schools that are HDSs for at least one year (with 242 school-years) and only

106 unique schools that are IDSs for at least one year (with 194 school-years) over the period of study (2011–2012 to 2018–2019). For the overall population of NYC school-years, 93 percent are MDSs, 4 percent are HDSs, and 3 percent are IDSs.[35] Among majority Black schools, there are 48 unique HDSs (59 school-years) and 7 unique IDSs (11 school-years), or 95 percent MDSs, 4 percent HDSs, and 1 percent IDSs. For majority Latinx schools, there are 67 unique HDSs (101 school-years) and 31 unique IDSs (42 school-years), or 94 percent MDSs, 4 percent HDSs, and 2 percent IDSs. And among schools with a high proportion of low socioeconomic status students, there are 42 unique HDSs (51 school-years) and 24 unique IDSs (27 school-years), or 92 percent MDSs, 4 percent HDSs, and 2 percent IDSs.[36]

Most IDSs and HDSs change categories at least once over the period of study, regardless of which group of schools they belong to. Approximately 90 percent of IDSs change to being MDSs for at least one year in the 2012–2018 period, and about 90 percent of HDSs also change to being MDSs for at least one year in the same period. Stated differently, only 10 percent of IDSs remain so for the entire period of study, about 30 percent were previously IDSs but changed to MDSs, around 30 percent became IDSs during this period, and approximately 50 percent changed more than once, with similar proportions for HDSs. IDSs maintain their IDS status across the seven-year period for an average of about two years (similar for HDSs), suggesting that positive or negative outlier schools in terms of discipline do not necessarily maintain their particular disciplinary environment over time. Because schools are classified as IDSs based on seven different criteria, it is unsurprising that schools may often change classification due to small movements in at least one of the discipline measures. This indicates the difficulty in achieving and maintaining IDS status but, at the same time, suggests that the IDS school-years in the analyses reflect schools that are genuinely excelling in inclusive disciplinary practices at a point in time and are not merely the result of statistical noise.

Characteristics of Inclusive Disciplinary Schools

Neighborhood Differences

IDSs and HDSs are located in generally different neighborhoods. IDSs tend to be located in neighborhoods that are more economically advantaged than those of MDSs and HDSs. IDSs are located in neighborhoods with lower serious crime and violent serious crime rates. The diversity and demographic composition of the neighborhoods in which IDSs and HDSs are located are quite similar with three exceptions: the proportion of the Black population, proportion of foreign-born population, and education level. There are no significant differences in the racial diversity or proportion of Latinx residents in the neighborhoods in which IDSs, MDSs, and HDSs are located. However, IDSs are situated in neighborhoods with a much lower percentage of Black residents (10 percent), compared to HDSs (29 percent) and MDSs (26 percent). Conversely, IDS neighborhoods have a larger foreign-born population (36 percent) relative to MDS (35 percent) and HDS (33 percent) neighborhoods. Neighborhoods where IDSs are located also have a higher proportion of the population with a bachelor's degree or higher. Three significant neighborhood characteristics that predict whether schools are IDSs or HDSs are crime, percentage of Latinx residents, and education level of neighborhoods. Schools in neighborhoods with higher proportions of Latinx population are more likely to be IDSs and less likely to be HDSs. Schools in neighborhoods with higher serious crime rates are less likely to be IDSs and HDSs. Schools in neighborhoods with higher education levels are less likely to be HDSs.

Student Composition Differences

There are significant differences in the students served by IDSs, MDSs, and HDSs. HDSs have a larger proportion of Black students (42 percent) than MDSs (36 percent) and IDSs (19 percent). However, there are no significant differences in the percentage of Latinx students in IDSs, MDSs, and HDSs. IDSs have a larger proportion of Asian, White, and other-race students relative to MDSs and HDSs. The most glaring difference between the demographic composition of IDSs and HDSs is in the proportion of students who are low socioeconomic status. In HDSs, roughly 88 percent of students are low socioeconomic status compared to 70 percent in IDSs. Similarly, HDSs also serve a higher proportion of students who are in temporary housing compared to MDSs and IDSs. HDSs (25 percent) also serve a higher proportion of students who are receiving special education services relative to IDSs (13 percent) and MDSs (21 percent). Additionally, IDSs tend to have higher proportions of students attending the school who live outside of the school neighborhood (census tract) compared to MDSs and HDSs. This suggests that IDSs are in-demand schools that may be attracting more White and advantaged students.

Schools with a greater proportion of Black students are less likely to be an IDS. In contrast, schools with higher percentages of other-race students are significantly more likely to be an IDS (but this significance disappears with the inclusion of neighborhood characteristics). Schools with higher percentages of low socioeconomic status students are more likely to be HDSs. Similarly, schools with higher proportions of students in temporary housing are less likely to be IDSs. Schools with a greater proportion of students who are receiving special education services are significantly more likely to be HDSs and less likely to be IDSs.

School Characteristic Differences

IDSs have more experienced teachers and school administrators than HDSs. There are significant differences among IDSs, MDSs, and HDSs in average years of teaching experience and the percentage of teachers who are Black or Latinx. IDSs have significantly more experienced teachers, suggesting that lower prevalence of and disparities in exclusionary discipline is related to having more experienced teachers. Schools with more experienced teachers are significantly more likely to be IDSs and less likely to be HDSs; each additional year of average teaching experience is associated with a 10 percent increase in the odds of that school being an IDS and a 9 percent decrease in the odds of that school being an HDS, rather than an MDS. IDSs also tend to have more experienced principals—an average of nineteen years for IDSs compared to eighteen years for MDSs and fifteen years for HDSs. Similar to principals, assistant principals of IDSs also tend to be significantly more experienced than assistant principals of MDSs or HDSs.

A key distinction between IDSs and HDSs is school climate (as reported on student and teacher surveys). School climate is significantly more positive in IDSs than MDSs or HDSs. Schools where students have better perceptions of school climate are significantly more likely to be IDSs, whereas schools with students who have worse perceptions of school climate are significantly more likely to be HDSs.

Results are mostly similar regardless of school group (all schools and predominantly Black or Latinx or low socioeconomic status), which provides evidence that the characteristics of IDSs are robust. The consistency of results across different operationalizations suggests that the criteria for IDSs identify a distinct set of schools with laudable disciplinary outcomes (both the prevalence of and disparities in ODRs and suspensions), regardless of the type of students they serve.

Predominantly Black IDS

Operationalizing IDSs using predominantly Black schools provides a measure well-aligned with the asset-based approach of IDSs—schools beating the school discipline odds that predominantly serve the students affected by discipline disparities.

For predominantly Black schools, there is generally a weaker relationship between neighborhood indicators and IDS/MDS/HDS status compared to the analysis for all schools. The neighborhood economic indicators have a lower magnitude and level of significance than for all schools, indicating that there is a weaker association between predominantly Black IDSs and economic advantage than there is for other IDSs. Stated differently, being in a better economic environment is less helpful for predominantly Black schools in becoming IDSs, compared to other schools. Another difference is that predominantly Black IDSs tend to be located in areas with higher levels of education, the opposite of our previous finding for all IDSs.

A notable difference is that, for all schools, IDSs tend to have a significantly lower proportion of Black and Latinx teachers, whereas when the sample is limited to predominantly Black schools, IDSs have significantly more teacher racial diversity compared to MDSs and HDSs. In addition, predominantly Black IDSs are also significantly more likely to have Black or Latinx assistant principals (previously, the difference for assistant principal racial diversity was insignificant).

DELVING DEEPER INTO INCLUSIVE DISCIPLINARY SCHOOLS

After identifying IDSs, the next step was to understand the inner workings of these schools. To do so, I recruited two of the identified IDSs in NYC to further unpack whether and how differences in educators' practices or differences in student behaviors or other salient differences (e.g., differences in resources at the school level) are instructive in school discipline outcomes. One of the schools was the rare predominantly Black IDS. My research team and I conducted individual interviews of principals, assistant principals, deans, teachers, guidance counselors, social workers, and school psychologists in each school. We quizzed school personnel on the ingredients of an IDS, with an emphasis on disciplinary practices and outcomes: What explains your low discipline rates? How do you support teachers to better navigate student misbehavior? How do other school personnel such as social workers and counselors contribute to the low prevalence of exclusionary discipline? We also conducted school observations.

Relationships, Relationships, Relationships

Looking into the black box of IDSs highlights the importance of culturally responsive practices and intentional relationship and community building in shaping students' disciplinary outcomes—not only teacher–student relationships but a host of relationships spanning the school ecosystem. The interpersonal relationships in schools have real and substantive implications for how perceived misbehavior is addressed. Relationships are foundational to the preventative approach to inclusive school discipline at both school sites. There is an intentional effort to build student–teacher, student–student, and school–family relationships, and these relationships are leveraged as a replacement for punitive or exclusionary practices.

IDSs foster strong relationships with families and parents. School personnel go above and beyond to ensure consistent and flexible communication and dialogue with parents through the disciplinary process. Proactive communication with parents to establish expectations encourages and promotes balanced accountability. Relationship building with parents, not just students, is a crucial plank of addressing inequality in school discipline. There is an emphasis on "letting parents know we care" and talking to parents about support at home with an eye toward syncing school and family norms and support. Often, parents may react to disciplinary infractions with "We don't see it at home." School leaders may invite parents to observe some behavior. In the wake of the COVID-19 pandemic, there was a divide between schools and families that could widen if not arrested by intentional initiatives.

Relationships are also important for community building within schools. Setting behavior expectations schoolwide and in each individual classroom was a key element of IDSs that was linked to relationship building. "Understanding the why" is an essential element of a nonpunitive approach. IDSs invest heavily in setting expectations at the start of the school year—not only expectations of teachers and assistant principals but also expectations for students and parents. Understanding roles and expectations of families and students is an often-overlooked element of the disciplinary process. School leaders underline the importance of expectation and norm setting at the beginning of the year. This is the primary emphasis in the first fifteen days. IDSs typically use the first month of the school year to establish routines, norms, and expectations. There is also an emphasis on sustained norm setting to shape behavioral expectations (orientation at the start of the year as well as when students return from breaks). Consistent reminders and dialoguing occur daily throughout the school with all staff members.

Relationship building is also connected to instruction focus. Authentic relationships lead to a willingness to engage in learning. Intentionally building relationships through prompts and collaborative activities is used in the classroom as a pedagogical strategy to increase engagement among students. Cultural congruence and cultural awareness also are key parts to building strong relationships.

Adult Well-Being

IDSs prioritizes supporting the health of both students *and* educators. There have been reports of higher levels of anxiety and depression among students as they grapple with the social isolation from the pandemic and learning how to do in-person schools again.[37] This has precipitated a heightened focus on supporting students. But IDSs also prioritize educators' mental health. Supporting educators in the disciplinary process is crucial—this includes coaching, modeling, professional development, and mental health support for teachers and school leaders. In supporting both student and educator health, IDSs financially prioritize mental health providers in specific roles (e.g., deans, social workers) and in partner organizations for both adults and students.

IDSs create happy teachers. School leaders may institute a system of check-in with their staff. Regular check-ins between principals and teachers are pivotal to prevent teachers from feeling overwhelmed, and they allow schools leaders to be proactive with support. One of the most important components of supporting teachers is communication. Leaders in IDSs are not afraid to have courageous conversations about biases in the classroom. At the same time, teachers feel well supported and are encouraged through training to get to the root cause of perceived student misbehavior. Training starts with preplanning, and the best training is through modeling. Simply put, teacher training and professional development are important elements of supporting educators in inclusive disciplinary schools.

Leaders of IDS schools also need support. If there was a wish list to reduce discipline disparities, principal coaching would be one of the first items. Principals need coaching on several dimensions of schooling related to school discipline including but not limited to: (a) relationship building, (b) communicating with parents and families, and (c) navigating tensions in the disciplinary process.[38]

Lifting Student Voices

Student voices and experiences are centered in IDSs. Student perspectives lead to actual changes in the school community and in teaching and learning, such as informing the professional learning and instructional vision. Attention to student voice also informs an intentional focus on belonging. There is a priority to "make school a place where kids want to be." This starts with a school leader who listens and engages. Student engagement is key. "Love" and "joy" are words school leaders of IDSs bandy about when describing the necessity of creating a caring environment. "We were kids before as well," and "They're still children, and sometimes, we criminalize them because we forget they're children" are sentiments that rang through conversations. The link between student engagement and empathy is clear as day. Culturally sustaining pedagogies are also related to lifting student voices. In IDSs, there is celebration of student and staff identities and stories—celebration of authenticity—and disruption of deficit beliefs about Black, Indigenous, Latinx, and Asian students.

CREATING INCLUSIVE DISCIPLINARY ENVIRONMENTS

The stubbornness of discipline disparities places increased emphasis on identifying, understanding, highlighting, and replicating effective approaches to reducing the use of exclusionary discipline. One of the main elements of disrupting discipline disparities is learning from success in local contexts. Districts should identify IDS and expand opportunities to share useful strategies and practices that can be immediately implemented.

Underscoring the Importance of School Climate and School Personnel

Examining inclusive disciplinary environments provides further evidence that teacher and school leader diversity, teacher experience, and school climate matter for school discipline. IDSs are more likely to be schools with an experienced teaching staff, led by Black or Latinx principals with positive school climates, underscoring the importance of the within-school process in the production of racial inequities in school discipline. Neighborhoods have little association with schools being IDSs when school characteristics are accounted for. In other words, HDSs are not necessarily schools in poor and crime-ridden neighborhoods but, rather, schools with less positive school climate, a higher proportion of students who are low socioeconomic status or receiving special education services, and less experienced teachers.

Creating a positive school climate is paramount to disrupting discipline disparities. Likewise, a diverse and experienced staff is crucial. IDSs have a diverse set of adults in the building. A more diverse school personnel is especially important for schools that serve predominantly Black students. School leaders are central to foster inclusive disciplinary practices. Without a supportive, visionary leader, we can't do any of these things. School leaders set a clear culture and climate that extend grace to understand students and view suspensions as a last resort.

Context Matters

The sociological context of districts and schools matters for school discipline. The state of school discipline in districts is partly reflective of the social and economic context of surrounding neighborhoods. Districts with more Black residents and residents of color are more likely to have a high prevalence of and disparities in suspensions. This is congruent with evidence of racial threat in school discipline as Whites respond via social control to the increasing proportion of residents of color.

Inclusive disciplinary environments at both the district and the school level suggests that we need to pay more attention to context. Particularly, the surrounding social and economic context in which discipline disparities are birthed and sustained in schools. There are several key lessons in identifying inclusive disciplinary environments at the district and school level. There are some notable differences between IDD and IDS worthy of further examination. Neighborhoods—education level—academic achievement. At the school level, most neighborhood characteristics did not significantly predict schools being IDSs. Neighborhood factors are much more predictive of IDD and HDD status. For instance, IDDs are predicted by average household income, the poverty rate, and the unemployment rate, whereas none of these variables had significance for IDSs. It may be that neighborhood characteristics matter more for district-level disciplinary outcomes than they do for individual schools within a district.

Inclusive Disciplinary Environments Are Not Necessarily High-Performing Environments

The exploration of inclusive disciplinary environments illustrates the complex relationship between improving school discipline and improving academic achievement. Schools may use suspensions to remove low-achieving students.[39] Academic challenges may also catalyze and foster student misbehavior, resulting in higher prevalence of exclusionary discipline.[40] There is a sense among educators that students struggling with the curriculum misbehave to escape instruction.

At the district level, high-performing districts are not the other side of the coin of IDDs. It is also noteworthy that in regression analyses, there is no significant relationship between district-level academic achievement (ELA and math scores) and IDD or HDD status. This suggests that IDDs are not necessarily the same districts that are high performers on standardized literacy and numeracy tests. At the school level, there are significant differences in the academic achievement—graduation rates and math and ELA proficiency—of IDSs, MDSs, and HDSs. MDSs have a higher graduation rate and percentage of students proficient in math and ELA than IDSs and HDSs. IDSs are performing slightly better academically than HDSs.

The link between disciplinary approach and student achievement is not linear or straightforward. Academic and student engagement are key considerations in solving the school discipline dilemma. Student learning is the ultimate goal of schools, and restoring instructional time that would have been lost to exclusion provides a foundation for academic improvement. Notwithstanding, there are other factors at play in boosting test scores such as teachers' instructional capacity and the academic supports and resources available for students. Inclusive disciplinary environments will be undermined and disparaged if academic achievement is not improved over time. Yet it is important to recognize that the strategies that foster inclusive disciplinary environments may not necessarily be the same strategies that improve academic achievement. As such, inclusive disciplinary environments will have to walk and chew gum at the same time (i.e., focus on improving discipline and improving academics as a two-pronged goal).

CHAPTER 6

Conclusion

The Black Future of School Discipline

At some point in history, educational stakeholders apparently became comfortable with school discipline resembling the criminal justice system. Consider the striking similarities in the statistics of who is incarcerated in society and who is suspended in schools.[1] The pathway toward improvement in school discipline cannot avoid honest conversations about the role of race and culture in education and society. The disciplinary experiences of Black students in K–12 schools are an urgent social justice issue. Black children—Black males, Black females, and Black students with disabilities—bear the brunt of a carceral society often due to structural factors rather than how they behave. Black and White students are being disciplined differently in schools. Millions of lost instructional days due to suspensions are linked to lower student achievement and adverse adult outcomes for Black students. Teachers are now becoming the refuge of advocates of law and order in school discipline. The demand for carcerality has replaced compassion in schools, and this may partly explain disparities in students' disciplinary outcomes. One of the central barriers to equal educational opportunity in the United States is racial disparities in school discipline.

The preceding chapters have (a) presented the Transforming School Discipline Strategic Framework (TSDSF) with research-based interventions and a sequence of concrete steps to help guide practitioners and policy makers in the quest to reduce racial inequality in exclusionary discipline, and (b) detailed the underlying rationale of an educator-focused approach intended to spark change in the disciplinary process in schools. The TSDSF provides a useful and actionable tool in the reimagination of a new state of school discipline. The TSDSF centers the evidence and is a pathway to implementing interventions with intentionality. By now, you will be quite familiar with the contours of the school discipline crisis. Lives and livelihoods are at stake while we figure out the answer to the pressing question of what we can do to reduce the prevalence of and disparities in exclusionary discipline, especially in a political climate of ambivalence and race neutrality. The transformation of school discipline will have to occur within a context of polarization.

Can you imagine a schooling system with no racial inequality in school discipline and what that would mean, more broadly, for inequality in education and society? Such a future would require a coordinated intergovernmental reform effort among federal, state, and local education agencies; greater investments in school discipline reforms; and enhanced school discipline data collection and analysis to eradicate discipline disparities.

In this concluding chapter, I offer a vision of the "Black future" of school discipline and outline roles that the federal government and states may play in shaping school discipline policies and practices to attain such progress. When I say "Black future" of school discipline, leaning on scholars of Afrofuturism, I mean a disciplinary process in schools that centers the wellness, joy, and advancement of Black students. I am applying the imaginative and liberatory ethos of Afrofuturism to the debacle of discipline disparities.[2] As eloquently noted by scholar Stephanie Toliver, "If BlackCrit asks, 'what does it mean to suffer?', Afrofuturism provides a way to consider how Black people might become free of suffering."[3] I articulate a list of needs in order to improve the disciplinary experiences and outcomes of Black students. I argue that the Black Future of School Discipline and the creation of inclusive disciplinary environments require ending race neutrality in the approach to school discipline policy, separating school safety from school discipline in policy discussions, and injecting accountability in disciplinary decisions. I call for leveraging of research evidence through research–practice partnerships. In the words of the great Otis Redding, "It's been a long, long time coming, but I know a change is gonna come." Indeed, the arc of this book—from the discussion of contributing factors in the introduction to imagining the transformation of school discipline—parallels the arc from Afropessimism to Afrofuturism in consideration of discipline disparities and reforms.

SAY IT LOUD . . .

Afrofuturism scholars such as Stephanie Toliver, Chezare Warren, and fahima ife have implored us to center Black students.[4] This is at the core of reimagining the disciplinary process in schools. It is important to align the contributors to disparities with interventions in order to disrupt, not perpetuate, the current anti-Black disciplinary systems in schools. Stephanie Toliver highlighted "how Afrofuturism acknowledges the antiblackness embedded in the USA."[5] We must understand discipline disparities as the product of a vicious cycle starting with low expectations and perceptions of adults in school buildings.[6] We must understand that anti-Blackness in school discipline manifests as a malaise among Black students. These understandings urge us to break the cycle by reframing student misbehavior as a justifiable resistance to anti-Black racism and hostile schooling environments instead of an innate propensity to misbehave or a result of traumatic non-school-related experiences out of educators' and school leaders' control. Instead of focusing on solutions that attempt to change Black student behavior, interventions ought to address educators' anti-Black bias and dehumanizing mind-sets, build an authentic and trusting relationship between educators and Black students, and change policies and practices that reinforce White, middle-class behavior standards.[7]

The divergence between what students (read: Black students) say about their disciplinary experiences and the growing demand of largely White teachers for greater discretion to exclude students indicates that something is awry in America's public schools.[8] Students are begging for empathy and understanding as well as the opportunity to be a student and learn from mistakes, whereas teachers are decrying disruptive students who are robbing their orderly peers from learning. Instead of protection in schools, Black students are afforded exclusion, with its attendant stigmatization and potential for recidivism. Are Black students getting a fair shot in public schools? Or are they being robbed of critical instructional time under the auspices of school discipline?

More than ever before, there is a need to apply Afrofuturism to disrupt discipline disparities. Afrofuturism urges a focus on creating Black healing, learning, and resistance spaces with Black students, educators, and families in schools, as education researchers Chezare Warren and Justin Coles advance as Black Education Spaces (BES) envisioned at the intersection of fugitive space and counterspace.[9] In this day and age, it is not beyond our ingenuity and available resources to find creative and inclusive ways to address student misbehavior within the school building. On the low and dark days, I question the will to imagine, create, and sustain inclusive disciplinary environments. As American Educational Research Association president Tyrone Howard said in his presidential speech in April 2024, "Hope is our focus and transformation is our goal."[10] How can we imagine a schooling experience without disparities in exclusionary discipline?

What might school discipline look like if educators adopt an Afrofuturism theoretical framework to their school discipline practices and explore an ideal school environment that fosters Black belonging, Black safety, Black validation, and Black reward?[11] Stewart calls for "deliberate turning toward Blackness" to make progress toward antiracism in student affairs.[12] A similar approach is needed in school discipline. The concept of inclusive disciplinary environments presented in this book provides an empirical starting point to conceptualize and build the Black Future of School Discipline. There is a necessity for deconstructing and reconstructing spaces that are welcoming to Black students.

WHAT WE NEED AND WHAT WE ARE FIGHTING FOR

In order to imagine disciplining students differently, we need to re-imagine the design and practices of school discipline. We need justice in the approach to school discipline.

We need to shift from understanding to disrupting. We need to shift from understanding inequality in school discipline to innovating in the programs, practices, and policies that can disrupt inequities in students' disciplinary outcomes.[13] A voluminous body of research has framed and exposed inequality in school discipline. The persistent and wicked disparities in students' disciplinary outcomes ought to suspend your belief in a just world.

We need to inject evidence into the polarizing debate on racial disparities in school discipline. This book takes the pivotal step of linking our understanding of discipline disparities to the strategies that can foster inclusive disciplinary districts and schools. We need to continue to rectify the misalignment between the solutions and contributors to discipline disparities.[14] We need strategy that iteratively synthesizes the wealth of scholarship on school discipline. The disruption of disparities in students' disciplinary outcomes is a complicated affair and requires work—strategic, sustained, and soul-fatiguing work.

We need remedies of compelling interest. School discipline luminary Russell Skiba and colleagues highlighted "the divide between best evidence and legal remedy."[15] They argued that "the area of racial disparities in discipline shows a distinct gap between the scientific knowledge base regarding racial disparities in discipline and the absence of a legal strategy accepted by the courts to address such disparities."[16] We need to switch from discrimination against to discrimination for Black students. We need to apply the strict scrutiny test to the strategy for school discipline reform and compelling governmental interest based on race to remedy discipline disparities. School discipline reforms cannot be race neutral or colorblind. Black and Brown students are not acting out but are the victims of race, racism, deficit thinking, anti-Blackness, and lack of representation in classrooms and schools. There is a crystallizing consensus on the limitations of race-neutral school discipline reforms and the need for an explicit focus on antiracist educational policy, programs, and leadership to reduce racial inequality in school discipline.[17] The benefits of policy and programmatic changes for the disciplinary experiences of Black students have been lacking due to lack of intentionality toward race in school discipline reforms.

We need race-conscious, evidence-based strategies to disrupt discipline disparities. Race matters in school discipline. The Transforming School Discipline Strategic Framework (TSDSF) takes a bold and concrete step in this direction to center evidence-based school discipline reforms that reduce both the overall rates of exclusionary discipline and inequities in how Black and White students are disciplined. The TSDSF synthesizes recent research on school discipline reforms in hopes of closing the gap between research and school discipline strategy. Whereas evidence of racial discrimination may be hard to come by, evidence of policy and programmatic changes that can reduce discipline disparities, as detailed in the TSDSF, is available and should be put to good use.

We need equity-centered research–practice partnerships to help in the disruption of discipline disparities. They can help with the uptake of research in districts' and schools' school discipline strategy, assist with the interpretation of data and monitoring of discipline disparities, and spark innovation in school discipline reforms through focused codesign teams with school personnel.

We need funding and accountability to sustain discipline reforms. The federal government and states have a major role here in shaping the local context of behavior management.

We need to pay down the relational debt in schools. Gloria Ladson Billings introduced the concept of debt to help explain differences in students' educational outcomes by race.[18] We can extend the notion of debt to help understand the differences in the rates of suspensions and expulsions for Black and White students. Discipline disparities are the product of a relational debt in today's schools. Students and teachers are disconnected. Students and school administrators are disconnected. And school administrators and teachers are barely seeing eye to eye.[19] The lack of relationships results in a poorer school climate and environments where students feel as if they don't belong and teachers feel as if they're not supported. The transformation of school discipline relies on a return to the core of authentic relationships and learning in schools—relationships among students, between students and teachers, between teachers and school leaders, and between school personnel and families.

We need to diversify the personnel in schools in the long run, but in the short run, we need resources to bolster the professional capacity of the current crop of educators. The operative question is whether a largely White body of teachers and school administrators can discipline students of color without discriminating against them. We need educators to see the humanity in Black children. If not, their fear, apprehension, and being scared of "dangerous" Black boys and girls lead to exclusion, to the detriment of the students they are committed to helping succeed.

We need a change in mind-set toward innovation and learning. We need to view suspensions and other forms of exclusionary discipline as outdated tools to manage student behavior. We need to upgrade our toolkit and revamp our playbook. This book has leveraged the research literature to provide a beacon for the underlying philosophy and strategies of a reimagined approach to school discipline. The mantra guiding this approach to school discipline is support, not suspend; educate rather than punish; and include rather than exclude. The approach is centered on returning schools to being places of learning, where all students are taught new skills such as conflict resolution, and places where teachers learn new skills to manage diverse classrooms.

We need action. We need district and school leaders, including superintendents, principals, directors of support, and others, to make disruptive decisions to stem the disproportionate flow of Black students, Black males, and Black students with disabilities to the office for further sanctioning and eliminate the inequities in the use of suspensions. Fewer suspensions are equivalent to more instructional days. And this matters for the students who are most suspended—Black students. This book is about disrupting discipline disparities. And we need disruption.

We need a better plan. The current approach to school discipline in most schools and districts nationwide is in need of a complete overhaul. Exclusion is not an efficacious response to student misbehavior; exclusionary discipline is being dispensed disproportionally, and exclusionary discipline harms students' short- and long-term outcomes. For all intents and purposes, public schools are places of learning. Yet school discipline policies and practices are excluding too many Black students from the opportunity to learn.

CONSTRUCTING THE BLACK FUTURE OF SCHOOL DISCIPLINE THROUGH POLICIES, PROGRAMS, AND PERSONNEL

I maintain that the solution starts with support. Teachers and school leaders are simply not adequately prepared to create relationships and connect with Black and Brown students they teach and develop. Why not try supporting teachers? Why not try plugging the well-documented gaps in teacher preparation? Why not provide more coaching and professional development to bolster teachers' lacking classroom management and cultural responsiveness skills? Why not try supporting students and allowing them some grace and space to develop into well-thinking, productive individuals? The research evidence tells us that support is perhaps the only viable path to a win–win situation. Support creates a path to happier, more efficacious teachers and returns the purpose of schooling to instruction and development for all rather than exclusion for some (read: Black students).

The ethos of the approach to school discipline reform should be characterized by the march toward: (a) the end of race-neutrality in school discipline, (b) separating school discipline from school safety, (c) accountability in school discipline, and (d) leveraging research to disrupt discipline disparities. These are key checkpoints on the road to the Black future of school discipline.

Toward the End of Race Neutrality in School Discipline

I am not ignorant of the real barriers and legal prohibitions on race-conscious school policies.[20] Notwithstanding, the Black Future of School Discipline prompts the consideration of the legal context of school discipline, particularly the barriers of shifting from race-neutral to race-conscious policies in the struggle to disrupt discipline disparities. It is important to highlight the race neutrality of school discipline policies. These barriers to race-conscious school discipline policies may vary across educational governance levels, namely at the federal, state, and school district levels. Indeed, as highlighted in the introduction, a wave of states such as Alabama, Kentucky, North Carolina, and West Virginia are considering or passing race-neutral policies, giving teachers wholesale discretion to remove "disruptive" students.

As highlighted by Skiba and colleagues, "Controversies surrounding school discipline are thus not about whether school administrators have the right and responsibility to address discipline and school safety, but rather how that is to be accomplished."[21] The questions of the Supreme Court justices as they consider the use of race in higher education admission policies underscore the importance of illustrating the manifestations of anti-Blackness in school discipline as outlined in chapter 1.[22] The effects of race and racism are unlikely to cease, yet the values of policy makers embodied in the policies they create seem to characterize anti-Blackness as a fad rather than a way of life in American society and schools. Indeed, even those arguing in favor of race-conscious policies in higher education believe "there is an endpoint in sight."[23] It also illustrates the misalignment between contributors to disparities in outcomes and proposed solutions when considering racialized policy issues such as school discipline. As noted by Skiba and colleagues, "Numerous criticisms of colorblind constitutionalism exist."[24] The empirical reality is becoming increasingly clear—the way to stop discrimination based on race is not race-neutral policies.

A solid consensus on the limitations of race-neutral school discipline reforms to address racial disparities in school discipline paves the way to address the need for an explicit focus on antiracist educational policy, programs, and leadership.[25] If racial equity is an explicit and expressed goal of school discipline reforms, race-neutral and colorblind language and disposition are inappropriate given that scholars have highlighted how colorblind ideology and language deepen the advantages of White students without the intended improvements in the disciplinary outcomes of Black students.[26] The goal of school discipline reforms is not simply to reduce the overall ODRs and suspensions, but to lower the rates at which Black students are referred to the office and suspended, which is a necessary component of disrupting racial inequality in exclusionary discipline. I maintain that race-neutral alternatives are simply not enough to reduce the disparities in students' disciplinary outcomes.

The Black Future of School Discipline compels us to center race in school discipline reforms. Tefera and colleagues examined three schools in the midst of "widespread discipline interventions and practices" and found that "these practices and interventions often failed to consider issues central to racial disproportionality in discipline."[27] Colorblind, or race-neutral or race-evasive, school discipline reforms will not disrupt discipline disparities. If the racial makeup of students in schools and school personnel is related to the inequities in students' disciplinary outcomes, then it is ludicrous to think that race does not matter in the efforts to dismantle said disproportionalities. The path to the disruption of persistent disparities in school discipline runs through race-conscious policies and practices.

Toward Separating School Discipline from School Safety

"In the end, I think it's one bill that really comes down to school safety," Beshear said. "At a time where we have seen some really scary incidents across the country. Now this is one, that I believe if carried out appropriately, can hopefully intervene before some of those things happen."[28] This description of House Bill 538 by Democratic governor of Kentucky Andy Beshear—a bill to address discretion in school discipline—perfectly epitomizes the conflation of school safety and school discipline. This book is about school discipline, not school safety. There is no lack of consensus on the need to keep children safe in schools. However, school safety is often conflated with school discipline. Allow me to outline the difference between the topics and their implications for school discipline reform.

To be sure, there is an overlap between school discipline and school safety when the severity of disciplinary infractions threatens the well-being of other students and staff. Teachers, assistant principals, principals, and support staff have a right to safety in their workplace. Student acts of violence against their peers and school personnel are absolutely unacceptable. And there should be commensurate consequences for this despicable behavior. Yes, the emotional safety of students is also an area of overlap between school safety and school discipline.

I maintain that while there are areas of overlap and interrelation, school discipline and school safety are separate policy issues. The primary goal of school discipline reforms is to disrupt racial inequality in how perceived misbehavior is addressed in schools. Simply put, Black and White students being disciplined differently is not a safety issue. The main prerogative of school discipline reforms cannot be to keep school personnel and staff safe. That should be the clear objective of school safety policy. Concerns for the safety of students, such as the horrific atrocities of the Covenant School shooting in Nashville in 2023, should not be conflated with and pitted against the concerns for the instructional time and educational opportunity robbed from Black students due to exclusionary discipline. To be clear, we cannot afford not to take threats against other students and staff seriously—not in the wake of too many school shootings in the past decade. But these severe incidents do not form the bulk of disciplinary infractions. And these are not the subjective offenses riddled with vulnerable decision points that lead to Black and White students being disciplined differently.

The conflation of school safety and school discipline results in school discipline policies aiming to make schools safer rather than restoring educational opportunity. Consequently, school safety policies such as hardening schools through school resource officers (SROs) and metal detectors are often advanced as a response to an uptick in behavioral challenges. To be clear, SROs are a school safety intervention rather than a school discipline reform. A 2019 report by the US Commission on Civil Rights using data from the 2017–2018 school year found that the number of SROs in schools has increased over time, and roughly half of all schools use SROs. Moreover, the school safety benefits of SROs (crime reduction) may come at a cost to school discipline (increase in suspension rates and disparities).[29] Serious offenses account for a minor proportion of disciplinary consequences yet seem to play a major role in school discipline reforms as school safety initiatives are advanced in lieu of structural changes to dismantle the racial inequality in how discretion is applied in the disciplinary process.

The separation of school safety from school discipline will hopefully bring clarity and a better approach to the two issues. It will draw a necessary distinction between resources for shatter-proof, gunshot-resistant windows and resources for additional coaching for top referrers. It will also create the clarity and space for a conversation on what a commensurate response should be for a student making a death threat. A ten-day suspension? Assignment to an alternative school? Expulsion? Counseling and intensive "tier 4" supports? And what comes next for such a student after appropriate disciplinary consequence? Have they forfeited their right to an education? Do they deserve to be cast away from the schooling system and left on their own to find themselves on the fringes of society? These are questions for which we can find better common-ground (and humane) answers if we stop conflating school safety with school discipline.

Alabama seems to have embarked on the path of separation of school safety and school discipline. The School Security Act addresses safety with inspections and assessments of schools' security needs, digitally mapping schools, and fostering key partnerships with the fire marshal and local law enforcement agencies. On the other hand, the Teachers' Bill of Rights (Senate Bill 157) pits teachers against school leaders, as discussed in the introduction of this book, but at least it separates school discipline from school safety. This is one of those rare instances where I would implore other states to follow Alabama's lead with regard to a separation of school safety and school discipline in the policy approach.

Toward Accountability in School Discipline

Even though federal policies such as No Child Left Behind (NCLB) and the Every Student Succeeds Act (ESSA) have infused test-based and market-based accountability into a variety of district and school-level processes, I maintain that the disciplinary process in schools is largely bereft of accountability. The road to discipline disparities is paved with paper tiger laws and wanton discretion among educators to remove rather than teach students. Consider the case of homeless students in Texas.[30] Despite a 2019 state law prohibiting schools from suspending homeless students for incidents not involving violence, weapons, or drugs or alcohol and the revelation that several districts such as Houston Independent School District did just that, there were no consequences from the Texas Education Agency (TEA). The TEA was not required to enforce the law. As such, enforcement measures should be a necessary corollary to school discipline policy changes.

School discipline needs greater accountability and oversight. Students are held accountable for their misbehavior through the code of conduct, but how are teachers and school administrators held accountable for their use (or misuse) of discretion in disciplinary decisions? Teachers have considerable authority and discretion in disciplinary decisions. Yet who holds teachers accountable if they are having a bad day and are quick to send a "disruptive" student to the principal's office? There is no real accountability for teachers' or school administrators' discretion in disciplinary decisions. There is a need for greater transparency in how the decisions to rob black students of instructional time under the guise of insubordination are made. There is a need for accountability in school discipline. Educators should be held to account for their use of discretion in disciplinary decisions in light of persistent racial disparities in students' disciplinary outcomes and growing evidence of bias in disciplinary decisions.

Yet, in the aftermath of the COVID-19 pandemic, a concerning trend across mostly Republican states—Alabama, West Virginia, Utah, and Kentucky—is taking root: the opposite of accountability in school discipline. As highlighted in the introduction, states are providing greater discretion to teachers in the name of protecting teachers. The rationale is generally "law and order," with teacher retention as the central underlying goal of school discipline policy changes. In Alabama, like many other states, where the pendulum is swinging toward exclusion via additional discretion for teachers, the Alabama Education Association argued that school administrators were not doing enough to address classroom disruption and teachers were being subjected to abuse while precious instructional time was being lost.[31] The growing role of teachers' unions in school discipline is on display, as most of the reforms are advocated for by a teachers' union that claims their members are under attack in the classroom. To be frank, I fear teachers' unions are making a mistake and putting themselves on the wrong side of history by prioritizing additional discretion, rather than additional support and training, in their advocacy for a response to student misbehavior.

Increasing teachers' autonomy and authority in disciplinary decisions without additional training is not supporting educators. Rather, it is giving them license to further fall victim to their bias and anti-Blackness.

A growing number of studies have called for limiting the discretion of teachers and school administrators, especially for minor infractions or subjective offenses.[32] Discretion, it seems, is a corollary to discipline disparities. Offenses driven in large part by educators' discretion such as defiance of authority, student incivility, or disorderly conduct account for a sizeable portion of all exclusionary discipline (roughly two-thirds).[33] The use of discretion in subjective perceived misbehavior is one of the key drivers of discipline disparities. The misconception that many fall prey to is that a law-and-order approach that allows for the removal of "disruptive" students to keep children safe and provide teachers with an orderly classroom will result in increased teacher retention and satisfaction. It won't. And in the quest to do so, many Black lives and livelihoods will be disrupted as the cycle of disproportionate exclusion repeats itself. There is a need for greater attention and examination of the role of discretion in school discipline policy.

Teachers cannot be judge, jury, and executioner. Indeed, Alabama's Teachers' Bill of Rights mentions resources for legal expenses in anticipation of retribution for not supporting educators or students. Here is an instance in which I would implore states not to follow Alabama. California, conversely, is leading the way in injecting accountability in school discipline by requiring teachers to track how they are supporting persistently disciplined students and publicizing parents' rights to appeal suspensions.

Toward Leveraging Research to Disrupt Discipline Disparities

Too many school discipline policy changes are often grounded in anecdotal stories rather than leveraging the wealth of research evidence on school discipline. A growing number of studies have called for limiting the discretion of teachers and school administrators, especially for minor infractions or subjective offenses.[34] Discretion, it seems, is a corollary to discipline disparities. Offenses driven in large part by educators' discretion such as defiance of authority, student incivility, or disorderly conduct account for a sizeable portion of all exclusionary discipline (roughly two-thirds).[35] The use of discretion in subjective perceived misbehavior is one of the key drivers of discipline disparities.

Yet this wave of post-pandemic state school discipline policies ignores research evidence that tells us that this wanton discretion is a pathway to bias in disciplinary decisions. There should be more, not fewer, guardrails on teachers' ability to exclude students from classrooms. The policy changes also fail to address the real issue in school discipline—Black and White students are disciplined differently. Their behavior is perceived differently. Black and White students can act in the same way with divergent disciplinary consequences. And most offenses are subjective rather than violence or harm to staff, themselves, or peers.

More importantly, these policy changes do not provide support for teachers or resources for evidence-based interventions. They do not fill gaps in classroom management or provide resources for professional development or coaching. In fact, these policy changes are stoking tensions in the interactions between teachers and school leaders in the disciplinary process. They will likely increase both the prevalence of and disparities in ODRs and suspensions and further rob students of color, particularly Black students, of instructional time as they catch up from the pandemic's learning loss. They will also likely worsen school climate and pit teachers against school leaders and students in schools. They may also fuel discord and conflict in districts as teachers can undermine school leaders' authority by going to the superintendent and the school board.

AN EXPANDED ROLE FOR STATES

There is room for states to play a greater role in the transformation of racial inequities in school discipline. States can provide support for districts and schools as they implement the TSDSF. States can play a more active role in the first two steps of the disruption sequence of the TSDSF: determining the state of school discipline and taking stock of and mapping current reform efforts. There is also an expanded role for states in providing a stricter oversight and more robust guidance on discipline disproportionalities. States also need to put their money where their mouth is with regard to school discipline reform. States can play a more active role in the training of district leaders, such as directors of student support, who oversee school districts' approach to school discipline. States can also support parents in the fight for educational opportunity rather than buttressing carcerality in schools.

There is a need for increased awareness among legislators along the political spectrum of the depth and breadth of the school discipline crisis. States such as Delaware have created the School Behavior and School Climate task force to examine school discipline data with an eye on reforms. These task forces can provide a rationale for investments in disrupting discipline disparities.

The collection of data to reveal the depth of discipline disparities is an area where both the federal and state governments can increase their involvement. States and districts should mandate the review and remedy of disproportionalities in students' disciplinary outcomes. Only nine states require districts to review school discipline data. In 2024 and beyond, it is pivotal that statewide data on the use of different suspension types (in-school suspensions and out-of-school suspensions) at the district and school level, disaggregated by the type of disciplinary infraction, and student characteristics should be collected and readily available for public consumption. This is foundational to the first step of the disruption sequence outlined in the TSDSF. States should also mandate the public release of school- and district-level data on disciplinary infractions and consequences disaggregated by student characteristics (e.g., race, special education status, intersectional identities) as part of an overall push for greater accountability in school discipline. States can also mandate monthly school discipline reports to the local school board to help foster a data culture within districts and keep key decision-makers abreast of the state of school discipline. These actions can help districts and schools to take the first step in the disruption sequence. Yet awareness is not enough, and the perusal of data is necessary but not sufficient to disrupt discipline disparities.

Disrupting discipline disparities requires investing in the school discipline–specific professional development of educators. Bolstering the professional capacity of educators to address school discipline is a central challenge of school discipline reforms given that educators are essential to the implementation of policies and programs. There is a need to create a structure of cascading supports where the district can support schools and school administrators can support teachers with a focus on the top 5 percent of referrers in each school. Districts and schools need resources to bolster the cascading system of supports for educators and students, not unfunded mandates or additional discretion to fuel exclusion. States can support districts by increasing the number of and diversifying school personnel. Personnel investments in restorative practices, including investing in restorative justice programs, hiring school-based restorative justice coordinators, hiring community members in support roles (e.g., paraprofessionals), and training, can easily cost tens or hundreds of millions of dollars (see the case of New York City).[36]

Simply put, a centerpiece of school discipline reform is training, including professional development and coaching. This training can entail interpretation of the language of school discipline (given that most districts cut and copy the state's guidance for disciplinary infractions and consequences) as well as a flow chart to foster consistency in disciplinary responses to perceived misbehavior across districts. Such guidance will help to ensure that infractions are commensurate with consequences and reduce the crevices in the disciplinary process where the uneven application of subjectivity gives rise to discipline disparities. Such guidance will eventually limit discretion at the school level and limit the pathways through which bias and stereotypes may infect disciplinary decisions.

Parents are becoming increasingly aware that the severity of the disciplinary consequences their children receive is linked to the color of their skin. Parents are increasingly demanding and advocating for their students' right to an education. States may launch a public relations campaign to inform parents of their rights and signal the state DOE's support to file civil rights complaints and monitor discrimination in disciplinary practices. This will eventually apply accountability pressure to districts and schools when they know states are paying keener attention to how students are excluded from classrooms and schools. Discrimination lawsuits, such as the complaint filed with the US DOE's Office for Civil Rights against Rockford Public School District in Illinois in June 2024, will also keep districts on their toes regarding the disproportionate use of exclusionary discipline.[37] Bills such as House Bill 207 in North Carolina (which was being considered in June 2024), which focuses on students' due-process rights, expunges suspensions under certain circumstances, and requires school administrators to justify exclusion and how student behavior violates codes of conduct, are a step in the right direction to ultimately increase accountability for the use of discretion in disciplinary decisions.

AN EXPANDED ROLE FOR THE FEDERAL GOVERNMENT

The ebbs and flows of federal directives have swung from the Obama administration's attention to racial disparities in school discipline to the Trump administration's rescindment of guidelines and now to the Biden administration's waffling stance (the type that releases guidelines the weekend before Memorial Day).[38] In 2014, the Department of Education and the Department of Justice released guidelines in the "Dear Colleague" letter that prompted a response by states and districts on school discipline policy. In 2018, this guidance was rescinded by the Trump administration. On a Friday afternoon in late May 2023, preceding the first Memorial Day weekend that eclipsed pre-COVID-19 pandemic travel numbers, the US Department of Education under the Biden administration released guidance on school discipline.[39] The timing of the release of the report was eerily similar to the Coleman Report, which was released on the weekend before the Fourth of July holiday in 1966. Whether the guidance letter has a similar impact on school discipline policy, practice, and discourse remains to be seen.

There is room for federal action to harness the power of discipline policy, incentivizing and cajoling states and districts to view suspensions as a nonoption or a last resort. There is a need for greater investment in school discipline data collection and analysis in order to better evaluate the progression of actions preceding disciplinary consequences and to monitor the effectiveness of alternative approaches to exclusionary discipline. We cannot overlook the role of resources in solving the school discipline crisis and federal government's importance in this regard. There is also a need for consistency at the federal level and a need to resist conflating school safety with school discipline.

In tandem with states, the federal government should ensure that discipline data from the infraction level up can be compared across districts.

The federal government can play a larger role in prohibiting suspensions. The retrenchment from bans on the use of suspensions in states such as Kentucky, Nevada, and West Virginia flies in the face of growing evidence of the effectiveness of these prohibitions on suspensions. Less than half of all states restrict suspensions. The evidence suggests this should be nationwide. The Black Future of School Discipline encompasses a ban on suspensions, particularly out-of-school suspensions for subjective offenses and attendance-related infractions. Out-of-school suspensions should be reserved for instances in which students pose a clear and imminent danger to peers, staff, or themselves. Districts and schools may also consider improving the processes and structures of in-school suspensions.

Without necessary funding, the federal government is de facto forfeiting its role in protecting the rights of students, particularly if discipline disparities continue to rob Black students of instructional time and equal educational opportunity. I argue that devoting resources to the transformation of racial inequality in school discipline is key. Reallocation (e.g., from hardening to supporting; instead of SROs/metal detectors, invest in guidance counselors and student support services) and an influx of resources are key pillars of the solutions. Scholars have called for increased funding through ESSA Title II Part A to fund professional learning.[40]

Relatedly, the federal government should provide adequate funding for the Office for Civil Rights. It will be pointless to encourage the filing of civil rights complaints regarding discrimination in school if they cannot be investigated in a timely and robust manner. If the Office for Civil Rights lacks resources and personnel, as it currently does, then school discipline complaints will likely fall by the wayside, and we will experience the opposite of injecting accountability into school discipline as states and districts sense there will be no repercussions for sustained disproportionalities in exclusionary discipline.[41] Therefore, the federal government should adequately fund the Education Department's Office for Civil Rights.

PARTNERING TO DISRUPT DISCIPLINE DISPARITIES

I hope research can provide actionable insights. I hope research can advance conceptual and empirical understandings of the "school discipline dilemma." I hope research can evolve from studies understanding the contributors to discipline disparities to studies on the ways in which schools disrupt racial inequality in exclusionary discipline. Indeed, greater use of research evidence is necessary to solve the school discipline crisis.[42]

The ultimate goal is to use research evidence in ways where school discipline policy, program and personnel-based changes materially improve the educational experiences and outcomes of Black students. Examining suspension patterns, policy, and surrounding discourse, as well as learning from exemplars, offers a ray of hope to someday disrupt discipline disparities. The use of research evidence in conversation with experiential knowledge and bold decision-making can disrupt discipline disparities sooner. The use of research evidence in school discipline has the potential to benefit youth by shaping policy and practice that reduces the use of exclusionary discipline, which, in turn, will change K–12 education outcomes (especially for Black students) and dismantle the school-to-prison pipeline.

Research–practice partnerships (RPPs) are posited as a vehicle to improve the use of research evidence and advance racial equity in education.[43] There is a crystallizing consensus on the importance of evidence to inform education policy and practice, as well as the complexities of research utilization.[44] Disrupting discipline disparities encompasses reimagining oppressive systems in education, focusing on students of color who have borne the brunt of discipline inequities, centering the local context, and designing new structures to advance racial equity.[45] As such, equity-centered RPPs provide a useful vehicle for transforming school discipline by connecting research evidence on school discipline to the decision-making process on school discipline policies and practices in local districts.

Equity-Centered RPPs as a Vehicle to Improve the Use of Research Evidence in School Discipline

Equity-centered RPPs are an evolving subset of RPPs loosely bound by equity principles and varying in partnership design and approaches to research–practice relations and strategies. Equity-centered RPPs hold significant potential to disrupt inequities in education and improve youth outcomes. Equity-centered RPPs can connect research evidence on school discipline to the decision-making process on school discipline policies and practices in local districts. At their core, equity-centered RPPs foster bidirectional learning at boundaries to catalyze and inform disruptive decisions.[46] RPPs provide hope for fostering conditions for not only the use of research evidence but also bidirectional learning to enhance and sustain school discipline reforms.

My experiences as a researcher in a place-based RPP focusing on school discipline in a mid-sized urban district in the southeastern United States have led to my belief that equity-centered RPPs can help reduce discipline disparities, although more empirical research is needed.[47] Now is the time to listen to the research evidence on school discipline and forge new ways of tapping into the experiential knowledge and expertise of practitioners to disrupt racial inequality in school discipline.

I contend that equity-centered RPPs can foster the conditions for learning and innovating that are necessary for the sustainable and dynamic transformation of racial inequality in school discipline. Equity-centered RPPs can help generate instrumental ideas for interventions that can disrupt racial inequality in school discipline in local contexts. RPPs foster a richer understanding of disparities in school discipline, provide a platform to craft effective solutions, and increase the use of research evidence in local decision-making. Equity-centered RPPs in school discipline can promote the use of research evidence, adult learning, and innovation in school discipline policy and practice. This will entail extending and deepening the thought partnership between district leaders and researchers to connect research evidence on school discipline to the decision-making process on school discipline policies and practices. Practitioners will need a partner to explore issues of whether school discipline reforms are working, for whom, and under what conditions.

Equity-centered RPPs provide a vehicle for researchers to play a re-envisioned role in disrupting discipline disparities. We must become accomplices and co-conspirators with district and school leaders with the intention of leveraging research to dismantle discipline inequities. This will require scrutinizing our ways of knowing as scholars and expanding our toolkits. It requires learning new methods, aligning our intentions with our scholarship, and expanding into new theories and literatures. It will require us recruiting like-minded scholars to collaborate. This will require doing the work in innovative ways, such as democratizing data collection and creating and curating spaces for district and school leaders to convene to interpret school discipline data and trends and brainstorm and share strategies to foster more inclusive disciplinary schools. Indeed, the disruption of discipline disparities is a mission, not a competition.

WHAT'S GOING ON

I conclude that I am no lawyer, but it is as clear as day that the disciplinary experiences and outcomes of Black children in America's schools are more than a civil rights issue. It is a civil rights travesty. I hope this book has made that clear. My dearly departed father, who left this earth while I prepared to write this book, taught me to speak the truth. He always reminded me to speak the truth and speak it well, cost it what it will. I hope that my children—a Black boy and a Black girl—will know that I tried my earnest and damnedest to speak truth to power. For their sake. For the lives of millions of Black children whose dreams and futures are suspended as the society of yesterday continues to shape the society of tomorrow. For equal rights and justice. For an opportunity to be Black children—to experience joy and belonging. For the chance to learn and escape the shackles of history and its contemporary chains. For the disruption of inequality in school discipline. For a fair chance in the United States. For the promise of *Brown v. Board of Education*. For educational opportunity. For excellence, knowing there is no distinction between equity and excellence.

To paraphrase Haile Selassie, until the discriminatory and exclusionary disciplinary process in schools is finally and permanently discredited and abandoned, equal educational opportunity will remain but a fleeting illusion to be pursued but never attained.

Notes

Introduction

1. The Office for Civil Rights in the US Department of Education defines exclusionary discipline as "the formal or informal removal, whether on a short-term or long-term basis, of a student from a class, school, or other educational program or activity for violating a school rule or code of conduct . . . includ[ing] detentions, in-school suspensions, out-of-school suspensions, suspensions from riding the school bus, expulsions, disciplinary transfers to alternative schools, referrals to law enforcement, and school related arrests." Office of Civil Rights, *Resource on Confronting Racial Discrimination in Student Discipline* (Washington, DC: US Department of Education, Office of Civil Rights, May 2023), https://www2.ed.gov/about/offices/list/ocr/docs/tvi-student-discipline-resource-202305.pdf.
2. "More Than 80 Percent of U.S. Public Schools Report Pandemic Has Negatively Impacted Student Behavior and Socio-Emotional Development," National Center for Education Statistics Annual Report, July 6, 2022, https://nces.ed.gov/whatsnew/press_releases/07_06_2022.asp.
3. "More Than 80 Percent of U.S. Public Schools Report Pandemic Has Negatively Impacted Student Behavior"; Kalyn Belsha, "Pandemic Effect: More Fights and Class Disruptions, New Data Show," *Chalkbeat*, July 6, 2022, https://www.chalkbeat.org/2022/7/6/23197094/student-fights-classroom-disruptions-suspensions-discipline-pandemic.
4. "More Than 80 Percent of U.S. Public Schools Report Pandemic Has Negatively Impacted Student Behavior"; Olivia Rios, Madison Watts, and Sarah Woll, *Building a Better Behavior Management Strategy for Students and Teachers: Key Findings from EAB's Student Behavior Survey* (Washington, DC: EAB, 2023), https://pages.eab.com/rs/732-GKV-655/images/EDIL-Student%20Behavior%20Executive%20Briefing-PDF.pdf.
5. Taylor Bayly, "Student Discipline Balancing Act: Addressing Bad Behavior Without Causing Harm," *The Bulletin*, August 13, 2023, https://www.bendbulletin.com/localstate/student-discipline-balancing-act-addressing-bad-behavior-without-causing-harm/article_94a3fa42-3637-11ee-a7c8-275fd8a17e4a.html.
6. Julianne Holt-Lunstad, *Our Epidemic of Loneliness and Isolation: The U.S. Surgeon General's Advisory on the Healing Effects of Social Connection and Community* (Washington, DC: Office of the Surgeon General, 2023), https://www.hhs.gov/sites/default/files/surgeon-general-social-connection-advisory.pdf.
7. Alex Zimmerman, "NYC School Suspensions Spiked 13% Last Year, Returning to Pre-pandemic Levels," *Chalkbeat*, January 8, 2024, https://www.chalkbeat.org/newyork/2024/01/08/nyc-school-suspensions-spike-to-pre-pandemic-levels/.
8. Eesha Pendharkar, "Here's How the Pandemic Changed School Discipline," *Education Week* 42, no. 16 (2022): 8–10; Richard O. Welsh, "School Discipline in the Age of COVID-19: Exploring Patterns, Policy, and Practice Considerations," *Peabody Journal of Education* 97, no. 3 (2022): 291–308.

9. Civil Rights Data Collection, *An Overview of Exclusionary Discipline Practices in Public Schools for the 2017–18 School Year* (Washington, DC: US Department of Education, Office of Civil Rights, June 2021), https://civilrightsdata.ed.gov/assets/downloads/crdc-exclusionary-school-discipline.pdf; Luis A. Rodriguez and Richard O. Welsh, "The Dimensions of School Discipline: Toward a Comprehensive Framework for Measuring Discipline Patterns and Outcomes in Schools," *AERA Open* 8 (2022), https://doi.org/10.1177/23328584221083669; Richard O. Welsh and Shafiqua Little, "The School Discipline Dilemma: A Comprehensive Review of Disparities and Alternative Approaches," *Review of Educational Research* 88, no. 5 (2018): 752–94, https://doi.org/10.3102/0034654318791582; Richard O. Welsh, "Schooling Levels and School Discipline: Examining the Variation in Disciplinary Infractions and Consequences Across Elementary, Middle, and High Schools," *Journal of Education for Students Placed at Risk (JESPAR)* 27, no. 3 (2022): 270–95, https://doi.org/10.1080/10824669.2022.2041998.
10. Carrie Hodousek, "Efforts to Address School Discipline Continue as New School Year Approaches," *WV MetroNews*, August 13, 2023, https://wvmetronews.com/2023/08/13/efforts-to-address-school-discipline-continue-as-new-school-year-approaches/.
11. Project Baltimore, "Civil Rights Attorney Ben Crump Joins Lawsuit Against Baltimore City Schools," *Fox 5 News*, July 6, 2022, https://foxbaltimore.com/news/project-baltimore/civil-rights-attorney-ben-crump-joins-lawsuit-against-baltimore-city-schools.
12. Anne Gregory, Russell J. Skiba, and Pedro A. Noguera, "The Achievement Gap and the Discipline Gap: Two Sides of the Same Coin?," *Educational Researcher* 39, no. 1 (2010): 59–68; Amanda E. Lewis and John B. Diamond, *Despite the Best Intentions: How Racial Inequality Thrives in Good Schools*, Transgressing Boundaries (New York: Oxford University Press, 2015); Daniel J. Losen et al., *Are We Closing the School Discipline Gap?* (Los Angeles: UCLA, The Civil Rights Project, February 23, 2015), https://escholarship.org/uc/item/2t36g571; Jayanti Owens and Sara S. McLanahan, "Unpacking the Drivers of Racial Disparities in School Suspension and Expulsion," *Social Forces* 98, no. 4 (2020): 1548–77, https://doi.org/10.1093/sf/soz095; Rodriguez and Welsh, "The Dimensions of School Discipline"; Welsh and Little, "The School Discipline Dilemma."
13. Civil Rights Data Collection, *An Overview of Exclusionary Discipline Practices in Public Schools*.
14. Civil Rights Data Collection, *An Overview of Exclusionary Discipline Practices in Public Schools*.
15. Civil Rights Data Collection, *An Overview of Exclusionary Discipline Practices in Public Schools*, 17.
16. United States Government Accountability Office, "Nationally, Black Girls Receive More Frequent and More Severe Discipline in School Than Other Girls," September 2024, https://www.gao.gov/assets/gao-24-106787.pdf.
17. Office of Civil Rights, *Resource on Confronting Racial Discrimination in Student Discipline*.
18. Anne Gregory et al., "An Examination of Restorative Interventions and Racial Equity in Out-of-School Suspensions," *School Psychology Review* 47, no. 2 (2018): 167–82, https://doi.org/10.17105/SPR-2017-0073.V47-2; Civil Rights Data Collection, *An Overview of Exclusionary Discipline Practices in Public Schools*; Russell J. Skiba et al., "Parsing Disciplinary Disproportionality: Contributions of Infraction, Student, and School Characteristics to Out-of-School Suspension and Expulsion," *American Educational Research*

Journal 51, no. 4 (2014): 640–70, https://doi.org/10.3102/0002831214541670; Welsh, "Schooling Levels and School Discipline."

19. Owens and McLanahan, "Unpacking the Drivers of Racial Disparities in School Suspension and Expulsion."
20. Erik J. Girvan et al., "The Relative Contribution of Subjective Office Referrals to Racial Disproportionality in School Discipline," *School Psychology Quarterly* 32, no. 3 (2017): 392–404, https://doi.org/10.1037/spq0000178; Keith Smolkowski et al., "Vulnerable Decision Points for Disproportionate Office Discipline Referrals: Comparisons of Discipline for African American and White Elementary School Students," *Behavioral Disorders* 41, no. 4 (2016): 178–95, https://doi.org/10.17988/bedi-41-04-178-195.1.
21. Rodriguez and Welsh, "The Dimensions of School Discipline."
22. H. Richard Milner IV, "Fifteenth Annual AERA Brown Lecture in Education Research: Disrupting Punitive Practices and Policies: Rac(e)ing Back to Teaching, Teacher Preparation, and Brown," *Educational Researcher* 49, no. 3 (2020): 147–60.
23. Nathan Barrett et al., "Disparities and Discrimination in Student Discipline by Race and Family Income," *Journal of Human Resources* 56, no. 3 (2021): 711–48, https://doi.org/10.3368/jhr.56.3.0118-9267R2; Jason A. Okonofua, David Paunesku, and Gregory M. Walton, "Brief Intervention to Encourage Empathic Discipline Cuts Suspension Rates in Half Among Adolescents," *Proceedings of the National Academy of Sciences* 113, no. 19 (2016): 5221–26, https://doi.org/10.1073/pnas.1523698113; Ying Shi and Maria Zhu, "Equal Time for Equal Crime? Racial Bias in School Discipline," *Economics of Education Review* 88 (2022): 102256, https://doi.org/10.1016/j.econedurev.2022.102256.
24. Barrett et al., "Disparities and Discrimination in Student Discipline by Race and Family Income"; Shi and Zhu, "Equal Time for Equal Crime?"; Skiba et al., "Parsing Disciplinary Disproportionality"; Welsh, "Schooling Levels and School Discipline."
25. Kaitlin P. Anderson, "Academic, Attendance, and Behavioral Outcomes of a Suspension Reduction Policy: Lessons for School Leaders and Policy Makers," *Educational Administration Quarterly* 56, no. 3 (2020): 435–71, https://doi.org/10.1177/0013161X19861138; Kaitlin P. Anderson and Gary W. Ritter, "Disparate Use of Exclusionary Discipline: Evidence on Inequities in School Discipline from a U.S. State," *Education Policy Analysis Archives* 25 (2017): 49, https://doi.org/10.14507/epaa.25.2787; Yolanda Anyon et al., "It's All About the Relationships: Educators' Rationales and Strategies for Building Connections with Students to Prevent Exclusionary School Discipline Outcomes," *Children & Schools* 40, no. 4 (2018): 221–30, https://doi.org/10.1093/cs/cdy017; Barrett et al., "Disparities and Discrimination in Student Discipline by Race and Family Income"; Erik J. Girvan et al., "The Relative Contribution of Subjective Office Referrals to Racial Disproportionality in School Discipline," *School Psychology Quarterly* 32, no. 3 (2017): 392–404, https://doi.org/10.1037/spq0000178; Anne Gregory et al., "An Examination of Restorative Interventions and Racial Equity in Out-of-School Suspensions," *School Psychology Review* 47, no. 2 (2018): 167–82, https://doi.org/10.17105/SPR-2017-0073.V47-2; Gary W. Ritter and Kaitlin P. Anderson, "Examining Disparities in Student Discipline: Mapping Inequities from Infractions to Consequences," *Peabody Journal of Education* 93, no. 2 (2018): 161–73, https://doi.org/10.1080/0161956X.2018.1435038; Michael Rocque, "Office Discipline and Student Behavior: Does Race Matter?," *American Journal of Education* 116, no. 4 (2010): 557–81, https://doi.org/10.1086/653629; Russell J. Skiba, Reece L. Peterson, and Tara Williams, "Office Referrals and Suspension: Disciplinary Intervention in Middle Schools," *Education and Treatment of Children* 20, no. 3 (1997): 295–315; Skiba et al., "Parsing Disciplinary Disproportionality"; Russell

J. Skiba et al., "Race Is Not Neutral: A National Investigation of African American and Latino Disproportionality in School Discipline," *School Psychology Review* 40, no. 1 (2011): 85–107, https://doi.org/10.1080/02796015.2011.12087730.

26. Jing Liu, Michael Hayes, and Seth Gershenson, "JUE Insight: From Referrals to Suspensions: New Evidence on Racial Disparities in Exclusionary Discipline," *Journal of Urban Economics* 141 (2022): 103453, https://doi.org/10.1016/j.jue.2022.103453; Rocque, "Office Discipline and Student Behavior"; Skiba et al., "Race Is Not Neutral."
27. Skiba et al., "Race Is Not Neutral"; Ritter and Anderson, "Examining Disparities in Student Discipline."
28. Daniel J. Losen and Amir Whitaker, *Lost Instruction: The Disparate Impact of the School Discipline Gap in California* (Los Angeles: UCLA, The Civil Rights Project, October 24, 2017), https://eric.ed.gov/?id=ED578997.
29. Daniel Losen and Paul Martinez, "Lost Opportunities: How Disparate School Discipline Continue to Drive Differences in the Opportunity to Learn," Learning Policy Institute, October 2020, https://learningpolicyinstitute.org/product/crdc-school-discipline-report.
30. Gregory, Skiba, and Noguera, "The Achievement Gap and the Discipline Gap"; Losen et al., *Are We Closing the School Discipline Gap?*
31. Miles Davison et al., "School Discipline and Racial Disparities in Early Adulthood," *Educational Researcher* 51, no. 3 (2022): 231–34, https://doi.org/10.3102/0013189X211061732; Paul Hemez, John J. Brent, and Thomas J. Mowen, "Exploring the School-to-Prison Pipeline: How School Suspensions Influence Incarceration During Young Adulthood," *Youth Violence and Juvenile Justice* 18, no. 3 (2020): 235–55, https://doi.org/10.1177/1541204019880945; Amity L. Noltemeyer, Rose Marie Ward, and Caven Mcloughlin, "Relationship Between School Suspension and Student Outcomes: A Meta-Analysis," *School Psychology Review* 44, no. 2 (2015): 224–41; Richard O. Welsh and Shafiqua Little, "Caste and Control in Schools: A Systematic Review of the Pathways, Rates and Correlates of Exclusion Due to School Discipline," *Children and Youth Services Review* 94 (2018): 315–39, https://doi.org/10.1016/j.childyouth.2018.09.031.
32. Andrew Bacher-Hicks, Stephen Billings, and David Deming, "The School to Prison Pipeline: Long-Run Impacts of School Suspensions on Adult Crime" (working paper, National Bureau of Economic Research, Cambridge, MA, September 2019), https://doi.org/10.3386/w26257; Tony Fabelo et al., *Breaking Schools' Rules: A Statewide Study of How School Discipline Relates to Students' Success and Juvenile Justice Involvement* (New York: Council of State Governments Justice Center, 2011), https://www.ojp.gov/ncjrs/virtual-library/abstracts/breaking-schools-rules-statewide-study-how-school-discipline; Joel Mittleman, "A Downward Spiral? Childhood Suspension and the Path to Juvenile Arrest," *Sociology of Education* 91, no. 3 (2018): 183–204, https://doi.org/10.1177/0038040718784603.
33. Lucy C. Sorensen, Shawn D. Bushway, and Elizabeth J. Gifford, "Getting Tough? The Effects of Discretionary Principal Discipline on Student Outcomes," *Education Finance and Policy* 17, no. 2 (2022): 255–84.
34. Michael Niño, Alexia Angton, Kathryn Norton-Smith, and Kayla Allison, "The Long Arm of School Punishment: The Role of School Suspension on Self-Rated Health from Adolescence to Midlife," *Socius* 10 (2024): 23780231241284942.
35. Kathleen H. Krause et al., "Report of Unfair Discipline at School and Associations with Health Risk Behaviors and Experiences—Youth Risk Behavior Survey, United States, 2023," *Morbidity and Mortality Weekly Report* 73, no. 4 (2024): 69–78, https://doi.org/10.15585/mmwr.su7304a8.

36. Juan Del Toro and Ming-Te Wang, "Vicarious Severe School Discipline Predicts Racial Disparities Among Non-Disciplined Black and White American Adolescents," *Child Development* 94, no. 6 (2023): 1762–78, https://doi.org/10.1111/cdev.13958; NaYoung Hwang and Domina Thurston, "Peer Disruption and Learning: Links Between Suspensions and the Educational Achievement of Non-Suspended Students," *Education Finance and Policy* 16, no. 3 (2021): 443–63.
37. Del Toro and Wang, "Vicarious Severe School Discipline Predicts Racial Disparities."
38. Del Toro and Wang, "Vicarious Severe School Discipline Predicts Racial Disparities."
39. Michael J. Petrilli, "Stop Appalling, Criminal Student Behavior: Drop 'Equity' and Bring Back Zero Tolerance," *The Hill*, April 22, 2024, https://thehill.com/opinion/education/4602618-stop-appalling-criminal-student-behavior-drop-equity-and-bring-back-zero-tolerance/.
40. Payton Muse, "'They're Going to Get Away with It': A Closer Look into School Discipline at Metro Schools," WZTV Nashville, August 7, 2023, https://fox17.com/news/local/nashville-tennessee-area-school-safety-suspension-expulsion-pepper-spray-teacher-assaults-theyre-going-to-get-away-with-it-a-closer-look-into-school-discipline-at-metro-schools-davidson-county-local-news.
41. Hwang and Thurston, "Peer Disruption and Learning."
42. Richard Welsh, "Why, Really, Are So Many Black Kids Suspended?," *Education Week*, August 19, 2021, https://www.edweek.org/leadership/opinion-why-really-are-so-many-black-kids-suspended/2021/08.
43. Josie Albertson-Grove, "After Brawl at St. Louis Park High, School Leaders Hear Parents' Worries," *Star Tribune*, January 24, 2024, https://www.startribune.com/after-brawl-at-st-louis-park-high-school-leaders-hear-parents-worries/600338221/.
44. Jasmine Ramirez, "San Diego Unified Looking into District's 'Restorative' Discipline Policy," *CBS8 San Diego*, February 28, 2023, https://www.cbs8.com/article/news/local/san-diego-unified-looking-into-districts-discipline-policy/509-ec0b95c6-1290-4c3b-937d-938d1a42d4eb.
45. John Williams III, "Carceral and Cathartic by Design: An Anti-Racism Historical Analysis of School Discipline in the U.S.," *Peabody Journal of Education* (2024): 142–65, https://doi.org/10.1080/0161956X.2024.2305034.
46. Sy Doan, Elizabeth D. Steiner, and Rakesh Pandey, "Teacher Well-Being and Intentions to Leave in 2024: Findings from the 2024 State of the American Teacher Survey," RAND, National Education Association, 2024, https://www.rand.org/content/dam/rand/pubs/research_reports/RRA1100/RRA1108-12/RAND_RRA1108-12.pdf.
47. Darby Beane, "Safety, Discipline, Future of the District Among Topics at 'Ideas for JCPS Student Success' Forum," *WDRB Louisville*, September 13, 2023, https://www.wdrb.com/news/safety-discipline-future-of-the-district-among-topics-at-ideas-for-jcps-student-success-forum/article_e58a4820-526c-11ee-bee9-a7bc09ccd16f.html.
48. Pendharkar, "Here's How the Pandemic Changed School Discipline"; Rachel M. Perera and Melissa Kay Diliberti, "Survey: Principals Say They Need Better-Trained Teachers and More Resources to Address Student Misbehavior," Brookings, June 8, 2023, https://www.brookings.edu/articles/survey-principals-say-they-need-better-trained-teachers-and-more-resources-to-address-student-misbehavior/; Rios, Watts, and Woll, *Building a Better Behavior Management Strategy for Students and Teachers*.
49. Louisiana Department of Education, "Governor Landry Joins State Superintendent to Unveil Recommendations to Support Teachers," May 22, 2024, https://louisianabelieves.com/newsroom/news-releases/release/2024/05/22/governor-landry-joins-state-

superintendent-to-unveil-recommendations-to-support-teachers; Louisiana Department of Education, "Let Teachers Teach," May 2024, https://louisianabelieves.com/docs/default-source/newsroom/let-teachers-teach-recommendations.pdf?sfvrsn=bbfd6e18_6/.

50. Richard O. Welsh, "Navigating Tensions in School Discipline: Examining School Leaders, Teachers, and the Conversion of Referrals into Suspensions," *American Journal of Education* 129, no. 2 (2023): 237–64, https://doi.org/10.1086/723064.
51. Holly Kurtz, "The Teachers Are Not All Right: Improving the Mental Well-Being of Teachers and Their Students," *Education Week*, August 7, 2024, https://www.edweek.org/research-center/reports/the-teachers-are-not-all-right-improving-the-mental-well-being-of-teachers-and-their-students/2024/08.
52. Doan, Steiner, and Pandey, "Teacher Well-Being and Intentions to Leave in 2024."
53. Kent McIntosh et al., "A 5-Point Intervention Approach for Enhancing Equity in School Discipline," OSEP Technical Assistance Center on Positive Behavioral Interventions and Supports, 2018, https://www.delawarepbs.org/wp-content/uploads/2020/07/McIntosh-Girvan-Horner-Smolkowski-Sugai-2018-A-5-Point-Intervention-Approach-for-Enhancing-Equity-in-School-Discipline.pdf.
54. Bayly, "Student Discipline Balancing Act."
55. Vicki Nishioka et al., *Are State Policy Reforms in Oregon Associated with Fewer School Suspensions and Expulsions?* (Washington, DC: Institute of Education Sciences, Regional Educational Laboratory Northwest, September 2020), https://files-eric-ed-gov.proxy.library.vanderbilt.edu/fulltext/ED607760.pdf.

Chapter 1

1. Ira Glasser and Alan H. Levine, "Bringing Student Rights to New York City's School System," *Journal of Law and Education* 1, no. 2 (1972), https://scholarcommons.sc.edu/cgi/viewcontent.cgi?article=1015&context=jled#:~:text=On%20January%2027%2C%201969%2C%20in,Lane%20High%20School%20in%20Brooklyn.
2. John L. Rury and Shirley Hill, "An End of Innocence: African-American High School Protest in the 1960s and 1970s," *History of Education* 42, no. 4 (2013): 486–508, https://doi.org/10.1080/0046760X.2013.819126; Alex Zimmerman, "NYC Is Capping Suspensions at 20 Days, a Major Victory for Discipline Reform Advocates," *Chalkbeat*, June 20, 2019, https://www.chalkbeat.org/newyork/2019/6/20/21108352/nyc-to-curb-suspensions-longer-than-20-days-a-major-victory-for-discipline-reform-advocates/.
3. Rebecca A. Cruz, Allison R. Firestone, and Janelle E. Rodl, "Disproportionality Reduction in Exclusionary School Discipline: A Best-Evidence Synthesis," *Review of Educational Research* 91, no. 3 (2021): 397–431, https://doi.org/10.3102/0034654321995255; Richard O. Welsh and Shafiqua Little, "The School Discipline Dilemma: A Comprehensive Review of Disparities and Alternative Approaches," *Review of Educational Research* 88, no. 5 (2018): 752–94, https://doi.org/10.3102/0034654318791582.
4. Neha Sobti and Richard O. Welsh, "Adding Color to My Tears: Toward a Theoretical Framework for Antiblackness in School Discipline," *Educational Researcher* 52, no. 8 (2023): 500–511.
5. Tera Eva Agyepong, *The Criminalization of Black Children: Race, Gender, and Delinquency in Chicago's Juvenile Justice System, 1899–1945* (Chapel Hill: University of North Carolina Press, 2018).
6. Nancy L. Arnez, "Implementation of Desegregation as a Discriminatory Process," *Journal of Negro Education* 47, no. 1 (1978): 28–45; Mark J. Chin, "Desegregated but Still Separated? The Impact of School Integration on Student Suspensions and Special Education

Classification," *Journal of Urban Economics* 141 (2024), https://doi.org/10.1016/j.jue.2021.103389; Brenda L. Townsend Walker, "Suspended Animation: A Legal Perspective of School Discipline and African American Learners in the Shadows of *Brown*," *Journal of Negro Education* 83, no. 3 (2014): 338–351.

7. Children's Defense Fund, *Children Out of School in America* (Cambridge, MA: Children's Defense Fund, 1975), https://digital.lib.utk.edu/collections/islandora/object/cdf%3A385#page/109/mode/2up.
8. Children's Defense Fund, *Children Out of School in America.*
9. Children's Defense Fund, *Children Out of School in America.*
10. Children's Defense Fund, *School Suspensions: Are They Helping Children?* (Cambridge, MA: Children's Defense Fund, 1975), https://files-eric-ed-gov.proxy.library.vanderbilt.edu/fulltext/ED113797.pdf.
11. Children's Defense Fund, *School Suspensions.*
12. Arnez, "Implementation of Desegregation as a Discriminatory Process"; Walker, "Suspended Animation."
13. Nathan Barrett et al., "Disparities and Discrimination in Student Discipline by Race and Family Income," *Journal of Human Resources* 56, no. 3 (2021): 711–48, https://doi.org/10.3368/jhr.56.3.0118-9267R2; Amanda E. Lewis and John B. Diamond, *Despite the Best Intentions: How Racial Inequality Thrives in Good Schools* (New York: Oxford University Press, 2015); Jing Liu, Emily K. Penner, and Wenjing Gao, "Troublemakers? The Role of Frequent Teacher Referrers in Expanding Racial Disciplinary Disproportionalities," *Educational Researcher* 52, no. 8 (June 14, 2023): 469–81, https://doi.org/10.3102/0013189X231179649; Ying Shi and Maria Zhu, "Equal Time for Equal Crime? Racial Bias in School Discipline," *Economics of Education Review* 88 (June 1, 2022): 102256, https://doi.org/10.1016/j.econedurev.2022.102256.
14. Children's Defense Fund, *School Suspensions*, 26.
15. Richard O. Welsh and Shafiqua Little, "Caste and Control in Schools: A Systematic Review of the Pathways, Rates and Correlates of Exclusion Due to School Discipline," *Children and Youth Services Review* 94 (2018): 315–39, https://doi.org/10.1016/j.childyouth.2018.09.031.
16. Jing Liu, Michael Hayes, and Seth Gershenson, "JUE Insight: From Referrals to Suspensions: New Evidence on Racial Disparities in Exclusionary Discipline," *Journal of Urban Economics* 141 (2022): 103453, https://doi.org/10.1016/j.jue.2022.103453; Richard O. Welsh and Luis A. Rodriguez, "The Plight of Persistently Disciplined Students: Examining Frequent Flyers and the Conversion of Office Discipline Referrals into Suspensions," *Educational Evaluation and Policy Analysis* 46, no. 1 (2023): 160–70, https://doi.org/10.3102/01623737231155155.
17. Welsh and Little, "The School Discipline Dilemma."
18. Johanna Lacoe and Matthew P. Steinberg, "Rolling Back Zero Tolerance: The Effect of Discipline Policy Reform on Suspension Usage and Student Outcomes," *Peabody Journal of Education* 93, no. 2 (2018): 207–27, https://doi.org/10.1080/0161956X.2018.1435047; Amity L. Noltemeyer, Rose Marie Ward, and Caven Mcloughlin, "Relationship Between School Suspension and Student Outcomes: A Meta-Analysis," *School Psychology Review* 44, no. 2 (2015): 224–40, https://doi.org/10.17105/spr-14-0008.1; Richard O. Welsh, "Schooling Levels and School Discipline: Examining the Variation in Disciplinary Infractions and Consequences Across Elementary, Middle, and High Schools," *Journal of Education for Students Placed at Risk* 27, no. 3 (2022): 270–95, https://doi.org/10.1080/10824669.2022.2041998.

19. Erik J. Girvan et al., "The Relative Contribution of Subjective Office Referrals to Racial Disproportionality in School Discipline," *School Psychology Quarterly* 32, no. 3 (2017): 392–404, https://doi.org/10.1037/spq0000178; Keith Smolkowski et al., "Vulnerable Decision Points for Disproportionate Office Discipline Referrals: Comparisons of Discipline for African American and White Elementary School Students," *Behavioral Disorders* 41, no. 4 (2016): 178–95, https://doi.org/10.17988/bedi-41-04-178-195.1.
20. Welsh and Rodriguez, "The Plight of Persistently Disciplined Students."
21. Walter S. Gilliam et al., *Do Early Educators' Implicit Biases Regarding Sex and Race Relate to Behavior Expectations and Recommendations of Preschool Expulsions and Suspensions?* (New Haven, CT: Yale University Child Study Center, 2016); Girvan et al., "The Relative Contribution of Subjective Office Referrals to Racial Disproportionality in School Discipline"; Jason A. Okonofua, David Paunesku, and Gregory M. Walton, "Brief Intervention to Encourage Empathic Discipline Cuts Suspension Rates in Half Among Adolescents," *Proceedings of the National Academy of Sciences* 113, no. 19 (2016): 5221–26, https://doi.org/10.1073/pnas.1523698113; Shoshana N. Jarvis and Jason A. Okonofua, "School Deferred: When Bias Affects School Leaders," *Social Psychological and Personality Science* 11, no. 4 (2020): 492–98, https://doi.org/10.1177/1948550619875150.
22. Maithreyi Gopalan et al., "Historical Patterns and Trends in Racial/Ethnic Disproportionality in School Discipline in the United States," *Socius* 10 (2024): 23780231241285105; Melanie Leung-Gagné et al., *Pushed Out: Trends and Disparities in Out-of-School Suspension* (Palo Alto, CA: Learning Policy Institute, 2022), https://doi.org/10.54300/235.277.
23. Leung-Gagné et al., *Pushed Out.*
24. Leung-Gagné et al., *Pushed Out.*
25. Leung-Gagné et al., *Pushed Out.*
26. Kaitlin P. Anderson, Anna J. Egalite, and Jonathan N. Mills, "Discipline Reform: The Impact of a Statewide Ban on Suspensions for Truancy," *Journal of Education for Students Placed at Risk* 24, no. 1 (2019): 68–91, https://doi.org/10.1080/10824669.2018.1537794; Blaire Cholewa et al., "Predictors and Academic Outcomes Associated with In-School Suspension," *School Psychology Quarterly* 33, no. 2 (2018): 191–99, https://doi.org/10.1037/spq0000213; Olivia Marcucci, "Parental Involvement and the Black–White Discipline Gap: The Role of Parental Social and Cultural Capital in American Schools," *Education and Urban Society* 52, no. 1 (2020): 143–68, https://doi.org/10.1177/0013124519846283; Noltemeyer, Ward, and Mcloughlin, "Relationship Between School Suspension and Student Outcomes"; Welsh, "Schooling Levels and School Discipline"; Jin Lee, "Potential Racial Threat on Student In-School Suspensions in Segregated US Neighborhoods," *Education and Urban Society* 55, no. 1 (2023): 3–33; Jason Jabbari and Odis Johnson, "The Collateral Damage of In-School Suspensions: A Counterfactual Analysis of High-Suspension Schools, Math Achievement and College Attendance," *Urban Education* 58, no. 5 (2023): 801–37, https://doi.org/10.1177/0042085920902256; Leung-Gagné et al., *Pushed Out.*
27. National Center for Education Statistics, *Digest of Education Statistics, Table 233.27* (Institute for Education Sciences, National Center for Education Statistics, 2022), https://nces.ed.gov/programs/digest/d22/tables/dt22_233.27.asp.
28. Leung-Gagné et al., *Pushed Out*; Welsh, "Schooling Levels and School Discipline"; Welsh and Little, "The School Discipline Dilemma."

29. Edward J. Smith and Shaun R. Harper, *Disproportionate Impact of K–12 School Suspension and Expulsion on Black Students in Southern States* (Philadelphia: University of Pennsylvania, Center for the Study of Race and Equity in Education, 2015).
30. Leung-Gagné et al., *Pushed Out.*
31. Leung-Gagné et al., *Pushed Out.*
32. US Department of Education, Office of Civil Rights (November 2023), "2020–21 Civil Rights Data Collection: Student Discipline and School Climate in U.S. Public Schools," https://www.ed.gov/sites/ed/files/about/offices/list/ocr/docs/crdc-discipline-school-climate-report.pdf?utm_content=&utm_medium=email&utm_name=&utm_source=govdelivery&utm_term=.
33. Jake Sussman and Andy Li, *North Carolina's Education System Stuck in Cycle of Racism* (Durham, NC: Southern Coalition for Social Justice, 2024), https://southerncoalition.org/report-north-carolinas-education-system-stuck-in-cycle-of-racism/.
34. Susan Tebben, "Report: Ohio School-to-Prison Pipeline Bolstered by 'Exclusionary Discipline,' Absenteeism," *Ohio Capital Journal*, August 23, 2024, https://ohiocapitaljournal.com/2024/08/23/report-ohio-school-to-prison-pipeline-bolstered-by-exclusionary-discipline-absenteeism/.
35. Council of Great City Schools, "Academic Key Performance Indicators," October 2024, https://www.cgcs.org/cms/lib/DC00001581/Centricity/Domain/35/Academic%20KPI%20Report%205%20Year%20Full%20Report%202024_10_07.pdf.
36. Alex Zimmerman, "Lengthy Suspensions Rose During the First Half of Last School Year, New Data Show," *Chalkbeat*, July 30, 2024, https://www.chalkbeat.org/newyork/2024/07/30/nyc-school-susperintendent-suspensions-tick-up/.
37. City of New York, "Mayor de Blasio Announces Roadmap to Reduce Punitive School Discipline and Make Schools Safer," November 2, 2015, http://www.nyc.gov/office-of-the-mayor/news/779-15/mayor-de-blasio-roadmap-reduce-punitive-school-discipline-make-schools-safer; Thalia Gonzalez, "Restorative Justice from the Margins to the Center: The Emergence of a New Norm in School Discipline," *Howard Law Journal* 60, no. 1 (2016): 267–308; NYC Public Schools, "Resilient Kids, Safer Schools," 2019, https://www.schools.nyc.gov/school-life/safe-schools/resilient-kids-safer-schools; Luis A. Rodriguez and Richard O. Welsh, "The Dimensions of School Discipline: Toward a Comprehensive Framework for Measuring Discipline Patterns and Outcomes in Schools," *AERA Open* 8 (2022): 23328584221083669, https://doi.org/10.1177/23328584221083669; Welsh and Little, "The School Discipline Dilemma."
38. Rodriguez and Welsh, "The Dimensions of School Discipline."
39. Alyssa Rafa, *50-State Comparison: State Policies on School Discipline* (Boulder, CO: Education Commission of the States, 2018), https://www.ecs.org/50-state-comparison-state-policies-on-school-discipline/; Matthew P. Steinberg and Johanna Lacoe, "Reforming School Discipline: School-Level Policy Implementation and the Consequences for Suspended Students and Their Peers," *American Journal of Education* 125, no. 1 (2018): 29–77, https://doi.org/10.1086/699811; Welsh and Little, "The School Discipline Dilemma."
40. Ashley C. Craig and David C. Martin, "Discipline Reform, School Culture, and Student Achievement" (working paper, IZA Discussion Papers, Bonn, 2023), https://www.econstor.eu/bitstream/10419/272533/1/dp15906.pdf.
41. Rodriguez and Welsh, "The Dimensions of School Discipline."
42. Christopher L. Busey, Kristen E. Duncan, and Tianna Dowie-Chin, "Critical What What? A Theoretical Systematic Review of 15 Years of Critical Race Theory Research in Social

Studies Education, 2004–2019," *Review of Educational Research* 93, no. 3 (2022): 412–53, https://doi.org/10.3102/00346543221105551.

43. Kimberle Williams Crenshaw, "Mapping the Margins: Intersectionality, Identity Politics, and Violence Against Women of Color," *Stanford Law Review* 43, no. 6 (1991): 1241–99; Kristian Edosomwan and John A. Williams III, "Double Jeopardy? Examining the Influence of Mathematics Tracking on In-School Suspensions Through an Intersectionality Framework," *School Science and Mathematics* 124, no. 2 (2023): 72–84, https://doi.org/10.1111/ssm.12607.
44. Kimberle Crenshaw, "Demarginalizing the Intersection of Race and Sex: A Black Feminist Critique of Antidiscrimination Doctrine, Feminist Theory and Antiracist Politics," *University of Chicago Legal Forum* 1989, no. 1 (1989): 8; Kamilah B. Legette and Yoli Anyon, "Just Go to the Office! An Intersectional Exploration of the Role of Race and Gender in Discipline Referral Reasons," *Race Ethnicity and Education* (2023): 1–21, https://doi.org/10.1080/13613324.2023.2192946.
45. Wendy Haight, Misa Kayama, and Priscilla Ann Gibson, "Out-of-School Suspensions of Black Youths: Culture, Ability, Disability, Gender, and Perspective," *Social Work* 61, no. 3 (2016): 235–43, https://doi.org/10.1093/sw/sww021.
46. These rates were calculated using longitudinal and administrative data provided by the NYC Department of Education (NYCDOE) spanning the period from 2011–2012 to 2021–2022. The analysis is limited to students in public middle and high schools, inclusive of schools of traditional grade configurations (grades 6–8 or 9–12) and combined grade configurations (grades K–8, 6–12, and K–12). Elementary schools were excluded due to the NYCPS having a different discipline code for elementary schools and the lack of comparable discipline data; charter and private schools were also excluded due to not being included in the NYCPS dataset. The NYCPS distinguishes between (a) superintendent's suspension and (b) principal's suspension, which primarily differ based on the level of severity of the alleged infraction as well as the duration under which the student is suspended. I report results from the combined total suspensions given that the overwhelming majority comprised principal suspensions (73–81 percent within a given school year). I aggregate disciplinary records to the city level to operationalize measures capturing the prevalence, disproportionality, and disparities in ODRs and suspensions in any given year. As a measure of prevalence of suspension, the *discipline rate* represents the proportion of students within a year who have experienced a suspension. The *discipline risk index* (Girvan et al., "The Relative Contribution of Subjective Office Referrals to Racial Disproportionality in School Discipline") provides a measure of disproportionality as it represents the proportion of students from a target racial or ethnic group (e.g., Black, Latinx) who have experienced the type of exclusionary disciplinary action being examined: number of students in target group disciplined divided by number of students in target group.
47. Welsh and Rodriguez, "The Plight of Persistently Disciplined Students."
48. Persistently referred students are students who receive more than one office discipline referral in a given school year, and persistently suspended students are students who receive more than one suspension in a given school year. Persistently disciplined rates are calculated using the rich, longitudinal administrative data for middle and high schools in NYC from the 2011–2012 to the 2021–2022 school years.
49. I examine the relationship between students' intersectional identities and the likelihood of students experiencing exclusionary discipline using student-level data comprising the analytic sample of middle and high school students. The probability that student i in

school *s* is disciplined during year *t* is modeled as a function of observable student characteristics and time-variant school characteristics. I run models separately for each of the two forms of exclusionary discipline of interest: (a) whether a student received an ODR, and (b) whether a student received a suspension in a given year. The specified model adjusts for year fixed effects and school fixed effects. In addition to the main model, I also compare the increased likelihood of exclusionary discipline for Black, Latinx, and White male SPED students with White female non-SPED students as the reference group to show the accumulative additional risk of ODR or suspension for students based on race, gender, and SPED. I then compare the likelihood of exclusionary discipline for Black, Latinx, and White male students with White female students as the reference group to show the additional risk of ODR or suspension associated with student race for male students. Next, I compare the likelihood of exclusionary discipline for Black and Latinx male students relative to White male students, and then do the same for female students, to compare the additional risk of ODR or suspension associated with race for both male and female students. Finally, I compare the likelihood of exclusionary discipline for Black male students with Black female students as the reference group to show the additional risk of ODR or suspension associated with student gender for Black students, and then do the same for Latinx and White students to compare the size of this additional risk across race.

50. Diana Lambert, "Victor Valley Union High School Violated Black Students Civil Rights, Says Federal Report," *EdSource*, August 17, 2022, https://edsource.org/updates/victor-valley-union-high-school-violated-black-students-civil-rights-says-federal-report.
51. Kaitlin P. Anderson, "Academic, Attendance, and Behavioral Outcomes of a Suspension Reduction Policy: Lessons for School Leaders and Policy Makers," *Educational Administration Quarterly* 56, no. 3 (2020): 435–71, https://doi.org/10.1177/0013161X19861138; Vicki Nishioka, Becca Merrill, and Havala Hanson, *Changes in Exclusionary and Nonexclusionary Discipline in Grades K–5 Following State Policy Reform in Oregon* (Institute of Education Sciences, Regional Educational Laboratory Northwest, February 2021), https://eric.ed.gov/?id=ED610682; Rafa, *50-State Comparison*; Richard O. Welsh, "Up the Down Escalator? Examining a Decade of School Discipline Reforms," *Children and Youth Services Review* 150 (2023): 106962, https://doi.org/10.1016/j.childyouth.2023.106962.
52. Ariel Gilreath, "Young Children Misbehave. Some Are Suspended for Acting Their Age," *The Hechinger Report*, April 2, 2024, http://hechingerreport.org/young-children-misbehave-some-are-suspended-for-acting-their-age/.
53. Rafa, *50-State Comparison.*
54. Bryan Kelley, Carlos Jamieson, and Zeke Perez Jr., *50-State Comparison: School Discipline Policies* (Boulder, CO: Education Commission of the States, May 17, 2021), https://www.ecs.org/50-state-comparison-school-discipline-policies/.
55. Gary W. Ritter, "Reviewing the Progress of School Discipline Reform," *Peabody Journal of Education* 93, no. 2 (2018): 133–38, https://doi.org/10.1080/0161956X.2018.1435034; Steinberg and Lacoe, "Reforming School Discipline"; Welsh and Little, "The School Discipline Dilemma."
56. Anne Gregory, Russell J. Skiba, and Kavitha Mediratta, "Eliminating Disparities in School Discipline: A Framework for Intervention," *Review of Research in Education* 41, no. 1 (2017): 253–78, https://doi.org/10.3102/0091732X17690499; Francis Huang and Yolanda Anyon, "The Relationship Between School Disciplinary Resolutions with School Climate and Attitudes Toward School," *Preventing School Failure: Alternative*

Education for Children and Youth 64, no. 3 (2020): 212–22, https://doi.org/10.1080/1045988X.2020.1722940; Welsh and Little, "The School Discipline Dilemma."

57. Initiative on Gender Justice & Opportunity, "School-Based Restorative Justice Legislative Trends," Georgetown Law Center on Poverty and Inequality, 2020, https://genderjusticeandopportunity.georgetown.edu/wp-content/uploads/2021/04/School-Based-RJ-Legislative-Trends-1-1.pdf.
58. Caitlynn Perez, "How Much Educators Say They Use Suspension, Expulsions, and Restorative Justice," *Education Week*, April 19, 2024, https://www.edweek.org/leadership/how-much-educators-say-they-use-suspensions-expulsions-and-restorative-justice/2024/04.
59. Richard O. Welsh, "Economics of Urban Education: Race, Resources, and Control in Schools," in Handbook of Urban Education, ed. H. Richard Milner and Kofi Lomotey, 2nd ed. (New York: Routledge, 2021); Welsh, "Schooling Levels and School Discipline."
60. Catherine Mata, "What Are We Learning from School Suspension Bans?," Brookings Institution, October 21, 2024, https://www.brookings.edu/articles/what-are-we-learning-from-school-suspension-bans/.
61. Jane Arnold Lincove, Catherine Mata, and Kalena E. Cortes, "The Effects of a Statewide Ban on School Suspensions," EdWorkingPaper: 24-1004, August 2024, Annenberg Institute at Brown University, https://doi.org/10.26300/rzkw-y763.
62. Anderson, "Academic, Attendance, and Behavioral Outcomes of a Suspension Reduction Policy."
63. Terry-Ann Craigie, "Do School Suspension Reforms Work? Evidence from Rhode Island," *Educational Evaluation and Policy Analysis* 44, no. 4 (2022): 667–88.
64. Lincove, Mata, and Cortes, "The Effects of a Statewide Ban on School Suspensions."
65. Nishioka, Merrill, and Hanson, *Changes in Exclusionary and Nonexclusionary Discipline in Grades K–5*.
66. Vicki Nishioka et al., *Are State Policy Reforms in Oregon Associated with Fewer School Suspensions and Expulsions?* (Washington, DC: Institute of Education Sciences, Regional Educational Laboratory Northwest, September 2020), https://files-eric-ed-gov.proxy.library.vanderbilt.edu/fulltext/ED607760.pdf.
67. Ayesha K. Hashim, Katharine O. Strunk, and Tasminda K. Dhaliwal, "Justice for All? Suspension Bans and Restorative Justice Programs in the Los Angeles Unified School District," *Peabody Journal of Education* 93, no. 2 (2018): 174–89, https://doi.org/10.1080/0161956X.2018.1435040; Craigie, "Do School Suspension Reforms Work?"; Lacoe and Steinberg, "Rolling Back Zero Tolerance"; Steinberg and Lacoe, "Reforming School Discipline."
68. Hashim, Strunk, and Dhaliwal, "Justice for All?"
69. E. Christine Baker-Smith, "Suspensions Suspended: Do Changes to High School Suspension Policies Change Suspension Rates?," *Peabody Journal of Education* 93, no. 2 (2018): 190–206, https://doi.org/10.1080/0161956X.2018.1435043.
70. Steinberg and Lacoe, "Reforming School Discipline."
71. Rui Wang, "The Impact of Suspension Reforms on Discipline Outcomes: Evidence from California High Schools," *AERA Open* 8 (2022): 23328584211068067.
72. Cruz, Firestone, and Rodl, "Disproportionality Reduction in Exclusionary School Discipline"; Miles Davison, Andrew M. Penner, and Emily K. Penner, "Restorative for All? Racial Disproportionality and School Discipline Under Restorative Justice," *American Educational Research Journal* 59, no. 4 (2022): 687–718, https://doi.org/10.3102/00028312211062613; Anne Gregory, Francis Huang, and Allison Rae

Ward-Seidel, "Evaluation of the Whole School Restorative Practices Project: One-Year Impact on Discipline Incidents," *Journal of School Psychology* 95 (2022): 58–71, https://doi.org/10.1016/j.jsp.2022.09.003; Ahhyun Lee and Nicholas A. Gage, "Updating and Expanding Systematic Reviews and Meta-Analyses on the Effects of School-Wide Positive Behavior Interventions and Supports," *Psychology in the Schools* 57, no. 5 (2020): 783–804, https://doi.org/10.1002/pits.22336.

73. Yolanda Anyon, Duan Zhang, and Cynthia Hazel, "Race, Exclusionary Discipline, and Connectedness to Adults in Secondary Schools," *American Journal of Community Psychology* 57, no. 3/4 (2016): 342–52, https://doi.org/10.1002/ajcp.12061; Thalia Gonzalez, "Keeping Kids in Schools: Restorative Justice, Punitive Discipline, and the School to Prison Pipeline," *Journal of Law and Education* 41, no. 2 (2012): 281–336; Anne Gregory and Kathleen Clawson, "The Potential of Restorative Approaches to Discipline for Narrowing Racial and Gender Disparities," in *Inequality in School Discipline: Research and Practice to Reduce Disparities*, ed. Russell J. Skiba, Kavitha Mediratta, and M. Karega Rausch (New York: Palgrave Macmillan US, 2016), 153–70; Sonia Jain et al., *Restorative Justice in Oakland Schools. Implementation and Impact: An Effective Strategy to Reduce Racially Disproportionate Discipline, Suspensions, and Improve Academic Outcomes* (Oakland Unified School District, 2014).

74. Anyon, Zhang, and Hazel, "Race, Exclusionary Discipline, and Connectedness to Adults in Secondary Schools"; Anne Gregory et al., "An Examination of Restorative Interventions and Racial Equity in Out-of-School Suspensions," *School Psychology Review* 47, no. 2 (2018): 167–82, https://doi.org/10.17105/SPR-2017-0073.V47-2.

75. Catherine Augustine et al., *Can Restorative Practices Improve School Climate and Curb Suspensions? An Evaluation of the Impact of Restorative Practices in a Mid-Sized Urban School District* (Santa Monica, CA: RAND, 2018), https://doi.org/10.7249/RR2840.

76. Catherine P. Bradshaw, Mary M. Mitchell, and Philip J. Leaf, "Examining the Effects of Schoolwide Positive Behavioral Interventions and Supports on Student Outcomes: Results from a Randomized Controlled Effectiveness Trial in Elementary Schools," *Journal of Positive Behavior Interventions* 12, no. 3 (2010): 133–48, https://doi.org/10.1177/1098300709334798; Paul Caldarella et al., "The Effects of School-Wide Positive Behavior Support on Middle School Climate and Student Outcomes," *RMLE Online* 35, no. 4 (2011): 1–14, https://doi.org/10.1080/19404476.2011.11462087; K. Brigid Flannery et al., "Effects of School-Wide Positive Behavioral Interventions and Supports and Fidelity of Implementation on Problem Behavior in High Schools," *School Psychology Quarterly* 29, no. 2 (2014): 111–24, https://doi.org/10.1037/spq0000039; Claudia G. Vincent et al., "Disciplinary Referrals for Culturally and Linguistically Diverse Students with and Without Disabilities: Patterns Resulting from School-Wide Positive Behavior Support," *Exceptionality* 19, no. 3 (2011): 175–90, https://doi.org/10.1080/09362835.2011.579936.

77. Bradshaw, Mitchell, and Leaf, "Examining the Effects of Schoolwide Positive Behavioral Interventions and Supports on Student Outcomes"; Nicholas A. Gage et al., "The Impact of School-Wide Positive Behavior Interventions and Supports on School Suspensions: A Statewide Quasi-Experimental Analysis," *Journal of Positive Behavior Interventions* 20, no. 4 (2018): 217–26, https://doi.org/10.1177/1098300718768204; Nicholas A. Gage et al., "A Quasi-Experimental Design Analysis of the Effects of School-Wide Positive Behavior Interventions and Supports on Discipline in Florida," *Journal of Positive Behavior Interventions* 21, no. 1 (2019): 50–61, https://doi.org/10.1177/1098300718768208; Claudia G. Vincent and Tary J. Tobin, "The Relationship Between Implementation

of School-Wide Positive Behavior Support (SWPBS) and Disciplinary Exclusion of Students from Various Ethnic Backgrounds with and Without Disabilities," *Journal of Emotional and Behavioral Disorders* 19, no. 4 (2011): 217–32, https://doi.org/10.1177/1063426610377329.

78. Cruz, Firestone, and Rodl, "Disproportionality Reduction in Exclusionary School Discipline"; Miles Davison et al., "School Discipline and Racial Disparities in Early Adulthood," *Educational Researcher* 51, no. 3 (2022): 231–34, https://doi.org/10.3102/0013189X211061732; Davison, Penner, and Penner, "Restorative for All?"; Gregory, Huang, and Ward-Seidel, "Evaluation of the Whole School Restorative Practices Project"; Nishioka, Merrill, and Hanson, *Changes in Exclusionary and Nonexclusionary Discipline in Grades K–5*.
79. Sean Darling-Hammond, "Fostering Belonging, Transforming Schools: The Impact of Restorative Practices," Learning Policy Institute, May 18, 2023, https://doi.org/10.54300/169.703.
80. Gregory, Huang, and Ward-Seidel, "Evaluation of the Whole School Restorative Practices Project."
81. Davison, Penner, and Penner, "Restorative for All?"
82. Cruz, Firestone, and Rodl, "Disproportionality Reduction in Exclusionary School Discipline."
83. Nishioka, Merrill, and Hanson, *Changes in Exclusionary and Nonexclusionary Discipline in Grades K–5*.
84. Wang, "The Impact of Suspension Reforms on Discipline Outcomes."
85. Michael J. Dumas and kihana miraya ross, "'Be Real Black for Me': Imagining Black-Crit in Education," *Urban Education* 51, no. 4 (2016): 415–42, https://doi.org/10.1177/0042085916628611; Savannah Shange, *Progressive Dystopia: Abolition, Antiblackness, and Schooling in San Francisco* (Durham, NC: Duke University Press, 2019); Damien M. Sojoyner, *First Strike: Educational Enclosures in Black Los Angeles* (Minneapolis: University of Minnesota Press, 2016).
86. Dumas and ross, "'Be Real Black for Me,'" 416–17; L. R. Gordon, ed., *Existence in Black* (New York: Routledge, 1997); F. B. Wilderson III, *Red, White & Black* (Durham, NC: Duke University Press, 2010).
87. Gholdy Muhammad, *Cultivating Genius: An Equity Framework for Culturally and Historically Responsive Literacy* (New York: Scholastic, 2020).
88. Amanda E. Lewis, *Race in the Schoolyard: Negotiating the Color Line in Classrooms and Communities* (New Brunswick, NJ: Rutgers University Press, 2003).
89. Eric Levenson et al., "Jacksonville Gunman in Racially Motivated Attack Legally Bought Two Weapons Earlier This Year, Sheriff Says," *CNN*, August 27, 2023, https://www.cnn.com/2023/08/27/us/jacksonville-florida-shooting-sunday/index.html.
90. The Associated Press, "The 2 Expelled Members of the 'Tennessee 3' Win Back Their State House Seats," *NPR*, August 4, 2023, https://www.npr.org/2023/08/04/1192068281/the-2-expelled-members-of-the-tennessee-3-win-back-their-state-house-seats.
91. Mary Whitfill Roeloffs, "Paramore's Haley Williams Accuses Tennessee Lawmakers of Racism over Snub of Allison Russell," *Forbes*, February 16, 2024, https://www.forbes.com/sites/maryroeloffs/2024/02/16/paramores-haley-williams-accuses-tennessee-lawmakers-of-racism-over-snub-of-allison-russell/.
92. Kirk Siegler, "Man Admits Racial Harassment of Utah Women's NCAA Basketball Team," *NPR*, May 7, 2024, https://www.npr.org/2024/05/07/1249735486/man-admits-racial-harassment-of-utah-womens-ncaa-basketball-team.

93. Jake Fenner, "LA Times Updates Controversial Op-ed That Called LSU's Women's Basketball Team 'Dirty Debutantes' . . . After Cries of Sexism and the Paper Deeming the Phrase Didn't Meet 'Editorial Standards,'" *Daily Mail*, March 31, 2024, https://www.dailymail.co.uk/sport/college-basketball/article-13257733/LA-Times-updates-controversial-op-ed-called-LSUs-womens-basketball-team-dirty-debutantes-cries-sexism-paper-deeming-phrase-didnt-meet-editorial-standards.html; Thomas Schlachter, "LA Times Edits Column and Apologizes After Drawing the Ire of LSU Coach Kim Mulkey," *CNN*, April 1, 2024, https://www.cnn.com/2024/04/01/sport/la-times-kim-mulkey-lsu-article-spt-intl/index.html; Danielle Cohen, "L.A. *Times* Writer Is Sorry for Calling LSU 'Dirty Debutantes,'" *The Cut*, April 2, 2024, https://www.thecut.com/article/la-times-writer-apologizes-lsu-column.html.
94. Minyvonne Burke, "Minneapolis Shooting Sparks Outrage as Suspect Is Charged but not Arrested," *NBC News*, October 26, 2024, https://www.nbcnews.com/news/us-news/minneapolis-man-charged-shooting-neighbor-not-arrested-prompting-anger-rcna177437.
95. Zack Linly, "White Man Charged with Murdering Black Woman Uber Driver over a Scam She Wasn't Responsible for," *NewsOne*, April 15, 2024, https://newsone.com/5158375/lo-letha-hall-murder-charges/.
96. Michael J. Dumas, "Against the Dark: Antiblackness in Education Policy and Discourse," *Theory into Practice* 55, no. 1 (2016): 11–19, https://doi.org/10.1080/00405841.2016.1116852.
97. Talia Richman, "Texas Lawmakers Could Make It Easier to Kick Students Out of Class," *Education Week*, April 14, 2023, https://www.edweek.org/leadership/texas-lawmakers-could-make-it-easier-to-kick-students-out-of-class/2023/04.
98. Jason A. Okonofua, Gregory M. Walton, and Jennifer L. Eberhardt, "A Vicious Cycle: A Social–Psychological Account of Extreme Racial Disparities in School Discipline," *Perspectives on Psychological Science* 11, no. 3 (2016): 381–98.
99. Izraelle I. McKinnon et al., "Experiences of Racism in School and Associations with Mental Health, Suicide Risk, and Substance Use Among High School Students—Youth Risk Behavior Survey, United States, 2023," *Morbidity and Mortality Weekly Report* 73, no. 4 (2024): 31–38, http://dx.doi.org/10.15585/mmwr.su7304a4.
100. McKinnon et al., "Experiences of Racism in School and Associations with Mental Health, Suicide Risk, and Substance Use Among High School Students."
101. Office of Public Affairs, "Justice Department Secures Agreement with Kansas School District Regarding School Discipline, Law Enforcement and Seclusion and Restraint," US Department of Justice, July 2, 2024, https://www.justice.gov/opa/pr/justice-department-secures-agreement-kansas-school-district-regarding-school-discipline-law.
102. Stacia Cedillo, "Beyond Inquiry: Towards the Specificity of Anti-Blackness Studies in STEM Education," *Canadian Journal of Science, Mathematics and Technology Education* 18, no. 3 (2018): 242–56, https://doi.org/10.1007/s42330-018-0025-0; Dumas and ross, "'Be Real Black for Me.'"
103. Pierre Bourdieu et al., *The Weight of the World: Social Suffering in Contemporary Society*, trans. Priscilla Parkhurst Ferguson (Stanford, CA: Stanford University Press, 1999); Cedillo, "Beyond Inquiry"; Crenshaw, "Demarginalizing the Intersection of Race and Sex"; W. E. B. Du Bois, *The Autobiography of W. E. B. Du Bois* (New York: International Publishers, 1968); Dumas, "Against the Dark"; Michael J. Dumas, "'Losing an Arm': Schooling as a Site of Black Suffering," *Race Ethnicity and Education* 17, no. 1 (2014): 1–29, https://doi.org/10.1080/13613324.2013.850412; Dumas and ross, "'Be Real Black for Me'"; Cheryl I. Harris, "Whiteness as Property," *Harvard Law Review*

106, no. 8 (1993): 1707–91, https://doi.org/10.2307/1341787; Karen D. Pyke, "What Is Internalized Racial Oppression and Why Don't We Study It? Acknowledging Racism's Hidden Injuries," *Sociological Perspectives* 53, no. 4 (2010): 551–72, https://doi.org/10.1525/sop.2010.53.4.551.

104. Subini Ancy Annamma et al., "Black Girls and School Discipline: The Complexities of Being Overrepresented and Understudied," *Urban Education* 54, no. 2 (2019): 211–42, https://doi.org/10.1177/0042085916646610; Anyon, Zhang, and Hazel, "Race, Exclusionary Discipline, and Connectedness to Adults in Secondary Schools"; Charles Bell, "'Maybe if They Let Us Tell the Story I Wouldn't Have Gotten Suspended': Understanding Black Students' and Parents' Perceptions of School Discipline," *Children and Youth Services Review* 110 (2020): 104757, https://doi.org/10.1016/j.childyouth.2020.104757; Jessika H. Bottiani, Catherine P. Bradshaw, and Tamar Mendelson, "A Multilevel Examination of Racial Disparities in High School Discipline: Black and White Adolescents' Perceived Equity, School Belonging, and Adjustment Problems," *Journal of Educational Psychology* 109, no. 4 (2017): 532–45, https://doi.org/10.1037/edu0000155; Dorothy A. Cheng, "Teacher Racial Composition and Exclusion Rates Among Black or African American Students," *Education and Urban Society* 51, no. 6 (2019): 822–47, https://doi.org/10.1177/0013124517748724; Justin A. Coles and Tunette Powell, "A BlackCrit Analysis on Black Urban Youth and Suspension Disproportionality as Anti-Black Symbolic Violence," *Race Ethnicity and Education* 23, no. 1 (2020): 113–33, https://doi.org/10.1080/13613324.2019.1631778; Ann Arnett Ferguson, *Bad Boys: Public Schools in the Making of Black Masculinity* (Ann Arbor: University of Michigan Press, 2000); Gilliam et al., *Do Early Educators' Implicit Biases Regarding Sex and Race Relate to Behavior Expectations?*; Charity Brown Griffin et al., "Racial Fairness, School Engagement, and Discipline Outcomes in African American High School Students: The Important Role of Gender," *School Psychology Review* 49, no. 3 (2020): 222–38, https://doi.org/10.1080/2372966X.2020.1726810; Haight, Kayama, and Gibson, "Out-of-School Suspensions of Black Youths"; Melanie Sberna Hinojosa, "Black-White Differences in School Suspension: Effect of Student Beliefs About Teachers," *Sociological Spectrum* 28, no. 2 (2008): 175–93, https://doi.org/10.1080/02732170701796429; Misa Kayama et al., "Use of Criminal Justice Language in Personal Narratives of Out-of-School Suspensions: Black Students, Caregivers, and Educators," *Children and Youth Services Review* 51 (2015): 26–35, https://doi.org/10.1016/j.childyouth.2015.01.020; Claire E. Kunesh and Amity Noltemeyer, "Understanding Disciplinary Disproportionality: Stereotypes Shape Pre-Service Teachers' Beliefs About Black Boys' Behavior," *Urban Education* 54, no. 4 (2019): 471–98, https://doi.org/10.1177/0042085915623337; Sharoni D. Little and La Verne A. Tolbert, "The Problem with Black Boys: Race, Gender, and Discipline in Christian and Private Elementary Schools," *Christian Education Journal* 15, no. 3 (2018): 408–21, https://doi.org/10.1177/0739891318805760; Erica Mattison and Mark S. Aber, "Closing the Achievement Gap: The Association of Racial Climate with Achievement and Behavioral Outcomes," *American Journal of Community Psychology* 40, no. 1 (2007): 1–12, https://doi.org/10.1007/s10464-007-9128-x; Edward W. Morris, "'Tuck in That Shirt!' Race, Class, Gender, and Discipline in an Urban School," *Sociological Perspectives* 48, no. 1 (2005): 25–48, https://doi.org/10.1525/sop.2005.48.1.25; Edward W. Morris and Brea L. Perry, "Girls Behaving Badly? Race, Gender, and Subjective Evaluation in the Discipline of African American Girls," *Sociology of Education* 90, no. 2 (2017): 127–48, https://doi.org/10.1177/0038040717694876; Jason A. Okonofua and Jennifer L. Eberhardt, "Two Strikes: Race and the Disciplining of Young Students," *Psychological*

Science 26, no. 5 (2015): 617–24, https://doi.org/10.1177/0956797615570365; Amanda D. Perez and Jason A. Okonofua, "The Good and Bad of a Reputation: Race and Punishment in K–12 Schools," *Journal of Experimental Social Psychology* 100 (2022): 104287, https://doi.org/10.1016/j.jesp.2022.104287; Erica L. M. Shirley and Dewey G. Cornell, "The Contribution of Student Perceptions of School Climate to Understanding the Disproportionate Punishment of African American Students in a Middle School," *School Psychology International* 33, no. 2 (2012): 115–34, https://doi.org/10.1177/0143034311406815; Smolkowski et al., "Vulnerable Decision Points for Disproportionate Office Discipline Referrals"; Frances Vavrus and KimMarie Cole, "'I Didn't Do Nothin": The Discursive Construction of School Suspension," *Urban Review* 34, no. 2 (2002): 87–111, https://doi.org/10.1023/A:1015375215801; David S. Yeager, "Loss of Institutional Trust Among Racial and Ethnic Minority Adolescents: A Consequence of Procedural Injustice and a Cause of Life-Span Outcomes," *Child Development* 88, no. 2 (2017): 658–76, https://doi.org/10.1111/cdev.12697.

105. Priscilla A. Gibson, "The Role of Race in the Out-of-School Suspensions of Black Students: The Perspectives of Students with Suspensions, Their Parents and Educators," *Children and Youth Services Review* 47 (2014): 274–82, https://doi.org/10.1016/j.childyouth.2014.09.020; Ramon Goings et al., "Using Double Consciousness as an Analytic Tool to Discuss the Decision Making of Black School Leaders in Disrupting the School-to-Prison Pipeline," *Taboo: The Journal of Culture and Education* 17, no. 4 (2018): 3, https://doi.org/10.31390/taboo.17.4.03; Muhammad Khalifa, "Can Blacks Be Racists? Black-on-Black Principal Abuse in an Urban School Setting," *International Journal of Qualitative Studies in Education* 28, no. 2 (2015): 259–82, https://doi.org/10.1080/09518398.2014.916002; Tunette Powell and Justin A. Coles, "'We Still Here': Black Mothers' Personal Narratives of Sense Making and Resisting Antiblackness and the Suspensions of Their Black Children," *Race Ethnicity and Education* 24, no. 1 (2021): 76–95, https://doi.org/10.1080/13613324.2020.1718076; Lawrence T. Winn and Maisha T. Winn, "Expectations and Realities: Education, the Discipline Gap, and the Experiences of Black Families Migrating to Small Cities," *Race and Social Problems* 7, no. 1 (2015): 73–83, https://doi.org/10.1007/s12552-014-9140-3.
106. Kaitlin P. Anderson and Gary W. Ritter, "Do School Discipline Policies Treat Students Fairly? Evidence from Arkansas," *Educational Policy* 34, no. 5 (2020): 707–34, https://doi.org/10.1177/0895904818802085; Barrett et al., "Disparities and Discrimination in Student Discipline by Race and Family Income"; Sheretta T. Butler-Barnes and Misha N. Inniss-Thompson, "'My Teacher Doesn't Like Me': Perceptions of Teacher Discrimination and School Discipline Among African-American and Caribbean Black Adolescent Girls," *Education Sciences* 10, no. 2 (2020): 44, https://doi.org/10.3390/educsci10020044; Dorinda J. Carter Andrews et al., "The Impossibility of Being 'Perfect and White': Black Girls' Racialized and Gendered Schooling Experiences," *American Educational Research Journal* 56, no. 6 (2019): 2531–72, https://doi.org/10.3102/0002831219849392.
107. Anyon, Zhang, and Hazel, "Race, Exclusionary Discipline, and Connectedness to Adults in Secondary Schools"; Bell, "'Maybe if They Let Us Tell the Story I Wouldn't Have Gotten Suspended.'"
108. Anne Gregory and Pharmicia M. Mosely, "The Discipline Gap: Teachers' Views on the Over-Representation of African American Students in the Discipline System," *Equity & Excellence in Education* 37, no. 1 (2004): 18–30, https://doi.org/10.1080/10665680490429280; Beth Sondel, Kerry Kretchmar, and Alyssa Hadley Dunn, "'Who Do These People Want Teaching Their Children?' White Saviorism, Colorblind Racism,

and Anti-Blackness in 'No Excuses' Charter Schools," *Urban Education* 57, no. 9 (2022): 1621–50, https://doi.org/10.1177/0042085919842618; Adai A. Tefera, Genevieve Siegel-Hawley, and Ashlee L. Sjogren, "The (In)Visibility of Race in School Discipline Across Urban, Suburban, and Exurban Contexts," *Teachers College Record* 124, no. 4 (2022): 151–79, https://doi.org/10.1177/01614681221093282.

109. Rebecca Epstein, Jamilia Blake, and Thalia González, "Girlhood Interrupted: The Erasure of Black Girls' Childhood" (Rochester, NY: SSRN Scholarly Paper, 2017), https://doi.org/10.2139/ssrn.3000695; Phillip Atiba Goff et al., "The Essence of Innocence: Consequences of Dehumanizing Black Children," *Journal of Personality and Social Psychology* 106, no. 4 (2014): 526–45, https://doi.org/10.1037/a0035663; Sobti and Welsh, "Adding Color to My Tears"; Welsh, "Schooling Levels and School Discipline."
110. Welsh, "Schooling Levels and School Discipline."
111. Epstein, Blake, and González, "Girlhood Interrupted"; Goff et al., "The Essence of Innocence," 526.
112. Alison N. Cooke and Amy G. Halberstadt, "Adultification, Anger Bias, and Adults' Different Perceptions of Black and White Children," *Cognition and Emotion* 35, no. 7 (2021): 1416–22.
113. Ferguson, *Bad Boys*; Gilliam et al., *Do Early Educators' Implicit Biases Regarding Sex and Race Relate to Behavior Expectations?*; Jarvis and Okonofua, "School Deferred"; Kamilah B. Legette, Amy G. Halberstadt, and Amber T. Majors, "Teachers' Understanding of Racial Inequity Predicts Their Perceptions of Students' Behaviors," *Contemporary Educational Psychology* 67 (2021): 102014; Okonofua and Eberhardt, "Two Strikes."
114. Barrett et al., "Disparities and Discrimination in Student Discipline by Race and Family Income"; Liu, Hayes, and Gershenson, "JUE Insight: From Referrals to Suspensions."
115. Gregory and Mosely, "The Discipline Gap"; Russell J. Skiba et al., "Race Is Not Neutral: A National Investigation of African American and Latino Disproportionality in School Discipline," *School Psychology Review* 40, no. 1 (2011): 85–107, https://doi.org/10.1080/02796015.2011.12087730.
116. Angela Y. Davis, *Are Prisons Obsolete?* (New York: Seven Stories, 2011).
117. Anne Gregory et al., "Good Intentions Are Not Enough: Centering Equity in School Discipline Reform," *School Psychology Review* 50, no. 2–3 (2021): 206–20, https://doi.org/10.1080/2372966X.2020.1861911; Welsh and Little, "The School Discipline Dilemma."
118. Welsh, "Up the Down Escalator?"
119. Jessika H. Bottiani et al., "Applying Double Check to Response to Intervention: Culturally Responsive Practices for Students with Learning Disabilities," *Insights on Learning Disabilities: From Prevailing Theories to Validated Practices* 9, no. 1 (2012): 93–108; Catherine P. Bradshaw et al., "Promoting Cultural Responsivity and Student Engagement Through Double Check Coaching of Classroom Teachers: An Efficacy Study," *School Psychology Review* 47, no. 2 (2018): 118–34, https://doi.org/10.17105/SPR-2017-0119.V47-2.
120. Christopher Redding, "A Teacher Like Me: A Review of the Effect of Student–Teacher Racial/Ethnic Matching on Teacher Perceptions of Students and Student Academic and Behavioral Outcomes," *Review of Educational Research* 89, no. 4 (2019): 499–535, https://doi.org/10.3102/0034654319853545.
121. Russell J. Skiba, "Interventions to Address Racial/Ethnic Disparities in School Discipline: Can Systems Reform Be Race-Neutral?," in *Race and Social Problems: Restructuring Inequality*, ed. Ralph L. Bangs and Larry E. Davis (New York: Springer, 2015); Skiba et al., "Race Is Not Neutral."

122. Gregory et al., "Good Intentions Are Not Enough."
123. Prudence L. Carter, "You Can't Fix What You Don't Look At: Acknowledging Race in Addressing Racial Discipline Disparities," *Urban Education* 52, no. 2 (2017): 207–35, https://doi.org/10.1177/0042085916660350.
124. Welsh and Little, "The School Discipline Dilemma."
125. Colombe Lemire, Michel Rousseau, and Carmen Dionne, "A Comparison of Fidelity Implementation Frameworks Used in the Field of Early Intervention," *American Journal of Evaluation* 44, no. 2 (2023): 236–52.
126. Kaitlin P. Anderson, "Inequitable Compliance: Implementation Failure of a Statewide Student Discipline Reform," *Peabody Journal of Education* 93, no. 2 (2018): 244–63.
127. Steinberg and Lacoe, "Reforming School Discipline."
128. Gage et al., "The Impact of School-Wide Positive Behavior Interventions and Supports on School Suspensions"; Jerin Kim et al., "Longitudinal Associations Between SWPBIS Fidelity of Implementation and Behavior and Academic Outcomes," *Behavioral Disorders* 43, no. 3 (2018): 357–69, https://doi.org/10.1177/0198742917747589; Welsh, "Up the Down Escalator?"
129. Christi Bergin et al., "Effectiveness of a Social-Emotional Learning Program for Both Teachers and Students," *AERA Open* 10 (2024): 23328584241281284.
130. Kelsey Morris and Adam Feinberg, "Collecting Fidelity Data to Support and Sustain PBIS/MTSS in Schools," Center on PBIS, University of Oregon, September 2022, https://www.pbis.org/resource/collecting-fidelity-data-to-support-and-sustain-pbis-mtss-in-schools.
131. Morris and Feinberg, "Collecting Fidelity Data to Support and Sustain PBIS/MTSS in Schools."
132. Flannery et al., "Effects of School-Wide Positive Behavioral Interventions and Supports."
133. Cruz, Firestone, and Rodl, "Disproportionality Reduction in Exclusionary School Discipline"; Thalia González, *Socializing Schools: Addressing Racial Disparities in Discipline Through Restorative Justice* (Rochester, NY: SSRN Scholarly Paper, 2015); Anne Gregory and Katherine R. Evans, *The Starts and Stumbles of Restorative Justice in Education: Where Do We Go from Here?* (Boulder: University of Colorado, National Education Policy Center, January 2020), https://eric.ed.gov/?id=ED605800.
134. Anne Gregory et al., "Closing the Racial Discipline Gap in Classrooms by Changing Teacher Practice," *School Psychology Review* 45, no. 2 (2016): 171–91, https://doi.org/10.17105/SPR45-2.171-191.
135. Anne Gregory, Francis L. Huang, and Allison Rae Ward-Seidel, "Adolescent Exposure to Restorative Practices and Their Perceptions of Support, Structure, and Bullying in the School Climate," *AERA Open* 10 (2024): 23328584241288525.
136. Abigail Gray et al., *Discipline in Context: Suspension, Climate, and PBIS in the School District of Philadelphia* (Philadelphia: Consortium for Policy Research in Education, October 2017), https://eric.ed.gov/?id=ED586779; Lauren Sartain, Elaine M. Allensworth, and Shanette Porter, *Suspending Chicago's Students: Differences in Discipline Practices Across Schools* (Chicago: University of Chicago, Consortium on Chicago School Research, September 2015).

Chapter 2

1. Richard O. Welsh, "School Discipline in the Age of COVID-19: Exploring Patterns, Policy, and Practice Considerations," *Peabody Journal of Education* 97, no. 3 (2022): 291–308, https://doi.org/10.1080/0161956X.2022.2079885; Eesha Pendharkar, "Here's How the

Pandemic Changed School Discipline," *Education Week*, November 28, 2022, https://www.edweek.org/leadership/heres-how-the-pandemic-changed-school-discipline/2022/11.

2. Simone Ispa-Landa, "Persistently Harsh Punishments Amid Efforts to Reform: Using Tools from Social Psychology to Counteract Racial Bias in School Disciplinary Decisions," *Educational Researcher* 47, no. 6 (2018): 384–90.
3. Richard O. Welsh and Shafiqua Little, "The School Discipline Dilemma: A Comprehensive Review of Disparities and Alternative Approaches," *Review of Educational Research* 88, no. 5 (2018): 752–94, https://doi.org/10.3102/0034654318791582.
4. Richard O. Welsh, "Up the Down Escalator? Examining a Decade of School Discipline Reforms," *Children and Youth Services Review* 150 (2023): 106962, https://doi.org/10.1016/j.childyouth.2023.106962; Rebecca A. Cruz, Allison R. Firestone, and Janelle E. Rodl, "Disproportionality Reduction in Exclusionary School Discipline: A Best-Evidence Synthesis," *Review of Educational Research* 91, no. 3 (2021): 397–431, https://doi.org/10.3102/0034654321995255.
5. John B. Diamond and Louis M. Gomez, "Disrupting White Supremacy and Anti-Black Racism in Educational Organizations," *Educational Researcher*, March 2023, 1–9, https://doi.org/10.3102/0013189X231161054.
6. "Suspended for . . . WHAT?," The Hechinger Report, 2024, http://hechingerreport.org/suspended-forwhat/.
7. Lindsay M. Fallon, Margarida Veiga, and George Sugai, "Strengthening MTSS for Behavior (MTSS-B) to Promote Racial Equity," *School Psychology Review* 52, no. 5 (2023): 518–33, https://doi.org/10.1080/2372966X.2021.1972333; Bryana H. French et al., "Toward a Psychological Framework of Radical Healing in Communities of Color," *Counseling Psychologist* 48, no. 1 (2020): 14–46, https://doi.org/10.1177/0011000019843506; Celeste M. Malone, Kirby Wycoff, and Erlanger A. Turner, "Applying a MTSS Framework to Address Racism and Promote Mental Health for Racial/Ethnic Minoritized Youth," *Psychology in the Schools* 59, no. 12 (2022): 2438–52, https://doi.org/10.1002/pits.22606; Gholdy Muhammad, *Cultivating Genius: An Equity Framework for Culturally and Historically Responsive Literacy* (New York: Scholastic, 2020); Michael D. Pullmann et al., "Reducing Racial and Ethnic Disproportionality in School Discipline Through an Assessment-to-Intervention Process: A Framework and Process," *Psychology in the Schools* 59, no. 12 (2022): 2486–505, https://doi.org/10.1002/pits.22651; Therese Sandomierski et al., "From 'Quick Fix' to Lasting Commitment: Using Root Cause Analysis to Address Disproportionate Discipline Outcomes," *Preventing School Failure* 66, no. 1 (2022): 1–13, https://doi.org/10.1080/1045988X.2021.1937025; Dean Spade, *Normal Life: Administrative Violence, Critical Trans Politics, and the Limits of Law* (Durham, NC: Duke University Press, 2015); Maisha T. Winn, *Justice on Both Sides: Transforming Education Through Restorative Justice* (Cambridge, MA: Harvard Education Press, 2020); Maisha T. Winn and Lawrence T. Winn, eds., *Restorative Justice in Education: Transforming Teaching and Learning Through the Disciplines* (Cambridge, MA: Harvard Education Press, 2021).
8. Anne Gregory, Russell J. Skiba, and Kavitha Mediratta, "Eliminating Disparities in School Discipline: A Framework for Intervention," *Review of Research in Education* 41, no. 1 (2017): 253–78, https://doi.org/10.3102/0091732X17690499.
9. Anne Gregory et al., "Good Intentions Are Not Enough: Centering Equity in School Discipline Reform," *School Psychology Review* 50, no. 2–3 (2021): 206–20, https://doi.org/10.1080/2372966X.2020.1861911.

10. Geoffrey D. Borman, Yeseul Choi, and Garret J. Hall, "The Impacts of a Brief Middle-School Self-Affirmation Intervention Help Propel African American and Latino Students Through High School," *Journal of Educational Psychology* 113, no. 3 (2021): 605–20, https://doi.org/10.1037/edu0000570; Anne Gregory et al., "Closing the Racial Discipline Gap in Classrooms by Changing Teacher Practice," *School Psychology Review* 45, no. 2 (2016): 171–91, https://doi.org/10.17105/SPR45-2.171-191; Anne Gregory et al., "Focused Classroom Coaching and Widespread Racial Equity in School Discipline," *AERA Open* 5, no. 4 (2019), https://doi.org/10.1177/2332858419897274; Clayton R. Cook et al., "Addressing Discipline Disparities for Black Male Students: Linking Malleable Root Causes to Feasible and Effective Practices," *School Psychology Review* 47, no. 2 (2018): 135–52, https://doi.org/10.17105/SPR-2017-0026.V47-2.
11. Kent McIntosh et al., "Using Discipline Data to Enhance Equity in School Discipline," *Intervention in School and Clinic* 53, no. 3 (2018): 146–52, https://doi.org/10.1177/1053451217702130.
12. María Reina Santiago-Rosario, Kent Mcintosh, and Ruthie Payno-Simmons, *Centering Equity Within the PBIS Framework: Overview and Evidence of Effectiveness* (Eugene: University of Oregon, Center on PBIS, Positive Behavioral Interventions and Supports, 2022), https://www.pbis.org/; Keith Smolkowski et al., "Vulnerable Decision Points for Disproportionate Office Discipline Referrals: Comparisons of Discipline for African American and White Elementary School Students," *Behavioral Disorders* 41, no. 4 (2016): 178–95.
13. McIntosh et al., "Using Discipline Data to Enhance Equity in School Discipline"; Adai A. Tefera, "Disrupting Disparities in School Discipline," *Phi Delta Kappan* 105, no. 7 (2024): 32–37, https://doi.org/10.1177/00317217241244903.
14. McIntosh et al., "Using Discipline Data to Enhance Equity in School Discipline."
15. Kent McIntosh et al., "Awareness Is Not Enough: A Double-Blind Randomized Controlled Trial of the Effects of Providing Discipline Disproportionality Data Reports to School Administrators," *Educational Researcher* 49, no. 7 (2020): 533–37, https://doi.org/10.3102/0013189X20939937.
16. Jing Liu, Emily K. Penner, and Wenjing Gao, "Troublemakers? The Role of Frequent Teacher Referrers in Expanding Racial Disciplinary Disproportionalities," *Educational Researcher* 52, no. 8 (2023): 469–81.
17. Luis A. Rodriguez and Richard O. Welsh, "The Dimensions of School Discipline: Toward a Comprehensive Framework for Measuring Discipline Patterns and Outcomes in Schools," *AERA Open* 8 (2022), https://doi.org/10.1177/23328584221083669.
18. Richard O. Welsh, "Economics of Urban Education: Race, Resources, and Control in Schools," in *Handbook of Urban Education*, ed. H. Richard Milner and Kofi Lomotey, 2nd ed. (New York: Routledge, 2021); Welsh, "Up the Down Escalator?"
19. Dewey G. Cornell, Korrie Allen, and Xitao Fan, "A Randomized Controlled Study of the Virginia Student Threat Assessment Guidelines in Kindergarten Through Grade 12," *School Psychology Review* 41, no. 1 (2012): 100–115, https://doi.org/10.1080/02796015.2012.12087378; Dewey Cornell and Peter Lovegrove, "Student Threat Assessment as a Method of Reducing Student Suspensions," in *Closing the School Discipline Gap: Equitable Remedies for Excessive Exclusion*, ed. Daniel J. Losen (New York: Teachers College Press, 2015); Dewey G. Cornell, Anne Gregory, and Xitao Fan, "Reductions in Long-Term Suspensions Following Adoption of the Virginia Student Threat Assessment Guidelines," *NASSP Bulletin* 95, no. 3 (2011): 175–94, https://doi.org/10.1177/0192636511415255.

20. Catherine P. Bradshaw, Mary M. Mitchell, and Philip J. Leaf, "Examining the Effects of Schoolwide Positive Behavioral Interventions and Supports on Student Outcomes: Results from a Randomized Controlled Effectiveness Trial in Elementary Schools," *Journal of Positive Behavior Interventions* 12, no. 3 (2010): 133–48, https://doi.org/10.1177/1098300709334798; Catherine P. Bradshaw, Tracy E. Waasdorp, and Philip J. Leaf, "Effects of School-Wide Positive Behavioral Interventions and Supports on Child Behavior Problems," *Pediatrics* 130, no. 5 (2012): 1136–45, https://doi.org/10.1542/peds.2012-0243; Catherine P. Bradshaw et al., "Promoting Cultural Responsivity and Student Engagement Through Double Check Coaching of Classroom Teachers: An Efficacy Study," *School Psychology Review* 47, no. 2 (2018): 118–34, https://doi.org/10.17105/SPR-2017-0119.V47-2.
21. Abigail Gray et al., "Discipline in Context: Suspension, Climate, and PBIS in the School District of Philadelphia. Research Report," *Consortium for Policy Research in Education*, 2017, https://repository.upenn.edu/server/api/core/bitstreams/0d78139b-74b2-4d11-8bb8-40f5695c0998/content.
22. Sean Darling-Hammond et al., "The Dynamic Nature of Student Discipline and Discipline Disparities," *Proceedings of the National Academy of Sciences* 120, no. 17 (April 25, 2023): e2120417120, https://doi.org/10.1073/pnas.2120417120.
23. Vicki Nishioka, *School Discipline Data Indicators: A Guide for Districts and Schools* (Regional Educational Laboratory Northwest: REL 2017-240, April 2017), https://eric.ed.gov/?id=ED573680.
24. Office of Special Education and Rehabilitative Services Blog, US Department of Education, "Discipline Discussions: The Impact and Harm of Exclusionary Discipline," https://sites.ed.gov/osers/2022/12/discipline-discussions-the-impact-and-harm-of-exclusionary-discipline/?utm_content=&utm_medium=email&utm_name=&utm_source=govdelivery&utm_term=; Center on PBIS, https://www.pbis.org/; School Discipline Lab, https://www.disciplinelab.com/; Equity Assistance Center-South, https://eacsouth.org/.
25. Vicki Nishioka, *Revising School Discipline Policies and Procedures to Promote Equity* (Portland, OR: Education Northwest, Regional Educational Laboratory Northwest, 2019), https://ies.ed.gov/ncee/edlabs/regions/northwest/pdf/facilitation-instr-policy-review.pdf; Vicki Nishioka and Aisling Nagel, *Planning and Facilitating Work Sessions to Improve School Discipline* (Portland, OR: Education Northwest, Regional Educational Laboratory Northwest, 2019), https://ies.ed.gov/ncee/edlabs/regions/northwest/pdf/introduction-rel-discipline-equity.pdf.
26. Rodriguez and Welsh, "The Dimensions of School Discipline."
27. Kelsey Morris and Adam Feinberg, "Collecting Fidelity Data to Support and Sustain PBIS/MTSS in Schools," Center on PBIS, University of Oregon, September 2022, www.pbis.org.
28. National Center on Safe Supportive Learning Environments, "Supportive School Discipline: A Snapshot from Safe Schools/Healthy Students Initiatives," 2012, https://safesupportivelearning.ed.gov/resources/supportive-school-discipline-snapshot-safe-schools healthy-students-initiatives.
29. Barbara Condliffe et al., *Study of Training in Multi-Tiered Systems of Support for Behavior: Impacts on Elementary School Students' Outcomes* (Washington, DC: US Department of Education, National Center for Education Evaluation and Regional Assistance, July 2022), 2, https://eric.ed.gov/?id=ED620902.

30. Kristine A. Camacho et al., "Advocating for Disciplinary Reform Through a Systematic Review of School Discipline Laws and State Guidance Across the United States," *School Psychology Review* (2024): 1–16.
31. Cook et al., "Addressing Discipline Disparities for Black Male Students"; Jason A. Okonofua et al., "A Scalable Empathic-Mindset Intervention Reduces Group Disparities in School Suspensions," *Science Advances* 8, no. 12 (2022): eabj0691, https://doi.org/10.1126/sciadv.abj0691.
32. Rachel M. Perera and Melissa Kay Diliberti, "Survey: Principals Say They Need Better-Trained Teachers and More Resources to Address Student Misbehavior," Brookings, June 8, 2023, https://www.brookings.edu/articles/survey-principals-say-they-need-better-trained-teachers-and-more-resources-to-address-student-misbehavior/.
33. Perera and Diliberti, "Survey: Principals Say They Need Better-Trained Teachers."
34. Gregory, Skiba, and Mediratta, "Eliminating Disparities in School Discipline."
35. Julie Greenberg, Hannah Putman, and Kate Walsh, *Training Our Future Teachers: Classroom Management* (Washington, DC: National Council on Teacher Quality, January 2014), https://www.nctq.org/dmsView/Future_Teachers_Classroom_Management_NCTQ_Report; National Council on Teacher Quality, *Teacher Prep Review: Classroom Management* (Washington, DC: National Council on Teacher Quality, 2020), https://www.nctq.org/review/standard/Classroom-Management.
36. Richard O. Welsh, "Administering Discipline: An Examination of the Factors Shaping School Discipline Practices," *Education and Urban Society* (2023): 1–34, https://doi.org/10.1177/00131245231208170.
37. Sarah D. Sparks, "A Classroom Management Training Helps New Teachers Send Fewer Kids to the Office," *Education Week*, April 15, 2024, https://www.edweek.org/teaching-learning/a-classroom-management-training-helps-new-teachers-send-fewer-kids-to-the-office/2024/04.
38. Gregory, Skiba, and Mediratta, "Eliminating Disparities in School Discipline."
39. Geneva Gay, *Culturally Responsive Teaching: Theory, Research, and Practice* (New York: Teachers College Press, 2018); Gregory, Skiba, and Mediratta, "Eliminating Disparities in School Discipline."
40. Office of Civil Rights, *Dear Colleague Letter on Implementation of IDEA Discipline Provisions* (Washington, DC: US Department of Education, July 19, 2022), https://sites.ed.gov/idea/files/dcl-implementation-of-idea-discipline-provisions.pdf.
41. Anne Gregory and Joshua Korth, "Teacher–Student Relationships and Behavioral Engagement in the Classroom," in *Handbook of Social Influences in School Contexts* (New York: Routledge, 2016); Andrew Kwok, "Classroom Management Actions of Beginning Urban Teachers," *Urban Education* 54, no. 3 (2019): 339–67, https://doi.org/10.1177/0042085918795017; Richard Welsh et al., "Conceptualization and Challenges: Examining District and School Leadership and Schools as Learning Organizations," *Learning Organization* 28, no. 4 (2021): 367–82, https://doi.org/10.1108/TLO-05-2020-0093.
42. Rebecca Epstein, Jamilia Blake, and Thalia González, *Girlhood Interrupted: The Erasure of Black Girls' Childhood* (Rochester, NY: SSRN Scholarly Paper, 2017), https://doi.org/10.2139/ssrn.3000695; Phillip Atiba Goff et al., "The Essence of Innocence: Consequences of Dehumanizing Black Children," *Journal of Personality and Social Psychology* 106, no. 4 (2014): 526–45, https://doi.org/10.1037/a0035663; Neha Sobti and Richard O. Welsh, "Adding Color to My Tears: Toward a Theoretical Framework for Antiblackness in School Discipline," *Educational Researcher* 52, no. 8 (2023): 500–511; Richard

O. Welsh, "Schooling Levels and School Discipline: Examining the Variation in Disciplinary Infractions and Consequences Across Elementary, Middle, and High Schools," *Journal of Education for Students Placed at Risk* 27, no. 3 (2022): 270–95, https://doi.org/10.1080/10824669.2022.2041998.

43. Liu, Penner, and Gao, "Troublemakers?"
44. Sy Doan, Elizabeth D. Steiner, Rakesh Pandey, "Teacher Well-Being and Intentions to Leave in 2024: Findings from the 2024 State of the American Teacher Survey," RAND, 2024, https://www.rand.org/content/dam/rand/pubs/research_reports/RRA1100/RRA1108-12/RAND_RRA1108-12.pdf.
45. Regional Educational Laboratory, *ESSA Tiers of Evidence: What You Need To Know* (Arlington, VA: American Institutes for Research, 2019), https://ies.ed.gov/ncee/edlabs/regions/midwest/pdf/blogs/RELMW-ESSA-Tiers-Video-Handout-508.pdf.
46. Kaitlin P. Anderson, "Academic, Attendance, and Behavioral Outcomes of a Suspension Reduction Policy: Lessons for School Leaders and Policy Makers," *Educational Administration Quarterly* 56, no. 3 (2020): 435–71; Kaitlin P. Anderson, Anna J. Egalite, and Jonathan N. Mills, "Discipline Reform: The Impact of a Statewide Ban on Suspensions for Truancy," *Journal of Education for Students Placed at Risk* 24, no. 1 (2019): 68–91; Terry-Ann Craigie, "Do School Suspension Reforms Work? Evidence from Rhode Island," *Educational Evaluation and Policy Analysis* 44, no. 4 (2022): 667–88; Benjamin W. Fisher and Deanna N. Devlin, "Cops and Counselors: How School Staffing Decisions Relate to Exclusionary Discipline Rates and Racial/Ethnic Disparities," *Race and Social Problems* 16, no. 1 (2024): 19–46; Ayesha K. Hashim, Katharine O. Strunk, and Tasminda K. Dhaliwal, "Justice for All? Suspension Bans and Restorative Justice Programs in the Los Angeles Unified School District," *Peabody Journal of Education* 93, no. 2 (2018): 174–89; Johanna Lacoe and Matthew P. Steinberg, "Rolling Back Zero Tolerance: The Effect of Discipline Policy Reform on Suspension Usage and Student Outcomes," *Peabody Journal of Education* 93, no. 2 (2018): 207–27; Matthew P. Steinberg and Johanna Lacoe, "Reforming School Discipline: School-Level Policy Implementation and the Consequences for Suspended Students and Their Peers," *American Journal of Education* 125, no. 1 (2018): 29–77; Rui Wang, "The Impact of Suspension Reforms on Discipline Outcomes: Evidence from California High Schools," *AERA Open* 8 (2022): 23328584211068067.
47. Catherine P. Bradshaw et al., "Altering School Climate Through School-Wide Positive Behavioral Interventions and Supports: Findings from a Group-Randomized Effectiveness Trial," *Prevention Science* 10 (2009): 100–115; Bradshaw, Mitchell, and Leaf, "Examining the Effects of Schoolwide Positive Behavioral Interventions and Supports on Student Outcomes"; Bradshaw, Waasdorp, and Leaf, "Effects of School-Wide Positive Behavioral Interventions and Supports on Child Behavior Problems"; Catherine P. Bradshaw, Tracy E. Waasdorp, and Philip J. Leaf, "Examining Variation in the Impact of School-Wide Positive Behavioral Interventions and Supports: Findings from a Randomized Controlled Effectiveness Trial," *Journal of Educational Psychology* 107, no. 2 (2015): 546, https://doi.org/10.1037/a0037630; Kent McIntosh et al., "Equity-Focused PBIS Approach Reduces Racial Inequities in School Discipline: A Randomized Controlled Trial," *School Psychology* 36, no. 6 (2021): 433.
48. Paul Caldarella et al., "The Effects of School-Wide Positive Behavior Support on Middle School Climate and Student Outcomes," *RMLE Online* 35, no. 4 (2011): 1–14; Nicholas A. Gage et al., "The Impact of School-Wide Positive Behavior Interventions and Supports on School Suspensions: A Statewide Quasi-Experimental Analysis," *Journal of Positive*

Behavior Interventions 20, no. 4 (2018): 217–26; Nicholas A. Gage et al., "A Quasi-Experimental Design Analysis of the Effects of School-Wide Positive Behavior Interventions and Supports on Discipline in Florida," *Journal of Positive Behavior Interventions* 21, no. 1 (2019): 50–61; Nicholas A. Gage et al., "The Effect of School-Wide Positive Behavior Interventions and Supports on Disciplinary Exclusions: A Conceptual Replication," *Behavioral Disorders* 46, no. 1 (2020): 42–53; Nicolette M. Grasley-Boy, Nicholas A. Gage, and Michael Lombardo, "Effect of SWPBIS on Disciplinary Exclusions for Students with and Without Disabilities," *Exceptional Children* 86, no. 1 (2019): 25–39; Ahhyun Lee et al., "The Impacts of School-Wide Positive Behavior Interventions and Supports on School Discipline Outcomes for Diverse Students," *Elementary School Journal* 121, no. 3 (2021): 410–29.

49. Joie Acosta et al., "Evaluation of a Whole-School Change Intervention: Findings from a Two-Year Cluster-Randomized Trial of the Restorative Practices Intervention," *Journal of Youth and Adolescence* 48 (2019): 876–90; Catherine H. Augustine et al., *Can Restorative Practices Improve School Climate and Curb Suspensions? An Evaluation of the Impact of Restorative Practices in a Mid-Sized Urban School District* (New York: RAND, 2018), https://doi.org/10.7249/RR2840; Anne Gregory, Francis Huang, and Allison Rae Ward-Seidel, "Evaluation of the Whole School Restorative Practices Project: One-Year Impact on Discipline Incidents," *Journal of School Psychology* 95 (2022): 58–71.
50. Francis L. Huang, Anne Gregory, and Allison Rae Ward-Seidel, "The Impact of Restorative Practices on the Use of Out-of-School Suspensions: Results from a Cluster Randomized Controlled Trial," *Prevention Science* 24, no. 5 (2023): 962–73.
51. Miles Davison, Andrew M. Penner, and Emily K. Penner, "Restorative for All? Racial Disproportionality and School Discipline Under Restorative Justice," *American Educational Research Journal* 59, no. 4 (2022): 687–718; Andrea Joseph, Rebecca Jean Hnilica, and Mary Hanson, "Using Restorative Practices to Reduce Racially Disproportionate School Suspensions: The Barriers School Leaders Should Consider During the First Year of Implementation," *Taboo: The Journal of Culture and Education* 20, no. 2 (2021): 6.
52. J. Parker Goyer et al., "Targeted Identity-Safety Interventions Cause Lasting Reductions in Discipline Citations Among Negatively Stereotyped Boys," *Journal of Personality and Social Psychology* 117, no. 2 (2019): 229; Jason A. Okonofua, David Paunesku, and Gregory M. Walton, "Brief Intervention to Encourage Empathic Discipline Cuts Suspension Rates in Half Among Adolescents," *Proceedings of the National Academy of Sciences* 113, no. 19 (2016): 5221–26; Okonofua et al., "A Scalable Empathic-Mindset Intervention Reduces Group Disparities in School Suspensions."
53. Kent McIntosh et al., "Effects of an Equity-Focused PBIS Approach to School Improvement on Exclusionary Discipline and School Climate," *Preventing School Failure: Alternative Education for Children and Youth* 65, no. 4 (2021): 354–61.
54. Cook et al., "Addressing Discipline Disparities for Black Male Students."
55. Kristine E. Larson et al., "Examining How Proactive Management and Culturally Responsive Teaching Relate to Student Behavior: Implications for Measurement and Practice," *School Psychology Review* 47, no. 2 (2018): 153–66.
56. Bradshaw et al., "Promoting Cultural Responsivity and Student Engagement Through Double Check Coaching of Classroom Teachers."
57. Cody Gion, Kent McIntosh, and Sarah Falcon, "Effects of a Multifaceted Classroom Intervention on Racial Disproportionality," *School Psychology Review* 51, no. 1 (2022): 67–83; Anne Gregory et al., "Eliminating the Racial Disparity in Classroom Exclusionary

Discipline," *Journal of Applied Research on Children: Informing Policy for Children at Risk* 5, no. 2 (2014): 12; Anne Gregory et al., "The Promise of a Teacher Professional Development Program in Reducing Racial Disparity in Classroom Exclusionary Discipline," *Closing the School Discipline Gap: Equitable Remedies for Excessive Exclusion* 168 (2015); Gregory et al., "Focused Classroom Coaching and Widespread Racial Equity in School Discipline"; Sophie S. Havighurst et al., "A Randomized Controlled Trial of an Emotion Socialization Intervention in Norwegian Kindergartens," *Early Education and Development* 35, no. 3 (2024): 454–75; Jason A. Okonofua, Amanda D. Perez, and Sean Darling-Hammond, "When Policy and Psychology Meet: Mitigating the Consequences of Bias in Schools," *Science Advances* 6, no. 42 (2020): eaba9479.

58. Gregory et al., "Closing the Racial Discipline Gap in Classrooms by Changing Teacher Practice"; Gregory et al., "Focused Classroom Coaching and Widespread Racial Equity in School Discipline."
59. Mark D. Weist et al., "A Randomized Controlled Trial on the Interconnected Systems Framework for School Mental Health and PBIS: Focus on Proximal Variables and School Discipline," *Journal of School Psychology* 94 (2022): 49–65.
60. Christi Bergin et al., "Effectiveness of a Social-Emotional Learning Program for Both Teachers and Students," *AERA Open* 10 (2024): 23328584241281284.
61. Kevin R. Binning et al., "Bolstering Trust and Reducing Discipline Incidents at a Diverse Middle School: How Self-Affirmation Affects Behavioral Conduct During the Transition to Adolescence," *Journal of School Psychology* 75 (2019): 74–88; Borman, Choi, and Hall, "The Impacts of a Brief Middle-School Self-Affirmation Intervention Help Propel African American and Latino Students Through High School," 605; Paul Caldarella et al., "Effects of Middle School Teachers' Praise-to-Reprimand Ratios on Students' Classroom Behavior," *Journal of Positive Behavior Interventions* 25, no. 1 (2023): 28–40; Goyer et al., "Targeted Identity-Safety Interventions Cause Lasting Reductions in Discipline Citations Among Negatively Stereotyped Boys."
62. Aydin Bal, Kemal Afacan, and Halil Ibrahim Cakir, "Culturally Responsive School Discipline: Implementing Learning Lab at a High School for Systemic Transformation," *American Educational Research Journal* 55, no. 5 (2018): 1007–50.
63. Cornell, Allen, and Fan, "A Randomized Controlled Study of the Virginia Student Threat Assessment Guidelines in Kindergarten Through Grade 12."
64. Cornell, Gregory, and Fan, "Reductions in Long-Term Suspensions Following Adoption of the Virginia Student Threat Assessment Guidelines."
65. Augustine et al., *Can Restorative Practices Improve School Climate and Curb Suspensions?*; Bradshaw, Mitchell, and Leaf, "Examining the Effects of Schoolwide Positive Behavioral Interventions and Supports on Student Outcomes"; Bradshaw, Waasdorp, and Leaf, "Effects of School-Wide Positive Behavioral Interventions and Supports on Child Behavior Problems"; Weist et al., "A Randomized Controlled Trial on the Interconnected Systems Framework for School Mental Health and PBIS."
66. Bradshaw et al., "Promoting Cultural Responsivity and Student Engagement Through Double Check Coaching of Classroom Teachers"; Gregory et al., "Closing the Racial Discipline Gap in Classrooms by Changing Teacher Practice."
67. There are two studies for restorative practices: Davison, Penner, and Penner, "Restorative for All?"; and Joseph, Hnilica, and Hanson, "Using Restorative Practices to Reduce Racially Disproportionate School Suspensions." There are six studies for PBIS: Caldarella et al., "The Effects of School-Wide Positive Behavior Support on Middle School Climate and Student Outcomes"; Gage et al., "The Effect of School-Wide Positive Behavior

Interventions and Supports on Disciplinary Exclusions"; Gage et al., "The Impact of School-Wide Positive Behavior Interventions and Supports on School Suspensions"; Gage et al., "A Quasi-Experimental Design Analysis of the Effects of School-Wide Positive Behavior Interventions and Supports on Discipline in Florida"; Grasley-Boy, Gage, and Lombardo, "Effect of SWPBIS on Disciplinary Exclusions for Students with and Without Disabilities"; Lee et al., "The Impacts of School-Wide Positive Behavior Interventions and Supports on School Discipline Outcomes for Diverse Students."

68. Anderson, "Academic, Attendance, and Behavioral Outcomes of a Suspension Reduction Policy"; Craigie, "Do School Suspension Reforms Work?"; Richard J. Murnane and John B. Willett, *Methods Matter: Improving Causal Inference in Educational and Social Science Research* (Oxford: Oxford University Press, 2010).
69. "Resource on Confronting Racial Discrimination in Student Discipline," US Department of Education Office for Civil Rights, US Department of Justice Civil Rights Division, May 2023, https://www.ed.gov/sites/ed/files/about/offices/list/ocr/docs/tvi-student-discipline-resource-202305.pdf.
70. Kaitlin P. Anderson, "Inequitable Compliance: Implementation Failure of a Statewide Student Discipline Reform," *Peabody Journal of Education* 93, no. 2 (2018): 244–63, https://doi.org/10.1080/0161956X.2018.1435052; Anderson, "Academic, Attendance, and Behavioral Outcomes of a Suspension Reduction Policy"; Anderson, Egalite, and Mills, "Discipline Reform"; E. Christine Baker-Smith, "Suspensions Suspended: Do Changes to High School Suspension Policies Change Suspension Rates?," *Peabody Journal of Education* 93, no. 2 (2018): 190–206, https://doi.org/10.1080/0161956X.2018.1435043; Craigie, "Do School Suspension Reforms Work?"; Fisher and Devlin, "Cops and Counselors"; Hashim, Strunk, and Dhaliwal, "Justice for All?"; Rebecca Hinze-Pifer and Lauren Sartain, "Rethinking Universal Suspension for Severe Student Behavior," *Peabody Journal of Education* 93, no. 2 (2018): 228–43, https://doi.org/10.1080/0161956X.2018.1435051; Lacoe and Steinberg, "Rolling Back Zero Tolerance"; Matthew A. Linick, Alicia N. Garcia, and Hannah Dunn-Grandpre, *The Effect of Discipline Reform Plans on Exclusionary Discipline Outcomes in Minnesota* (Washington, DC: Institute of Education Sciences, Regional Educational Laboratory Midwest, 2021), https://eric.ed.gov/?id=ED614777; Vicki Nishioka et al., *Are State Policy Reforms in Oregon Associated with Fewer School Suspensions and Expulsions?* (Washington, DC: Institute of Education Sciences, Regional Educational Laboratory Northwest, September 2020), https://files-eric-ed-gov/?id=ED607760.pdf; Vicki Nishioka, Becca Merrill, and Havala Hanson, *Changes in Exclusionary and Nonexclusionary Discipline in Grades K–5 Following State Policy Reform in Oregon* (Washington, DC: Institute of Education Sciences, Regional Educational Laboratory Northwest, February 2021), https://eric.ed.gov/?id=ED610682; Steinberg and Lacoe, "Reforming School Discipline."
71. Steinberg and Lacoe, "Reforming School Discipline."
72. Trevor Fronius et al., *Restorative Justice in U.S. Schools: A Research Review* (San Francisco: WestEd, February 2016), https://eric.ed.gov/?id=ED596786.
73. Thalia Gonzalez, "Restorative Justice from the Margins to the Center: The Emergence of a New Norm in School Discipline," *Howard Law Journal* 60, no. 1 (2016): 267–308.
74. Sonia Jain et al., *Restorative Justice in Oakland Schools. Implementation and Impact: An Effective Strategy to Reduce Racially Disproportionate Discipline, Suspensions, and Improve Academic Outcomes* (Oakland, CA: Oakland Unified School District, 2014).

75. Fania Davis, "Discipline with Dignity: Oakland Classrooms Try Healing Instead of Punishment," *Reclaiming Children and Youth* 23, no. 1 (2014): 38–41; Fronius et al., *Restorative Justice in U.S. Schools.*
76. Davis, "Discipline with Dignity."
77. Acosta et al., "Evaluation of a Whole-School Change Intervention"; Augustine et al., *Can Restorative Practices Improve School Climate and Curb Suspensions?*; Bradshaw et al., "Altering School Climate Through School-Wide Positive Behavioral Interventions and Supports"; Bradshaw, Mitchell, and Leaf, "Examining the Effects of Schoolwide Positive Behavioral Interventions and Supports on Student Outcomes"; Bradshaw, Waasdorp, and Leaf, "Effects of School-Wide Positive Behavioral Interventions and Supports on Child Behavior Problems"; Bradshaw, Waasdorp, and Leaf, "Examining Variation in the Impact of School-Wide Positive Behavioral Interventions and Supports," 546–57; Gregory, Huang, and Ward-Seidel, "Evaluation of the Whole School Restorative Practices Project"; Huang, Gregory, and Ward-Seidel, "The Impact of Restorative Practices on the Use of Out-of-School Suspensions"; McIntosh et al., "Equity-Focused PBIS Approach Reduces Racial Inequities in School Discipline."
78. Caldarella et al., "The Effects of School-Wide Positive Behavior Support on Middle School Climate and Student Outcomes"; Davison, Penner, and Penner, "Restorative for All?"; Gage et al., "The Impact of School-Wide Positive Behavior Interventions and Supports on School Suspensions"; Gage et al., "A Quasi-Experimental Design Analysis of the Effects of School-Wide Positive Behavior Interventions and Supports on Discipline in Florida"; Gage et al., "The Effect of School-Wide Positive Behavior Interventions and Supports on Disciplinary Exclusions"; Grasley-Boy, Gage, and Lombardo, "Effect of SWPBIS on Disciplinary Exclusions for Students with and Without Disabilities"; Joseph, Hnilica, and Hanson, "Using Restorative Practices to Reduce Racially Disproportionate School Suspensions"; Lee et al., "The Impacts of School-Wide Positive Behavior Interventions and Supports on School Discipline Outcomes for Diverse Students."
79. Weist et al., "A Randomized Controlled Trial on the Interconnected Systems Framework for School Mental Health and PBIS."
80. Acosta et al., "Evaluation of a Whole-School Change Intervention"; Caldarella et al., "The Effects of School-Wide Positive Behavior Support on Middle School Climate and Student Outcomes"; Mary M. Mitchell and Catherine P. Bradshaw, "Examining Classroom Influences on Student Perceptions of School Climate: The Role of Classroom Management and Exclusionary Discipline Strategies," *Journal of School Psychology* 51, no. 5 (2013): 599–610, https://doi.org/10.1016/j.jsp.2013.05.005; Russell J. Skiba and Jeffrey R. Sprague, "Safety Without Suspensions," *Educational Leadership* 66, no. 1 (September 2008): 38–43.
81. Francis Huang and Yolanda Anyon, "The Relationship Between School Disciplinary Resolutions with School Climate and Attitudes Toward School," *Preventing School Failure: Alternative Education for Children and Youth* 64, no. 3 (2020): 212–22, https://doi.org/10.1080/1045988X.2020.1722940; Jain et al., *Restorative Justice in Oakland Schools.*
82. Lilyana Ortega, "Outcomes of a Restorative Circles Program in a High School Setting," *Psychology of Violence* 6, no. 3 (2016), https://doi.org/10.1037/vio0000048.
83. Jain et al., *Restorative Justice in Oakland Schools.*
84. Augustine et al., *Can Restorative Practices Improve School Climate and Curb Suspensions?*
85. Welsh and Little, "The School Discipline Dilemma," 773.

86. Jason A. Okonofua, Gregory M. Walton, and Jennifer L. Eberhardt, "A Vicious Cycle: A Social–Psychological Account of Extreme Racial Disparities in School Discipline," *Perspectives on Psychological Science* 11, no. 3 (2016): 381–98, https://doi.org/10.1177/1745691616635592.
87. Santiago-Rosario, Mcintosh, and Payno-Simmons, *Centering Equity Within the PBIS Framework*.
88. Yolanda Anyon, Duan Zhang, and Cynthia Hazel, "Race, Exclusionary Discipline, and Connectedness to Adults in Secondary Schools," *American Journal of Community Psychology* 57, no. 3/4 (2016): 342–52, https://doi.org/10.1002/ajcp.12061; Bradshaw et al., "Promoting Cultural Responsivity and Student Engagement Through Double Check Coaching of Classroom Teachers"; Cook et al., "Addressing Discipline Disparities for Black Male Students"; Cornell, Allen, and Fan, "A Randomized Controlled Study of the Virginia Student Threat Assessment Guidelines in Kindergarten Through Grade 12."
89. Okonofua et al., "A Scalable Empathic-Mindset Intervention Reduces Group Disparities in School Suspensions."
90. Goyer et al., "Targeted Identity-Safety Interventions Cause Lasting Reductions in Discipline Citations Among Negatively Stereotyped Boys"; Okonofua, Paunesku, and Walton, "Brief Intervention to Encourage Empathic Discipline Cuts Suspension Rates in Half Among Adolescents"; Okonofua et al., "A Scalable Empathic-Mindset Intervention Reduces Group Disparities in School Suspensions."
91. Okonofua et al., "A Scalable Empathic-Mindset Intervention Reduces Group Disparities in School Suspensions."
92. McIntosh et al., "Equity-Focused PBIS Approach Reduces Racial Inequities in School Discipline"; McIntosh et al., "Effects of an Equity-Focused PBIS Approach to School Improvement on Exclusionary Discipline and School Climate."
93. Cook et al., "Addressing Discipline Disparities for Black Male Students."
94. Gion, McIntosh, and Falcon, "Effects of a Multifaceted Classroom Intervention on Racial Disproportionality"; Anne Gregory, "Effects of a Professional Development Program on Behavioral Engagement of Students in Middle and High School," *Psychology in the Schools* 51, no. 2 (2014): 143–63, https://doi.org/10.1002/pits.21741; Gregory et al., "Eliminating the Racial Disparity in Classroom Exclusionary Discipline"; Gregory et al., "Focused Classroom Coaching and Widespread Racial Equity in School Discipline"; Okonofua et al., "A Scalable Empathic-Mindset Intervention Reduces Group Disparities in School Suspensions."
95. Gregory et al., "Focused Classroom Coaching and Widespread Racial Equity in School Discipline"; Gregory et al., "Closing the Racial Discipline Gap in Classrooms by Changing Teacher Practice."
96. Gregory et al., "Closing the Racial Discipline Gap in Classrooms by Changing Teacher Practice."
97. Gregory et al., "Eliminating the Racial Disparity in Classroom Exclusionary Discipline"; Matthew P. Steinberg and Johanna Lacoe, "What Do We Know About School Discipline Reform? Assessing the Alternatives to Suspensions and Expulsions," *Education Next* 17, no. 1 (December 22, 2017): 44–53.
98. Bradshaw et al., "Promoting Cultural Responsivity and Student Engagement Through Double Check Coaching of Classroom Teachers."
99. CASEL, "Fundamentals of SEL," Collaborative for Academic, Social, and Emotional Learning, https://casel.org/fundamentals-of-sel/.

100. David M. Osher et al., "Avoid Simple Solutions and Quick Fixes: Lessons Learned from a Comprehensive Districtwide Approach to Improving Student Behavior and School Safety," *Journal of Applied Research on Children* 5, no. 2 (2014), http://digitalcommons.library.tmc.edu/childrenatrisk/vol5/iss2/16.
101. Bergin et al., "Effectiveness of a Social-Emotional Learning Program for Both Teachers and Students."
102. CASEL, "Key Implementation Insights from the Collaborating Districts Initiative," Collaborative for Academic, Social, and Emotional Learning, June 2017, https://casel.org/casel-gateway-key-insights-from-cdi/?view=1.
103. María Reina Santiago-Rosario and Kent McIntosh, "Increasing Disciplinary Equity by Teaching Neutralizing Routines to Teachers and Students," in *Motivating the SEL Field Forward Through Equity*, Advances in Motivation and Achievement, vol. 21, ed. Nicholas Yoder and Alexandra Skoog-Hoffman (Leeds, UK: Emerald, 2021) 127–42, https://doi.org/10.1108/S0749-742320210000021010; Smolkowski et al., "Vulnerable Decision Points for Disproportionate Office Discipline Referrals"; Sean C. Austin, Kent McIntosh, and Erik J. Girvan, "National Patterns of Vulnerable Decision Points in School Discipline," *Journal of School Psychology* 102 (February 1, 2024): 101259, https://doi.org/10.1016/j.jsp.2023.101259.
104. Kristin Cipollone, Emily Brown Hoffman, and Maria Sciuchetti, "Compliance and Control: The Hidden Curriculum of Social-Emotional Learning," *Perspectives on Early Childhood Psychology and Education* 6, no. 1 (November 21, 2022), https://doi.org/10.58948/2834-8257.1005; Kara Ieva and Jordon Beasley, "Dismantling Racism Through Collaborative Consultation: Promoting Culturally Affirming Educator SEL," *Theory Into Practice* 61, no. 2 (April 3, 2022): 236–49, https://doi.org/10.1080/00405841.2022.2036049; Chynna S. McCall, Monica E. Romero, Wenxi Yang, and Tanya Weigand, "A Call for Equity-Focused Social-Emotional Learning," *School Psychology Review* 52, no. 5 (September 3, 2023): 586–607, https://doi.org/10.1080/2372966X.2022.2093125; Stephanie R. Forman, James Lamar Foster, and Jessica G. Rigby, "School Leaders' Use of Social-Emotional Learning to Disrupt Whiteness," *Educational Administration Quarterly* 58, no. 3 (August 1, 2022): 351–85, https://doi.org/10.1177/0013161X211053609.
105. Juyeon Lee, Valerie B. Shapiro, and Bo-Kyung Elizabeth Kim, "Universal School-Based Social and Emotional Learning (SEL) for Diverse Student Subgroups: Implications for Enhancing Equity Through SEL," *Prevention Science* 24, no. 5 (July 1, 2023): 1011–22, https://doi.org/10.1007/s11121-023-01552-y.
106. Jessika H. Bottiani, Catherine P. Bradshaw, and Tamar Mendelson, "A Multilevel Examination of Racial Disparities in High School Discipline: Black and White Adolescents' Perceived Equity, School Belonging, and Adjustment Problems," *Journal of Educational Psychology* 109, no. 4 (2017): 532–45, https://doi.org/10.1037/edu0000155.
107. Gholdy Muhammad, *Unearthing Joy: A Guide to Culturally and Historically Responsive Curriculum and Instruction* (New York: Scholastic, 2023); Muhammad, *Cultivating Genius*.
108. Bal, Afacan, and Cakir, "Culturally Responsive School Discipline"; Borman, Choi, and Hall, "The Impacts of a Brief Middle-School Self-Affirmation Intervention Help Propel African American and Latino Students Through High School"; Caldarella et al., "The Effects of School-Wide Positive Behavior Support on Middle School Climate and Student Outcomes."

109. Borman, Choi, and Hall, "The Impacts of a Brief Middle-School Self-Affirmation Intervention Help Propel African American and Latino Students Through High School."
110. Binning et al., "Bolstering Trust and Reducing Discipline Incidents at a Diverse Middle School."
111. Goyer et al., "Targeted Identity-Safety Interventions Cause Lasting Reductions in Discipline Citations Among Negatively Stereotyped Boys."
112. Geoffrey D. Borman et al., "Self-Affirmation Effects Are Produced by School Context, Student Engagement with the Intervention, and Time: Lessons from a District-Wide Implementation," *Psychological Science* 29, no. 11 (November 1, 2018): 1773–84, https://doi.org/10.1177/0956797618784016; Borman, Choi, and Hall, "The Impacts of a Brief Middle-School Self-Affirmation Intervention Help Propel African American and Latino Students Through High School"; Zezhen Wu, Thees F. Spreckelsen, and Geoffrey L. Cohen, "A Meta-Analysis of the Effect of Values Affirmation on Academic Achievement," *Journal of Social Issues* 77, no. 3 (2021): 702–50, https://doi.org/10.1111/josi.12415.
113. Anne Gregory, Francis L. Huang, and Allison Rae Ward-Seidel, "Adolescent Exposure to Restorative Practices and Their Perceptions of Support, Structure, and Bullying in the School Climate," *AERA Open* 10 (2024): 23328584241288525.
114. Richard O. Welsh, "Navigating Tensions in School Discipline: Examining School Leaders, Teachers, and the Conversion of Referrals into Suspensions," *American Journal of Education* 129, no. 2 (2023): 237–64.
115. Richard O. Welsh and Luis A. Rodriguez, "The Plight of Persistently Disciplined Students: Examining Frequent Flyers and the Conversion of Office Discipline Referrals into Suspensions," *Educational Evaluation and Policy Analysis* 46, no. 1 (2024): 160–70.
116. H. Richard Milner, *The Race Card: Leading the Fight for Truth in America's Schools* (Thousand Oaks, CA: Corwin, 2023).
117. Tefera, "Disrupting Disparities in School Discipline"; Welsh, "Administering Discipline"; Welsh and Little, "The School Discipline Dilemma."

Chapter 3

1. Leslie T. Fenwick, *Jim Crow's Pink Slip: The Untold Story of Black Principal and Teacher Leadership* (Cambridge, MA: Harvard Education Press, 2022); Linda C. Tillman, "(Un) Intended Consequences? The Impact of the Brown v. Board of Education Decision on the Employment Status of Black Educators," *Education and Urban Society* 36, no. 3 (2004): 280–303, https://doi.org/10.1177/0013124504264360.
2. Fenwick, *Jim Crow's Pink Slip*; Leslie T. Fenwick, "Otherwise Qualified: The Untold Story of Brown and Black Educators' Professional Superiority," Brown Lecture, 2023, https://www-aera-net.proxy.library.vanderbilt.edu/Events-Meetings/Annual-Brown-Lecture-in-Education-Research.
3. Nathan Barrett et al., "Disparities and Discrimination in Student Discipline by Race and Family Income," *Journal of Human Resources* 56, no. 3 (2021): 711–48, https://doi.org/10.3368/jhr.56.3.0118-9267R2; Erik J. Girvan et al., "The Relative Contribution of Subjective Office Referrals to Racial Disproportionality in School Discipline," *School Psychology Quarterly* 32, no. 3 (2017): 392–404, https://doi.org/10.1037/spq0000178; Kamilah B. Legette and Yoli Anyon, "Just Go to the Office! An Intersectional Exploration of the Role of Race and Gender in Discipline Referral Reasons," *Race Ethnicity and Education* (2023): 1–21, https://doi.org/10.1080/13613324.2023.2192946; Richard O. Welsh, "Schooling Levels and School Discipline: Examining the Variation in Disciplinary

Infractions and Consequences Across Elementary, Middle, and High Schools," *Journal of Education for Students Placed at Risk* 27, no. 3 (2022): 270–95, https://doi.org/10.1080/10824669.2022.2041998

4. Legette and Anyon, "Just Go to the Office!"; Neha Sobti and Richard O. Welsh, "Adding Color to My Tears: Toward a Theoretical Framework for Antiblackness in School Discipline," *Educational Researcher* 52, no. 8 (2023): 500–511, https://doi.org/10.3102/0013189X231191448.
5. Shafiqua J. Little and Richard O. Welsh, "Rac(e)ing to Punishment? Applying Theory to Racial Disparities in Disciplinary Outcomes," *Race Ethnicity and Education* 25, no. 4 (2022): 564–84, https://doi.org/10.1080/13613324.2019.1599344; Sobti and Welsh, "Adding Color to My Tears."
6. Welsh, "Schooling Levels and School Discipline."
7. Russell J. Skiba et al., "Parsing Disciplinary Disproportionality: Contributions of Infraction, Student, and School Characteristics to Out-of-School Suspension and Expulsion," *American Educational Research Journal* 51, no. 4 (2014): 640–70, https://doi.org/10.3102/0002831214541670; Richard O. Welsh and Shafiqua Little, "The School Discipline Dilemma: A Comprehensive Review of Disparities and Alternative Approaches," *Review of Educational Research* 88, no. 5 (October 1, 2018): 752–94, https://doi.org/10.3102/0034654318791582.
8. Cresean Hughes et al., "'Value in Diversity': School Racial and Ethnic Composition, Teacher Diversity, and School Punishment," *Social Science Research* 92 (2020): 102481, https://doi.org/10.1016/j.ssresearch.2020.102481.
9. David E. DeMatthews et al., "Guilty as Charged? Principals' Perspectives on Disciplinary Practices and the Racial Discipline Gap," *Educational Administration Quarterly* 53, no. 4 (2017): 519–55, https://doi.org/10.1177/0013161X17714844.
10. K. Jurée Capers, "The Role of Desegregation and Teachers of Color in Discipline Disproportionality," *Urban Review* 51, no. 5 (2019): 789–815, https://doi.org/10.1007/s11256-019-00505-6; Christopher Redding, "A Teacher Like Me: A Review of the Effect of Student–Teacher Racial/Ethnic Matching on Teacher Perceptions of Students and Student Academic and Behavioral Outcomes," *Review of Educational Research* 89, no. 4 (2019): 499–535, https://doi.org/10.3102/0034654319853545; Olivia Marcucci and Rowhea Elmesky, "Advancing Culturally Relevant Discipline: An Ethnographic Microanalysis of Disciplinary Interactions with Black Students," *Urban Education* 58, no. 6 (2023): 1118–50, https://doi.org/10.1177/0042085920909165.
11. Capers, "The Role of Desegregation and Teachers of Color in Discipline Disproportionality."
12. H. Richard Milner, "Fifteenth Annual AERA Brown Lecture in Education Research: Disrupting Punitive Practices and Policies: Rac(e)ing Back to Teaching, Teacher Preparation, and Brown," *Educational Researcher* 49, no. 3 (2020): 147–60, https://doi.org/10.3102/0013189X20907396; Jayanti Owens, "Double Jeopardy: Teacher Biases, Racialized Organizations, and the Production of Racial/Ethnic Disparities in School Discipline," *American Sociological Review* 87, no. 6 (2022): 1007–48, https://doi.org/10.1177/00031224221135810; Richard O. Welsh, "Economics of Urban Education: Race, Resources, and Control in Schools," in *Handbook of Urban Education*, ed. H. Richard Milner and Kofi Lomotey, 2nd ed. (New York: Routledge, 2021).
13. Owens, "Double Jeopardy"; Welsh, "Economics of Urban Education."

14. National Center for Education Statistics, *Characteristics of Public School Teachers*, Condition of Education (Washington, DC: US Department of Education, Institute of Education Sciences, 2023), https://nces.ed.gov/programs/coe/indicator/clr.
15. National Center for Education Statistics, *Racial/Ethnic Enrollment in Public Schools*, Condition of Education (Washington, DC: US Department of Education, Institute of Education Sciences, May 2024), https://nces.ed.gov/programs/coe/indicator/cge/racial-ethnic-enrollment.
16. National Center for Education Statistics, *Characteristics of Public and Private School Principals*, Condition of Education (Washington, DC: US Department of Education, Institute of Education Sciences, November 2023), https://nces.ed.gov/programs/coe/indicator/cls/public-school-principals.
17. Catherine P. Bradshaw, Mary M. Mitchell, and Philip J. Leaf, "Examining the Effects of Schoolwide Positive Behavioral Interventions and Supports on Student Outcomes: Results from a Randomized Controlled Effectiveness Trial in Elementary Schools," *Journal of Positive Behavior Interventions* 12, no. 3 (2010): 133–48, https://doi.org/10.1177/1098300709334798; Constance A. Lindsay and Cassandra M. D. Hart, "Exposure to Same-Race Teachers and Student Disciplinary Outcomes for Black Students in North Carolina," *Educational Evaluation and Policy Analysis* 39, no. 3 (2017): 485–510, https://doi.org/10.3102/0162373717693109; Little and Welsh, "Rac(e)ing to Punishment?"; Marcucci and Elmesky, "Advancing Culturally Relevant Discipline"; Welsh and Little, "The School Discipline Dilemma"; Richard O. Welsh and Shafiqua Little, "Caste and Control in Schools: A Systematic Review of the Pathways, Rates and Correlates of Exclusion Due to School Discipline," *Children and Youth Services Review* 94 (2018): 315–39, https://doi.org/10.1016/j.childyouth.2018.09.031; Frances Vavrus and KimMarie Cole, "'I Didn't Do Nothin'": The Discursive Construction of School Suspension," *Urban Review* 34, no. 2 (2002): 87–111, https://doi.org/10.1023/A:1015375215801.
18. Richard O. Welsh and Neha Sobti, "Moving from Pathology to Politicized Care: Examining Black School Leaders' Perspectives on School Discipline," *Journal of School Leadership* 33, no. 6 (2023): 579–606, https://doi.org/10.1177/10526846231174153; Richard O. Welsh, "School Leadership, Race, and School Discipline: Examining the Relationship Between School Leader-Student Racial Congruence and the Likelihood of Exclusionary Discipline," *Race and Justice* (2024): 21533687241227176, https://doi.org/10.1177/21533687241227176.
19. David S. Kirk, "Unraveling the Contextual Effects on Student Suspension and Juvenile Arrest: The Independent and Interdependent Influences of School, Neighborhood, and Family Social Controls," *Criminology* 47, no. 2 (2009): 479–520, https://doi.org/10.1111/j.1745-9125.2009.00147.x.
20. Kirk, "Unraveling the Contextual Effects on Student Suspension and Juvenile Arrest."
21. Decoteau J. Irby, "Trouble at School: Understanding School Discipline Systems as Nets of Social Control," *Equity & Excellence in Education* 47, no. 4 (2014): 513–30, https://doi.org/10.1080/10665684.2014.958963; Simone Ispa-Landa, "Racial and Gender Inequality and School Discipline: Toward a More Comprehensive View of School Policy," *Social Currents* 4, no. 6 (2017): 511–17, https://doi.org/10.1177/2329496517704876; Aaron Kupchik, *Homeroom Security: School Discipline in an Age of Fear* (New York: New York University Press, 2010); Pedro A. Noguera, "Schools, Prisons, and Social Implications of Punishment: Rethinking Disciplinary Practices," *Theory Into Practice* 42, no. 4 (2003): 341–50, https://doi.org/10.1207/s15430421tip4204_12; Kelly Welch and Allison Ann

Payne, "Racial Threat and Punitive School Discipline," *Social Problems* 57, no. 1 (2010): 25–48, https://doi.org/10.1525/sp.2010.57.1.25; Kelly Welch and Allison Ann Payne, "Latino/a Student Threat and School Disciplinary Policies and Practices," *Sociology of Education* 91, no. 2 (2018): 91–110, https://doi.org/10.1177/0038040718757720.

22. Rebecca A. Cruz and Allison R. Firestone, "On Reducing Disparities in Office Discipline Referrals: A Systematic Review of Underlying Theories," *Whiteness and Education* 9, no. 1 (2024): 82–104.
23. Heidi M. Gansen, "Disciplining Difference(s): Reproducing Inequalities Through Disciplinary Interactions in Preschool," *Social Problems* 68, no. 3 (2021): 740–60, https://doi.org/10.1093/socpro/spaa011; Kirk, "Unraveling the Contextual Effects on Student Suspension and Juvenile Arrest"; Amanda E. Lewis and John B. Diamond, *Despite the Best Intentions: How Racial Inequality Thrives in Good Schools* (New York: Oxford University Press, 2015); Carla Shedd, *Unequal City: Race, Schools, and Perceptions of Injustice* (New York: Russell Sage Foundation, 2015), https://www.jstor.org/stable/10.7758/9781610448529.
24. Irby, "Trouble at School."
25. Welch and Payne, "Latino/a Student Threat and School Disciplinary Policies and Practices."
26. Donald P. Haider-Markel, Chelsie L. M. Bright, and Steven M. Sylvester, "Staying in Class: Representative Bureaucracy and Student Praise and Punishment," *Journal of Policy Studies* 37, no. 2 (2022): 27–40, https://doi.org/10.52372/jps37203; Irby, "Trouble at School."
27. Irby, "Trouble at School."
28. Julia T. Atiles, Talley M. Gresham, and Isaac Washburn, "Values and Beliefs Regarding Discipline Practices: How School Culture Impacts Teacher Responses to Student Misbehavior," *Educational Research Quarterly* 40, no. 3 (2017): 3–24; Jamilia J. Blake et al., "Does Student–Teacher Racial/Ethnic Match Impact Black Students' Discipline Risk? A Test of the Cultural Synchrony Hypothesis," in *Inequality in School Discipline: Research and Practice to Reduce Disparities*, ed. Russell J. Skiba, Kavitha Mediratta, and M. Karega Rausch (New York: Palgrave Macmillan, 2016); Bradshaw, Mitchell, and Leaf, "Examining the Effects of Schoolwide Positive Behavioral Interventions and Supports on Student Outcomes"; Ann Arnett Ferguson, *Bad Boys: Public Schools in the Making of Black Masculinity*, Law, Meaning, and Violence (Ann Arbor: University of Michigan Press, 2000); Anne Gregory and Pharmicia M. Mosely, "The Discipline Gap: Teachers' Views on the Over-Representation of African American Students in the Discipline System," *Equity & Excellence in Education* 37, no. 1 (2004): 18–30, https://doi.org/10.1080/10665680490429280; Dorothy Hines-Datiri, "When Police Intervene: Race, Gender, and Discipline of Black Male Students at an Urban High School," *Journal of Cases in Educational Leadership* 18, no. 2 (2015): 122–33, https://doi.org/10.1177/1555458915584676; Jeffrey L. Jordan and Bulent Anil, "Race, Gender, School Discipline, and Human Capital Effects," *Journal of Agricultural and Applied Economics* 41, no. 2 (2009): 419–29, https://doi.org/10.1017/S1074070800002893; Lindsay and Hart, "Exposure to Same-Race Teachers and Student Disciplinary Outcomes for Black Students in North Carolina"; Jason A. Okonofua and Jennifer L. Eberhardt, "Two Strikes: Race and the Disciplining of Young Students," *Psychological Science* 26, no. 5 (2015): 617–24, https://doi.org/10.1177/0956797615570365; Jason A. Okonofua, David Paunesku, and Gregory M. Walton, "Brief Intervention to Encourage Empathic Discipline Cuts Suspension Rates in Half Among Adolescents," *Proceedings of the*

National Academy of Sciences 113, no. 19 (2016): 5221–26, https://doi.org/10.1073/pnas.1523698113.

29. Atiles, Gresham, and Washburn, "Values and Beliefs Regarding Discipline Practices"; Blake et al., "Does Student–Teacher Racial/Ethnic Match Impact Black Students' Discipline Risk?"; Bradshaw, Mitchell, and Leaf, "Examining the Effects of Schoolwide Positive Behavioral Interventions and Supports on Student Outcomes"; Vincent Cho, Katrina Borowiec, and Kaitlyn F. Tuthill, "Organizational Problem-Solving and School Discipline: Comparing the Roles of Schoolwide Behavior Management Technologies," *Journal of Educational Administration* 59, no. 3 (2021): 302–17, https://doi.org/10.1108/JEA-10-2020-0229; Ferguson, *Bad Boys*; Gregory and Mosely, "The Discipline Gap"; Hines-Datiri, "When Police Intervene"; Josh Kinsler, "Understanding the Black–White School Discipline Gap," *Economics of Education Review*, Special Issue: Economic Returns to Education, 30, no. 6 (2011): 1370–83, https://doi.org/10.1016/j.econedurev.2011.07.004; Lindsay and Hart, "Exposure to Same-Race Teachers and Student Disciplinary Outcomes for Black Students in North Carolina"; Okonofua and Eberhardt, "Two Strikes"; Okonofua, Paunesku, and Walton, "Brief Intervention to Encourage Empathic Discipline Cuts Suspension Rates in Half Among Adolescents"; Russell J. Skiba et al., "Race Is Not Neutral: A National Investigation of African American and Latino Disproportionality in School Discipline," *School Psychology Review* 40, no. 1 (2011): 85–107, https://doi.org/10.1080/02796015.2011.12087730; Skiba et al., "Parsing Disciplinary Disproportionality"; Cheryl Staats, *Implicit Racial Bias and School Discipline Disparities* (Columbus: Ohio State University, Kirwan Institute for the Study of Race and Ethnicity, 2014).
30. Anne Gregory, Russell J. Skiba, and Pedro A. Noguera, "The Achievement Gap and the Discipline Gap: Two Sides of the Same Coin?," *Educational Researcher* 39, no. 1 (2010): 59–68; Marcucci and Elmesky, "Advancing Culturally Relevant Discipline"; Sharon L. Nichols, "Teachers' and Students' Beliefs About Student Belonging in One Middle School," *Elementary School Journal* 106, no. 3 (2006): 255–71, https://doi.org/10.1086/501486.
31. Lindsey M. O'Brennan, Catherine P. Bradshaw, and Michael J. Furlong, "Influence of Classroom and School Climate on Teacher Perceptions of Student Problem Behavior," *School Mental Health* 6, no. 2 (2014): 125–36, https://doi.org/10.1007/s12310-014-9118-8.
32. Capers, "The Role of Desegregation and Teachers of Color in Discipline Disproportionality"; Milner, "Fifteenth Annual AERA Brown Lecture in Education Research."
33. Jason A. Grissom, Jill Nicholson-Crotty, and Sean Nicholson-Crotty, "Race, Region, and Representative Bureaucracy," *Public Administration Review* 69, no. 5 (2009): 911–19, https://doi.org/10.1111/j.1540-6210.2009.02040.x; Lindsay and Hart, "Exposure to Same-Race Teachers and Student Disciplinary Outcomes for Black Students in North Carolina."
34. Blake et al., "Does Student–Teacher Racial/Ethnic Match Impact Black Students' Discipline Risk?"; Hughes et al., "'Value in Diversity.'"
35. Stephen B. Holt and Seth Gershenson, "The Impact of Demographic Representation on Absences and Suspensions," *Policy Studies Journal* 47, no. 4 (2019): 1069–99, https://doi.org/10.1111/psj.12229; Lindsay and Hart, "Exposure to Same-Race Teachers and Student Disciplinary Outcomes for Black Students in North Carolina"; Matthew Shirrell, Travis J. Bristol, and Tolani A. Britton, "The Effects of Student–Teacher Ethnoracial Matching on Exclusionary Discipline for Asian American, Black, and Latinx Students:

Evidence from New York City," *Educational Evaluation and Policy Analysis* 46, no. 3 (June 19, 2023): 01623737231175461, https://doi.org/10.3102/01623737231175461.

36. Walter S. Gilliam et al., *Do Early Educators' Implicit Biases Regarding Sex and Race Relate to Behavior Expectations and Recommendations of Preschool Expulsions and Suspensions?* (New Haven, CT: Yale University Child Study Center, 2016); Welsh and Little, "Caste and Control in Schools."
37. Owens, "Double Jeopardy."
38. DeMatthews et al., "Guilty as Charged?"; Joanne W. Golann and Ashley Jones, "How Principals Balance Control and Care in Urban School Discipline," *Urban Education* 59, no. 1 (2021): 31–62, https://doi.org/10.1177/00420859211046824; Abigail Gray et al., *Discipline in Context: Suspension, Climate, and PBIS in the School District of Philadelphia* (Philadelphia: Consortium for Policy Research in Education, October 2017), https://eric.ed.gov/?id=ED586779; Brianna L. Kennedy, Amy S. Murphy, and Adam Jordan, "Title I Middle School Administrators' Beliefs and Choices About Using Corporal Punishment and Exclusionary Discipline," *American Journal of Education* 123, no. 2 (2017): 243–80, https://doi.org/10.1086/689929; Kinsler, "Understanding the Black–White School Discipline Gap"; Gathogo Mukuria, "Disciplinary Challenges: How Do Principals Address This Dilemma?," *Urban Education* 37, no. 3 (2002): 432–52, https://doi.org/10.1177/00485902037003007; Ani N. Shabazian, "Voices That Matter: Chief Administrative Officers' Role in the Student Discipline Gap," *Urban Education* 55, no. 1 (2020): 66–94, https://doi.org/10.1177/0042085916651319; Skiba et al., "Parsing Disciplinary Disproportionality"; Lucy C. Sorensen, Shawn D. Bushway, and Elizabeth J. Gifford, "Getting Tough? The Effects of Discretionary Principal Discipline on Student Outcomes," *Education Finance and Policy* 17, no. 2 (2022): 255–84, https://doi.org/10.1162/edfp_a_00341; Kathryn E. Wiley, "A Tale of Two Logics: School Discipline and Racial Disparities in a 'Mostly White' Middle School," *American Journal of Education* 127, no. 2 (2021): 163–92, https://doi.org/10.1086/712084; John A. Williams III et al., "The Discipline Gatekeeper: Assistant Principals' Experiences with Managing School Discipline in Urban Middle Schools," *Urban Education* 58, no. 8 (2023): 1543–71, https://doi.org/10.1177/0042085920908913.
39. Gray et al., *Discipline in Context*; Mukuria, "Disciplinary Challenges"; Skiba et al., "Parsing Disciplinary Disproportionality"; Russell J. Skiba, Heather Edl, and M. Karega Rausch, "How Do Principals Feel About Discipline? The Disciplinary Practices Survey" (presented at the Annual Convention of the American Educational Research Association, Chicago, 2007).
40. Gray et al., *Discipline in Context*; Kennedy, Murphy, and Jordan, "Title I Middle School Administrators' Beliefs and Choices About Using Corporal Punishment and Exclusionary Discipline"; Mukuria, "Disciplinary Challenges."
41. Skiba et al., "Parsing Disciplinary Disproportionality."
42. Nora M. Findlay, "Discretion in Student Discipline: Insight into Elementary Principals' Decision Making," *Educational Administration Quarterly* 51, no. 3 (2015): 472–507, https://doi.org/10.1177/0013161X14523617.
43. Kennedy, Murphy, and Jordan, "Title I Middle School Administrators' Beliefs and Choices About Using Corporal Punishment and Exclusionary Discipline."
44. Kennedy, Murphy, and Jordan, "Title I Middle School Administrators' Beliefs and Choices About Using Corporal Punishment and Exclusionary Discipline."
45. Barrett et al., "Disparities and Discrimination in Student Discipline by Race and Family Income"; Ying Shi and Maria Zhu, "Equal Time for Equal Crime? Racial Bias in

School Discipline," *Economics of Education Review* 88 (2022): 102256, https://doi.org/10.1016/j.econedurev.2022.102256; Skiba et al., "Parsing Disciplinary Disproportionality"; Sobti and Welsh, "Adding Color to My Tears"; Welsh, "Schooling Levels and School Discipline."

46. Shi and Zhu, "Equal Time for Equal Crime?"
47. Shoshana N. Jarvis and Jason A. Okonofua, "School Deferred: When Bias Affects School Leaders," *Social Psychological and Personality Science* 11, no. 4 (2020): 492–98.
48. Wiley, "A Tale of Two Logics."
49. Andrew Bacher-Hicks, Stephen B. Billings, and David J. Deming, "The School to Prison Pipeline: Long-Run Impacts of School Suspensions on Adult Crime," National Bureau of Economic Research, September 2019, https://www.nber.org/papers/w26257.
50. Brendan Bartanen and Jason A. Grissom, "School Principal Race, Teacher Racial Diversity, and Student Achievement," *Journal of Human Resources* 58, no. 2 (2023): 666–712, https://doi.org/10.3368/jhr.58.4.0218-9328R2; Golann and Jones, "How Principals Balance Control and Care in Urban School Discipline."
51. Bartanen and Grissom, "School Principal Race, Teacher Racial Diversity, and Student Achievement."
52. EAB, "Breaking Bad Behavior: The Rise of Classroom Disruptions in Early Grades and How Districts Are Responding," District Leadership Forum, 2019, https://pages.eab.com/rs/732-GKV-655/images/BreakingBadBehaviorStudy.pdf; Arianna Prothero, "How to Manage Discord over Student Discipline," *Education Week*, October 16, 2019, https://www.edweek.org/leadership/how-to-manage-discord-over-student-discipline/2019/10.
53. DeMatthews et al., "Guilty as Charged?"; Skiba, Edl, and Rausch, "How Do Principals Feel About Discipline?"
54. EAB, "Breaking Bad Behavior."
55. Richard O. Welsh, "Navigating Tensions in School Discipline: Examining School Leaders, Teachers, and the Conversion of Referrals into Suspensions," *American Journal of Education* 129, no. 2 (2023): 237–64, https://doi.org/10.1086/723064; Richard O. Welsh, "Administering Discipline: An Examination of the Factors Shaping School Discipline Practices," *Education and Urban Society* (2023): 1–34, https://doi.org/10.1177/00131245231208170.
56. Melissa R. Jenkins et al., "Regional Trends and the Role of School Support Staff in Suspensions of Students with Disabilities," *Children and Youth Services Review* 141 (2022): 106622, https://doi.org/10.1016/j.childyouth.2022.106622; Susan C. Whiston et al., "School Counseling Outcome: A Meta-Analytic Examination of Interventions," *Journal of Counseling & Development* 89, no. 1 (2011): 37–55, https://doi.org/10.1002/j.1556-6678.2011.tb00059.x.
57. Eric Madfis, Paul Hirschfield, and Lynn A. Addington, "School Securitization and Its Alternatives: The Social, Political, and Contextual Drivers of School Safety Policy and Practice," *School Psychology Review* 50, no. 2–3 (July 3, 2021): 191–205, https://doi.org/10.1080/2372966X.2020.1855063.
58. Charles Bartholomew, *Preventing the School-to-Prison Pipeline: A Public Health Approach for School Psychologists, Counselors, and Social Workers* (New York: Routledge, 2023), https://doi.org/10.4324/9781003284383; Madfis, Hirschfield, and Addington, "School Securitization and Its Alternatives."
59. Jenkins et al., "Regional Trends and the Role of School Support Staff in Suspensions of Students with Disabilities"; Whiston et al., "School Counseling Outcome."

60. Jenkins et al., "Regional Trends and the Role of School Support Staff in Suspensions of Students with Disabilities"; Christine Mulhern, "Beyond Teachers: Estimating Individual Guidance Counselors' Effects on Educational Attainment" (working paper, EdWorking-Paper, Annenberg Institute at Brown University, August 2022), https://doi.org/10.26300/SJXM-ZW40; Whiston et al., "School Counseling Outcome."
61. Jacqueline Agresta, "Professional Role Perceptions of School Social Workers, Psychologists, and Counselors," *Children & Schools* 26, no. 3 (2004): 151–63, https://doi.org/10.1093/cs/26.3.151; Ali Esparza and Amy Milsom, "Discipline in Schools: Exploring the Role of the School Counselor," *Journal of Counselor Leadership and Advocacy* 11, no. 1 (2024): 60–74, https://doi.org/10.1080/2326716X.2023.2297998; Laura H. Godbold, "Middle School Guidance Counselors: Are There Enough?," ERIC, May 9, 1994, https://eric.ed.gov/?id=ED374385; Charles W. Humes and Thomas H. Hohenshil, "Elementary Counselors, School Psychologists, School Social Workers: Who Does What?," *Elementary School Guidance & Counseling* 22, no. 1 (1987): 37–45.
62. Godbold, "Middle School Guidance Counselors."
63. Godbold, "Middle School Guidance Counselors."
64. Humes and Hohenshil, "Elementary Counselors, School Psychologists, School Social Workers."
65. Chenoa S. Woods and Thurston Domina, "The School Counselor Caseload and the High School-to-College Pipeline," *Teachers College Record* 116, no. 10 (2014): 1–30, https://doi.org/10.1177/016146811411601006.
66. Jenkins et al., "Regional Trends and the Role of School Support Staff in Suspensions of Students with Disabilities"; Caitlin Kearney et al., "Student-to-School Counselor Ratios: A Meta-Analytic Review of the Evidence," *Journal of Counseling & Development* 99, no. 4 (2021): 418–28, https://doi.org/10.1002/jcad.12394; Mulhern, "Beyond Teachers"; Richard T. Lapan, Sara A. Whitcomb, and Nancy M. Aleman, "Connecticut Professional School Counselors: College and Career Counseling Services and Smaller Ratios Benefit Students," *Professional School Counseling* 16, no. 2 (2012): 2156759X0001600206, https://doi.org/10.1177/2156759X0001600206; Whiston et al., "School Counseling Outcome."
67. Meghan M. Mitchell, Gaylene Armstrong, and Todd Armstrong, "Disproportionate School Disciplinary Responses: An Exploration of Prisonization and Minority Threat Hypothesis Among Black, Hispanic, and Native American Students," *Criminal Justice Policy Review* 31, no. 1 (February 1, 2020): 80–102, https://doi.org/10.1177/0887403418813672.
68. Katherine C. Cowan et al., "A Framework for Safe and Successful Schools: Updated," National Association of School Psychologists, March 2015, https://eric-ed-gov.proxy.library.vanderbilt.edu/?id=ED612657; Esparza and Milsom, "Discipline in Schools."
69. Thurston Domina et al., "The Impact of School Counselor Resources in Elementary and Middle Grades," *Professional School Counseling* 26, no. 1a (March 1, 2022): 2156759X221086746, https://doi.org/10.1177/2156759X221086746.
70. Randall Reback, "Noninstructional Spending Improves Noncognitive Outcomes: Discontinuity Evidence from a Unique Elementary School Counselor Financing System," *Education Finance and Policy* 5, no. 2 (April 1, 2010): 105–37, https://doi.org/10.1162/edfp.2010.5.2.5201; Peg Donohue et al., "The Impacts of School Counselor Ratios on Student Outcomes: A Multistate Study," *Professional School Counseling* 26, no. 1 (May 1, 2022): 2156759X221137283, https://doi.org/10.1177/2156759X221137283; Kearney et al., "Student-to-School Counselor Ratios."

71. Richard T. Lapan, "Missouri Professional School Counselors: Ratios Matter, Especially in High-Poverty Schools," *Professional School Counseling* 16, no. 2 (2012): 2156759X0001600207, https://doi.org/10.1177/2156759X0001600207.
72. Scott E. Carrell and Susan A. Carrell, "Do Lower Student to Counselor Ratios Reduce School Disciplinary Problems?," *BE Journal of Economic Analysis & Policy* 5, no. 1 (2006): 0000101515153806451463.
73. Scott E. Carrell and Mark Hoekstra, "Are School Counselors an Effective Education Input?," *Economics Letters* 125, no. 1 (2014): 66–69.
74. Reback, "Noninstructional Spending Improves Noncognitive Outcomes."
75. Edwin Hernandez, Enrique Espinoza, and Jewel Patterson, "School Counselors Involvement and Opportunities to Advocate Against Racialized Punitive Practices," *Teaching and Supervision in Counseling* 3, no. 2 (July 16, 2021), https://doi.org/10.7290/tsc030210.
76. Alizé B. Hill and Toyan Harper, "'They Slow Me Down': Peer Relationships, School Fights, and the Criminalization of Black Adolescent Development Through School Discipline Policies," *Youth & Society* (September 3, 2024), https://doi.org/10.1177/0044118X241273356.
77. Yolanda Anyon et al., "It's All About the Relationships: Educators' Rationales and Strategies for Building Connections with Students to Prevent Exclusionary School Discipline Outcomes," *Children & Schools* 40, no. 4 (October 2018): 221–30, https://doi.org/10.1093/cs/cdy017.
78. Agresta, "Professional Role Perceptions of School Social Workers, Psychologists, and Counselors"; Humes and Hohenshil, "Elementary Counselors, School Psychologists, School Social Workers"; Bonnie K. Nastasi et al., "Mental Health Programming and the Role of School Psychologists," *School Psychology Review* 27, no. 2 (1998): 217–32, https://doi.org/10.1080/02796015.1998.12085910.
79. Agresta, "Professional Role Perceptions of School Social Workers, Psychologists, and Counselors"; Katie Eklund et al., "Examining the Role of School Psychologists as Providers of Mental and Behavioral Health Services," *Psychology in the Schools* 57, no. 4 (2020): 489–501, https://doi.org/10.1002/pits.22323; David S. Goh, J. Teslow, and Gerald B. Fuller, "The Practice of Psychological Assessment Among School Psychologists," *Professional Psychology* 12, no. 6 (1981): 696–706, https://doi.org/10.1037/0735-7028.12.6.696; Humes and Hohenshil, "Elementary Counselors, School Psychologists, School Social Workers"; Nastasi et al., "Mental Health Programming and the Role of School Psychologists"; Margo R. Ross, Sharon Rose Powell, and Maurice J. Elias, "New Roles for School Psychologists: Addressing the Social and Emotional Learning Needs of Students," *School Psychology Review* 31, no. 1 (2002): 43–52, https://doi.org/10.1080/02796015.2002.12086141; Shannon M. Suldo, Allison Friedrich, and Jessica Michalowski, "Personal and Systems-Level Factors That Limit and Facilitate School Psychologists' Involvement in School-Based Mental Health Services," *Psychology in the Schools* 47, no. 4 (2010): 354–73, https://doi.org/10.1002/pits.20475.
80. Kizzy Albritton, Kenia Cruz, and Cierra Townsend, "Disrupting the Preschool to Prison Pipeline: School Psychologists as Change Agents," *Communique: National Association of School Psychologists* 49, no. 4 (December 1, 2020): 4–7, https://go.gale.com/ps/i.do?p=AONE&sw=w&issn=0164775X&v=2.1&it=r&id=GALE%7CA646812244&sid=googleScholar&linkaccess=abs; Heather E. Ormiston, Malena A. Nygaard, and Olivia C. Heck, "The Role of School Psychologists in the Implementation of Trauma-Informed Multi-Tiered Systems of Support in Schools," *Journal of Applied School Psychology* 37,

no. 4 (November 12, 2020): 319–51, https://doi.org/10.1080/15377903.2020.1848955; Kizzy Albritton, Rachel Stein, and Kenia Cruz, "Embracing the Promise and Potential of Preschool-Age Black Boys: Strength-Based Opportunities for Early Childhood School Psychologists," *School Psychology Review* 52, no. 3 (May 4, 2023): 343–56, https://doi.org/10.1080/2372966X.2021.1977586.

81. Jenkins et al., "Regional Trends and the Role of School Support Staff in Suspensions of Students with Disabilities."
82. Elisa S. Shernoff et al., "Expanding the Role of School Psychologists to Support Early Career Teachers: A Mixed-Method Study," *School Psychology Review* 45, no. 2 (2016): 226–49.
83. Bradley Petry and Nadine Serbonich, "Achieving and Maintaining Change in Urban Schools: The Role of the School Psychologist," *Communique* 46, no. 6 (March 1, 2018): 10–13, https://go.gale.com/ps/i.do?p=AONE&sw=w&issn=0164775X&v=2.1&it=r&id=GALE%7CA547746063&sid=googleScholar&linkaccess=abs.
84. Agresta, "Professional Role Perceptions of School Social Workers, Psychologists, and Counselors"; Nadine M. Finigan-Carr and Wendy E. Shaia, "School Social Workers as Partners in the School Mission," *Phi Delta Kappan* 99, no. 7 (2018): 26–30, https://doi.org/10.1177/0031721718767856; Megan Callahan Sherman, "The School Social Worker: A Marginalized Commodity Within the School Ecosystem," *Children & Schools* 38, no. 3 (2016): 147–51, https://doi.org/10.1093/cs/cdw016.
85. Sherman, "The School Social Worker."
86. Sherman, "The School Social Worker."
87. Jenkins et al., "Regional Trends and the Role of School Support Staff in Suspensions of Students with Disabilities."
88. Susan McCarter, "The School-to-Prison Pipeline: A Primer for Social Workers," *Social Work* 62, no. 1 (January 1, 2017): 53–61, https://doi.org/10.1093/sw/sww078; Sarah K. Ura and Ana d'Abreu, "Racial Bias, Social–Emotional Competence, and Teachers' Evaluation of Student Behavior," *Children & Schools* 44, no. 1 (January 1, 2022): 17–26, https://doi.org/10.1093/cs/cdab028.
89. James P. Huguley et al., "Just Discipline in Schools: An Integrated and Interdisciplinary Approach," *Children & Schools* 42, no. 3 (July 1, 2020): 195–99, https://doi.org/10.1093/cs/cdaa012.
90. Reema Amin, "NYC's Plan to Hire 500 Full-Time Social Workers Is Still Short of the Need: Analysis," *Chalkbeat*, June 10, 2021, https://www.chalkbeat.org/newyork/2021/6/10/22528533/nycs-plan-to-hire-500-full-time-social-workers-is-still-short-of-the-need-analysis/.
91. The primary sources of data include information on students and schools drawn from NYC Department of Education (NYCDOE) administrative records from 2011–2012 to 2018–2019 for public middle and high schools. NYCDOE school discipline records provide student-level information on reported infractions that resulted in an ODR or suspension. The school-level dataset includes information about the number, race, experience, education, and gender of school support staff by group (guidance counselors, social workers, and school psychologists) as well as information of students and other school staff (school leaders and teachers).
92. I utilize administrative and survey data on schools, staff, and students from 2011–2012 to 2021–2022 made available through the Research Alliance for NYC Public Schools. Due to availability of school discipline records, the analysis is restricted to elementary, middle, and high schools with traditional grade configurations (grades K–5, 6–8, or 9–12)

and combined grade configurations (grades K–8, K–12, or 6–12) representing over 1,900 unique schools and over 20,000 unique school years. For each staff type, I operationalize staff demographics to include percentage of staff who are Black or Latinx as well as percentage who are male. Average years of experience and education level (percentage with a master's or more advanced degree) serve as measures of staff qualifications.

93. Hughes et al., "'Value in Diversity.'"
94. Luis A. Rodriguez, Richard O. Welsh, and Chelsea Daniels, "School Climate, Teacher Characteristics, and School Discipline: Evidence From New York City," *AERA Open* 10 (2024): 23328584241263860.
95. Shuyang Wang et al., "Linking Teacher Quality and School Discipline Disproportionality," *Journal of Education Human Resources* 41, no. 4 (2023): 729–62, https://doi.org/10.3138/jehr-2021-0057; John A. Williams III, Felicia D. Persky, and Jennifer N. Johnson, "Does Longevity Matter? Teacher Experience and the Suspension of Black Middle School," *Journal of Urban Learning, Teaching, and Research* 14 (2018): 50–62.
96. Wang et al., "Linking Teacher Quality and School Discipline Disproportionality"; Williams, Persky, and Johnson, "Does Longevity Matter?"; Michael S. Hayes, Jing Liu, and Seth Gershenson, "Who Refers Whom? The Effects of Teacher Characteristics on Disciplinary Office Referrals," *Economics of Education Review* 93 (2023): 102376.
97. Daniel J. Losen et al., "Disturbing Inequities: Exploring the Relationship Between Racial Disparities in Special Education Identification and Discipline," *Journal of Applied Research on Children* 5, no. 2 (2014), https://doi.org/10.58464/2155-5834.1224.
98. Betty Achinstein and Rodney T. Ogawa, "New Teachers of Color and Culturally Responsive Teaching in an Era of Educational Accountability: Caught in a Double Bind," *Journal of Educational Change* 13, no. 1 (2012): 1–39, https://doi.org/10.1007/s10833-011-9165-y; Charlotte E. Wolff et al., "Keeping an Eye on Learning: Differences Between Expert and Novice Teachers' Representations of Classroom Management Events," *Journal of Teacher Education* 66, no. 1 (2015): 68–85, https://doi.org/10.1177/0022487114549810.
99. Shanna E. Hirsch et al., "Professional Learning and Development in Classroom Management for Novice Teachers: A Systematic Review," *Education and Treatment of Children* 44, no. 4 (2021): 291–307, https://doi.org/10.1007/s43494-021-00042-6; Tim Pressley, Hannah Croyle, and Madison Edgar, "Different Approaches to Classroom Environments Based on Teacher Experience and Effectiveness," *Psychology in the Schools* 57, no. 4 (2020): 606–26, https://doi.org/10.1002/pits.22341; Wolff et al., "Keeping an Eye on Learning."
100. The project utilizes administrative and survey data of schools, staff, and students from 2012 to 2022 made available through the Research Alliance for NYC Schools. Due to availability of school discipline records, the analysis is restricted to middle and high schools with traditional grade configurations (grades 6–8 or 9–12) and combined grade configurations (grades 6–12) representing over 900 unique schools.
101. Welsh and Little, "The School Discipline Dilemma."
102. Bradley W. Davis et al., "Conceptualizing Principal–Student Racial Congruence," *Journal of School Leadership* 26, no. 4 (2016): 554–79, https://doi.org/10.1177/105268461602600401; Wesley Edwards, Rachel Boggs, and Pedro Reyes, "Student-Principal Racial/Ethnic Match, Geographic Locale, and Student Disciplinary Outcomes," *Journal of School Leadership* 33, no. 3 (2023): 313–39, https://doi.org/10.1177/10526846221134009; Lindsay and Hart, "Exposure to Same-Race Teachers and Student Disciplinary Outcomes for Black Students in North Carolina."

103. Capers, "The Role of Desegregation and Teachers of Color in Discipline Disproportionality"; Lewis and Diamond, *Despite the Best Intentions*; Marcucci and Elmesky, "Advancing Culturally Relevant Discipline"; Milner, "Fifteenth Annual AERA Brown Lecture in Education Research."
104. Lora Henderson Smith et al., "The Discipline Gap in Context: The Role of School Racial and Ethnic Diversity and Within School Positionality on Out-of-School Suspensions," *Journal of School Psychology* 98 (2023): 61–77, https://doi.org/10.1016/j.jsp.2023.02.006.
105. Christopher Redding, "Are Homegrown Teachers Who Graduate from Urban Districts More Racially Diverse, More Effective, and Less Likely to Exit Teaching?," *American Educational Research Journal* 59, no. 5 (2022): 939–74, https://doi.org/10.3102/00028312221078018; Angela Valenzuela, *Grow Your Own Educator Programs: A Review of the Literature with an Emphasis on Equity-Based Approaches* (Austin: University of Texas at Austin, IDRA EAC-South, 2017), https://eric.ed.gov/?id=ED582731.
106. William H. Marinell and Vanessa M. Coca, *Who Stays and Who Leaves? Findings from a Three-Part Study of Teacher Turnover in NYC Middle Schools* (New York: New York University Steinhardt, Research Alliance for New York City Schools, March 2013), https://eric.ed.gov/?id=ED540818.
107. Dorinda J. Carter Andrews, Gail Richmond, and Joanne E. Marciano, "The Teacher Support Imperative: Teacher Education and the Pedagogy of Connection," *Journal of Teacher Education* 72, no. 3 (2021): 267–70.
108. Kelly Allen et al., "What Schools Need to Know About Fostering School Belonging: A Meta-Analysis," *Educational Psychology Review* 30, no. 1 (2018): 1–34, https://doi.org/10.1007/s10648-016-9389-8; Linda Darling-Hammond, "Teacher Education and the American Future," *Journal of Teacher Education* 61, no. 1–2 (2010): 35–47, https://doi.org/10.1177/0022487109348024; Etta R. Hollins, ed., *Rethinking Field Experiences in Preservice Teacher Preparation: Meeting New Challenges for Accountability* (New York: Routledge, 2015).
109. Gordana Djigic and Snezana Stojiljkovic, "Classroom Management Styles, Classroom Climate and School Achievement," *Procedia – Social and Behavioral Sciences* 29 (2011): 819–28, https://doi.org/10.1016/j.sbspro.2011.11.310; Andrew Kwok, "Classroom Management Actions of Beginning Urban Teachers," *Urban Education* 54, no. 3 (2019): 339–67, https://doi.org/10.1177/0042085918795017.
110. Dorinda J. Carter Andrews et al., "Decentering Whiteness in Teacher Education: Addressing the Questions of Who, With Whom, and How," *Journal of Teacher Education* 72, no. 2 (2021): 134–37, https://doi.org/10.1177/0022487120987966.
111. Colleen L. Eddy et al., "Does Teacher Emotional Exhaustion and Efficacy Predict Student Discipline Sanctions?," *School Psychology Review* 49, no. 3 (2020): 239–55, https://doi.org/10.1080/2372966X.2020.1733340.
112. Yoon-Suk Hwang et al., "A Systematic Review of Mindfulness Interventions for In-Service Teachers: A Tool to Enhance Teacher Wellbeing and Performance," *Teaching and Teacher Education* 64 (2017): 26–42, https://doi.org/10.1016/j.tate.2017.01.015; Anne Milatz, Marko Lüftenegger, and Barbara Schober, "Teachers' Relationship Closeness with Students as a Resource for Teacher Wellbeing: A Response Surface Analytical Approach," *Frontiers in Psychology* 6 (2015), https://doi.org/10.3389/fpsyg.2015.01949; Susanne Owen, "Professional Learning Communities: Building Skills, Reinvigorating the Passion, and Nurturing Teacher Wellbeing and 'Flourishing' Within Significantly Innovative Schooling Contexts," *Educational Review* 68, no. 4 (2016): 403–19, https://doi.

org/10.1080/00131911.2015.1119101; Jantine L. Spilt, Helma M. Y. Koomen, and Jochem T. Thijs, "Teacher Wellbeing: The Importance of Teacher–Student Relationships," *Educational Psychology Review* 23, no. 4 (2011): 457–77, https://doi.org/10.1007/s10648-011-9170-y.

Chapter 4

1. Mary M. Mitchell, Catherine P. Bradshaw, and Philip J. Leaf, "Student and Teacher Perceptions of School Climate: A Multilevel Exploration of Patterns of Discrepancy," *Journal of School Health* 80, no. 6 (2010): 271–79, https://doi.org/10.1111/j.1746-1561.2010.00501.x; Ming-Te Wang and Jessica L. Degol, "School Climate: A Review of the Construct, Measurement, and Impact on Student Outcomes," *Educational Psychology Review* 28, no. 2 (2016): 315–52, https://doi.org/10.1007/s10648-015-9319-1.
2. Ruth Berkowitz et al., "A Research Synthesis of the Associations Between Socioeconomic Background, Inequality, School Climate, and Academic Achievement," *Review of Educational Research* 87, no. 2 (2017): 425–69, https://doi.org/10.3102/0034654316669821; Jonathan Cohen et al., "School Climate: Research, Policy, Practice, and Teacher Education," *Teachers College Record* 111, no. 1 (2009): 180–213, https://doi.org/10.1177/016146810911100108; Amrit Thapa et al., "A Review of School Climate Research," *Review of Educational Research* 83, no. 3 (2013): 357–85, https://doi.org/10.3102/0034654313483907.
3. Berkowitz et al., "A Research Synthesis of the Associations Between Socioeconomic Background, Inequality, School Climate, and Academic Achievement."
4. Nicholas A. Gage et al., "Student Perceptions of School Climate as Predictors of Office Discipline Referrals," *American Educational Research Journal* 53, no. 3 (2016): 492–515, https://doi.org/10.3102/0002831216637349; Francis L. Huang and Dewey Cornell, "The Relationship of School Climate with Out-of-School Suspensions," *Children and Youth Services Review* 94 (2018): 378–89, https://doi.org/10.1016/j.childyouth.2018.08.013; Mitchell, Bradshaw, and Leaf, "Student and Teacher Perceptions of School Climate"; Office of Civil Rights and Civil Rights Division, *Joint Dear Colleague Letter* (Washington, DC: US Department of Education and US Department of Justice, January 8, 2014), https://www2.ed.gov/about/offices/list/ocr/letters/colleague-201401-title-vi.html; Russell J. Skiba et al., "Parsing Disciplinary Disproportionality: Contributions of Infraction, Student, and School Characteristics to Out-of-School Suspension and Expulsion," *American Educational Research Journal* 51, no. 4 (2014): 640–70, https://doi.org/10.3102/0002831214541670.
5. Anne Gregory et al., "An Examination of Restorative Interventions and Racial Equity in Out-of-School Suspensions," *School Psychology Review* 47, no. 2 (2018): 167–82, https://doi.org/10.17105/SPR-2017-0073.V47-2; Anne Gregory and Katherine R. Evans, "The Starts and Stumbles of Restorative Justice in Education: Where Do We Go from Here?" (Boulder: University of Colorado, National Education Policy Center, January 2020), https://eric.ed.gov/?id=ED605800; Allison Ann Payne and Kelly Welch, "Transforming School Climate and Student Discipline: The Restorative Justice Promise for Peace," in *Restorative Justice: Promoting Peace and Wellbeing*, ed. Gabriel Velez and Theo Gavrielides (New York: Springer International, 2022), 61–78, https://doi.org/10.1007/978-3-031-13101-1_4.
6. George G. Bear et al., "School-Wide Practices Associated with School Climate in Elementary, Middle, and High Schools," *Teaching and Teacher Education* 63 (2017): 372–83, https://doi.org/10.1016/j.tate.2017.01.012; Anna Heilbrun, Dewey Cornell,

and Timothy Konold, "Authoritative School Climate and Suspension Rates in Middle Schools: Implications for Reducing the Racial Disparity in School Discipline," *Journal of School Violence* 17, no. 3 (2018): 324–38, https://doi.org/10.1080/15388220.2017.1368395; Lindsey M. O'Brennan, Catherine P. Bradshaw, and Michael J. Furlong, "Influence of Classroom and School Climate on Teacher Perceptions of Student Problem Behavior," *School Mental Health* 6, no. 2 (2014): 125–36, https://doi.org/10.1007/s12310-014-9118-8; Matthew P. Steinberg, Elaine Allensworth, and David W. Johnson, *What Conditions Jeopardize and Support Safety in Urban Schools? The Influence of Community Characteristics, School Composition and School Organizational Practices on Student and Teacher Reports of Safety in Chicago* (Los Angeles: UCLA, Civil Rights Project/Proyecto Derechos Civiles, April 6, 2013), https://escholarship.org/uc/item/2mx8c60x; Courtney A. Zulauf-McCurdy and Katherine M. Zinsser, "How Teachers' Perceptions of the Parent–Teacher Relationship Affect Children's Risk for Early Childhood Expulsion," *Psychology in the Schools* 58, no. 1 (2021): 69–88; Luis A. Rodriguez and Richard O. Welsh, "The Ties That Bind: An Examination of School-Family Relationships and Middle School Discipline in New York City," *Educational Researcher* 53, no. 2 (2024): 85–99.

7. Yolanda Anyon, Duan Zhang, and Cynthia Hazel, "Race, Exclusionary Discipline, and Connectedness to Adults in Secondary Schools," *American Journal of Community Psychology* 57, no. 3/4 (2016): 342–52, https://doi.org/10.1002/ajcp.12061; Jessika H. Bottiani, Catherine P. Bradshaw, and Tamar Mendelson, "A Multilevel Examination of Racial Disparities in High School Discipline: Black and White Adolescents' Perceived Equity, School Belonging, and Adjustment Problems," *Journal of Educational Psychology* 109, no. 4 (2017): 532–45, https://doi.org/10.1037/edu0000155; Francis Huang and Yolanda Anyon, "The Relationship Between School Disciplinary Resolutions with School Climate and Attitudes Toward School," *Preventing School Failure* 64, no. 3 (2020): 212–22, https://doi.org/10.1080/1045988X.2020.1722940; Timothy Konold et al., "Racial/Ethnic Differences in Perceptions of School Climate and Its Association with Student Engagement and Peer Aggression," *Journal of Youth and Adolescence* 46, no. 6 (2017): 1289–1303, https://doi.org/10.1007/s10964-016-0576-1; Kristine E. Larson, "A Multilevel Analysis of Racial Discipline Disproportionality: A Focus on Student Perceptions of Academic Engagement and Disciplinary Environment," *Journal of School Psychology* 77 (2019): 152–67, https://doi.org/10.1016/j.jsp.2019.09.003; Mitchell, Bradshaw, and Leaf, "Student and Teacher Perceptions of School Climate."
8. Gregory et al., "An Examination of Restorative Interventions and Racial Equity in Out-of-School Suspensions"; Heilbrun, Cornell, and Konold, "Authoritative School Climate and Suspension Rates in Middle Schools"; Huang and Cornell, "The Relationship of School Climate with Out-of-School Suspensions."
9. National School Climate Council, "What Is School Climate?," 2007, https://schoolclimate.org/about/our-approach/what-is-school-climate/.
10. Cohen et al., "School Climate"; Thapa et al., "A Review of School Climate Research."
11. National Center on Safe and Supportive Learning Environments: School Climate Improvement, https://safesupportivelearning.ed.gov/school-climate-improvement.
12. Cohen et al., "School Climate," 182.
13. Thapa et al., "A Review of School Climate Research."
14. Kathleen Moritz Rudasill et al., "Systems View of School Climate: A Theoretical Framework for Research," *Educational Psychology Review* 30, no. 1 (2018): 35–60, https://doi.org/10.1007/s10648-017-9401-y.

15. Dewey Cornell and Francis Huang, "Authoritative School Climate and High School Student Risk Behavior: A Cross-Sectional Multi-Level Analysis of Student Self-Reports," *Journal of Youth and Adolescence* 45, no. 11 (2016): 2246–59, https://doi.org/10.1007/s10964-016-0424-3; Huang and Anyon, "The Relationship Between School Disciplinary Resolutions with School Climate and Attitudes Toward School."
16. Marisa E. Marraccini et al., "Measuring Student Perceptions of School Climate: A Systematic Review and Ecological Content Analysis," *School Mental Health* 12, no. 2 (2020): 195–221, https://doi.org/10.1007/s12310-019-09348-8; Mary M. Mitchell and Catherine P. Bradshaw, "Examining Classroom Influences on Student Perceptions of School Climate: The Role of Classroom Management and Exclusionary Discipline Strategies," *Journal of School Psychology* 51, no. 5 (2013): 599–610, https://doi.org/10.1016/j.jsp.2013.05.005; Wang and Degol, "School Climate."
17. Rudasill et al., "Systems View of School Climate."
18. Rudasill et al., "Systems View of School Climate," 46.
19. Rudasill et al., "Systems View of School Climate."
20. Rudasill et al., "Systems View of School Climate," 46.
21. Urie Bronfenbrenner, "The Developing Ecology of Human Development: Paradigm Lost or Paradigm Regained," in *Biennial Meeting of the Society for Research in Child Development* (Kansas City, MO, 1989).
22. Juliette Berg et al., *The Intersection of School Climate and Social and Emotional Development* (Washington, DC: American Institutes for Research, 2017); David Osher et al., "The Contribution of School and Classroom Disciplinary Practices to the School-to-Prison Pipeline," in *Handbook of Classroom Management*, ed. Edward J. Sabornie and Dorothy L. Espelage, 3rd ed. (New York: Routledge, 2022).
23. Sean C. Austin et al., "Examining Differential Effects of an Equity-Focused Schoolwide Positive Behavioral Interventions and Supports Approach on Teachers' Equity in School Discipline," *Journal of School Psychology* 104 (2024): 101284, https://doi.org/10.1016/j.jsp.2024.101284; Keith Smolkowski et al., "Vulnerable Decision Points for Disproportionate Office Discipline Referrals: Comparisons of Discipline for African American and White Elementary School Students," *Behavioral Disorders* 41, no. 4 (2016): 178–95, https://doi.org/10.17988/bedi-41-04-178-195.1.
24. Erik J. Girvan et al., "The Relative Contribution of Subjective Office Referrals to Racial Disproportionality in School Discipline," *School Psychology Quarterly* 32, no. 3 (2017): 392–404, https://doi.org/10.1037/spq0000178.
25. Osher et al., "The Contribution of School and Classroom Disciplinary Practices to the School-to-Prison Pipeline"; Richard O. Welsh, "Administering Discipline: An Examination of the Factors Shaping School Discipline Practices," *Education and Urban Society* (2023): 1–34, https://doi.org/10.1177/00131245231208170; Richard O. Welsh and Luis A. Rodriguez, "The Plight of Persistently Disciplined Students: Examining Frequent Flyers and the Conversion of Office Discipline Referrals into Suspensions," *Educational Evaluation and Policy Analysis* 46, no. 1 (2023): 160–70, https://doi.org/10.3102/01623737231155155.
26. Berg et al., *The Intersection of School Climate and Social and Emotional Development*; Osher et al., "The Contribution of School and Classroom Disciplinary Practices to the School-to-Prison Pipeline"; Welsh and Rodriguez, "The Plight of Persistently Disciplined Students."
27. Frances Vavrus and KimMarie Cole, "'I Didn't Do Nothin'': The Discursive Construction of School Suspension," *Urban Review* 34, no. 2 (2002): 87–111, https://

doi.org/10.1023/A:1015375215801; Welsh, "Administering Discipline." Disciplinary moments capture the progression of the teacher–student interactions to disciplinary consequences.

28. Cohen et al., "School Climate"; Rudasill et al., "Systems View of School Climate." Safety and discipline are two of the preeminent themes in the extant literature on school climate. Safety typically encompasses physical safety, whereas discipline is synonymous with order and adhering to rules and norms. In their literature synthesis, Cohen and colleagues highlighted the importance of socioemotional safety, and Rudasill and colleagues pinpointed safety as one of the three core elements of school climate. The "fairness with which discipline is used in schools" is a particularly salient element of safety when considering the relationship between school climate and school discipline.
29. Cohen et al., "School Climate"; Thapa et al., "A Review of School Climate Research."
30. Charity Brown Griffin, Jamelia N. Harris, and Sherrie L. Proctor, "Intersectionality and School Racial Climate to Create Schools as Sites of Fairness and Liberation for Black Girls," *Journal of School Psychology* 104 (2024): 101282.
31. Griffin, Harris, and Proctor, "Intersectionality and School Racial Climate."
32. Adam Voight et al., "The Racial School Climate Gap: Within-School Disparities in Students' Experiences of Safety, Support, and Connectedness," *American Journal of Community Psychology* 56, no. 3 (2015): 252–67, https://doi.org/10.1007/s10464-015-9751-x.
33. Anyon, Zhang, and Hazel, "Race, Exclusionary Discipline, and Connectedness to Adults in Secondary Schools"; Konold et al., "Racial/Ethnic Differences in Perceptions of School Climate and Its Association with Student Engagement and Peer Aggression."
34. Bottiani, Bradshaw, and Mendelson, "A Multilevel Examination of Racial Disparities in High School Discipline."
35. Voight et al., "The Racial School Climate Gap."
36. Jessika H. Bottiani, Catherine P. Bradshaw, and Tamar Mendelson, "Inequality in Black and White High School Students' Perceptions of School Support: An Examination of Race in Context," *Journal of Youth and Adolescence* 45 (2016): 1176–91.
37. Sarah A. Fefer and Kayla Gordon, "Exploring Perceptions of School Climate Among Secondary Students with Varying Discipline Infractions," *International Journal of School & Educational Psychology* 8, no. 3 (2020): 174–83, https://doi.org/10.1080/21683603.2018.1541033; Gage et al., "Student Perceptions of School Climate as Predictors of Office Discipline Referrals"; Anne Gregory, Dewey Cornell, and Xitao Fan, "The Relationship of School Structure and Support to Suspension Rates for Black and White High School Students," *American Educational Research Journal* 48, no. 4 (2011): 904–34, https://doi.org/10.3102/0002831211398531; Heilbrun, Cornell, and Konold, "Authoritative School Climate and Suspension Rates in Middle Schools"; Huang and Cornell, "The Relationship of School Climate with Out-of-School Suspensions"; Erica Mattison and Mark S. Aber, "Closing the Achievement Gap: The Association of Racial Climate with Achievement and Behavioral Outcomes," *American Journal of Community Psychology* 40, no. 1 (2007): 1–12, https://doi.org/10.1007/s10464-007-9128-x.
38. Cornell and Huang, "Authoritative School Climate and High School Student Risk Behavior"; Fefer and Gordon, "Exploring Perceptions of School Climate Among Secondary Students with Varying Discipline Infractions"; Gregory, Cornell, and Fan, "The Relationship of School Structure and Support to Suspension Rates for Black and White High School Students"; Heilbrun, Cornell, and Konold, "Authoritative School Climate and Suspension Rates in Middle Schools"; Huang and Cornell, "The Relationship of School Climate with Out-of-School Suspensions"; Jung-Sook Lee, "The Effects of the

Teacher–Student Relationship and Academic Press on Student Engagement and Academic Performance," *International Journal of Educational Research* 53 (2012): 330–40, https://doi.org/10.1016/j.ijer.2012.04.006.

39. Gregory, Cornell, and Fan, "The Relationship of School Structure and Support to Suspension Rates for Black and White High School Students."
40. Bottiani, Bradshaw, and Mendelson, "A Multilevel Examination of Racial Disparities in High School Discipline"; Mattison and Aber, "Closing the Achievement Gap"; Steinberg, Allensworth, and Johnson, *What Conditions Jeopardize and Support Safety in Urban Schools?*
41. Bottiani, Bradshaw, and Mendelson, "A Multilevel Examination of Racial Disparities in High School Discipline"; Huang and Cornell, "The Relationship of School Climate with Out-of-School Suspensions."
42. Bear et al., "School-Wide Practices Associated with School Climate in Elementary, Middle, and High Schools"; Bottiani, Bradshaw, and Mendelson, "A Multilevel Examination of Racial Disparities in High School Discipline"; Fefer and Gordon, "Exploring Perceptions of School Climate Among Secondary Students with Varying Discipline Infractions"; Gage et al., "Student Perceptions of School Climate as Predictors of Office Discipline Referrals"; Gregory, Cornell, and Fan, "The Relationship of School Structure and Support to Suspension Rates for Black and White High School Students"; Heilbrun, Cornell, and Konold, "Authoritative School Climate and Suspension Rates in Middle Schools"; Huang and Cornell, "The Relationship of School Climate with Out-of-School Suspensions."
43. Huang and Anyon, "The Relationship Between School Disciplinary Resolutions with School Climate and Attitudes Toward School."
44. The US Department of Education National Center on Safe and Supportive Learning Environments, https://safesupportivelearning.ed.gov/school-climate-improvement.
45. Melanie Asmar, "New Data Shows Denver Schools Are More Closely Following Discipline Rules," *Chalkbeat*, April 15, 2024, https://www.chalkbeat.org/colorado/2024/04/16/new-data-shows-denver-schools-better-following-discipline-rules/.
46. Huang and Anyon, "The Relationship Between School Disciplinary Resolutions with School Climate and Attitudes Toward School."
47. Data came from the NYC Public Schools (NYCPS), which runs the largest school district in the United States with over 1 million students enrolled in the public school system each year. For this analyses, student-level and school-level data were used for the population of public middle and high schools spanning the period from 2011–2012 to 2018–2019, whereas elementary schools were excluded due to the NYCPS having a different discipline code for elementary schools and the lack of comparable discipline data; charter and private schools were also excluded due to not being included in the NYCPS dataset. The analysis is inclusive of schools of traditional grade configurations (grades 6–8 or 9–12) and combined grade configurations (grades K–8, 6–12, and K–12). This resulted in 1875 unique schools, 7685 school years, 1,167,306 unique students, and 3,988,302 student years (i.e., the number of unique student-level observations in our dataset across all years) being included in our analysis. Our analytic sample included 40 percent Latinx students, 27 percent Black students, 17 percent Asian students, 14 percent White students, 2 percent other race students, 92 percent low socioeconomic status students, 15 percent Limited English Proficiency students, 23 percent students receiving special education services, and 8 percent students living in temporary housing.
48. Marraccini et al., "Measuring Student Perceptions of School Climate."

49. Cohen et al., "School Climate"; Thapa et al., "A Review of School Climate Research."
50. The overall student survey completion rate in our sample is approximately 73 percent, ranging from 71 to 74 percent across the years 2011–2012 to 2018–2019. The overall response rate is about 68 percent for Black students, 78 percent for White students, 72 percent for Latinx students, 81 percent for Asian students, and 56 percent for other race students, with no substantial variation between years. To reduce the dimensionality of the data, we conduct an exploratory factor analysis for student survey items. Based on visual examination of the scree plot and the Kaiser-Guttman stopping criteria, we retained two factors based on student survey items representing (1) students' perception of risky peer student behavior within school; and (2) students' perception of the overall school environment. Almost all of the student and school variables have small but statistically significant average differences between students who completed the survey and those who did not. The student and school characteristics with the largest standardized differences include students receiving special education services, the proportion of students at a school who receive special education services, the average attendance rate, the graduation rate, and the math and ELA proficiency rates. Overall, it appears that the students in our sample who responded to the survey come from backgrounds and attend schools where it is more likely that they will have better perceptions of school climate, so it is possible that we slightly under sample students with worse perceptions of school climate.
51. We use two school climate constructs consistent with the above: (a) a peer student behavior construct that measures student perceptions of social interactions and relationships between students, and (b) an overall school environment construct that measures student perceptions of safety and inclusive relationships between school staff and students. Our school climate constructs also align with the NYCPS conceptualization of school climate (which the NYCPS refers to as "school quality"), which includes six elements of climate (rigorous instruction, collaborative teachers, supportive environment, effective school leadership, strong family–community ties, and trust), with all of the relevant survey questions in our two constructs falling under the NYCPS supportive environment heading.
52. O'Brennan, Bradshaw, and Furlong, "Influence of Classroom and School Climate on Teacher Perceptions of Student Problem Behavior."
53. The school-level analytic sample for this study consists of 1,091 unique middle and high schools across all years—approximately 29 percent are traditional middle schools, 44 percent traditional high schools, and 27 percent are schools serving other combined grade configurations. Schools with higher suspension rates are staffed by teachers with lower years of teaching experience as well as a larger share of Black teachers. On average, these schools serve a higher share of students who are Black and Latinx, eligible for free or reduced-price lunch (FRPL), living in temporary housing, and receiving special education services with discernibly lower proficiency in math and ELA at the middle school level and rates of graduation at the high school level. As for the teacher survey data, 80 to 83 percent of teachers responded to the NYC School Survey overall in any given year while three-fourths of all schools had at least 74 percent of teachers respond each year.
54. During the years under study, the New York City School Survey underwent a number of revisions. Our analyses are limited to survey items that remained the same between 2012 and 2018. The survey data we use for this study span the 2011–2012 through 2018–2019 school years and represent more than 270,000 teacher-year responses. Due to NYCPS policy, responses are anonymized at the individual teacher level but remain linkable to other forms of data—teacher demographics and background information,

student suspensions—at the school level, which serves as the unit of analysis for this study. The NYC School Survey is administered annually to teachers and intends to capture teachers' opinions across six broad reporting categories within an overarching framework for school improvement: (1) rigorous instruction; (2) collaboration between teachers; (3) aspects for whether the school is a supportive environment; (4) effective school leadership; (5) ties between the school, families, and general community; and (6) trust between teachers, administrators, and parents. Each year, the NYC School Survey for teachers consists of anywhere between twenty to thirty Likert scale questions; however, to extend the extant school discipline literature, which has primarily utilized cross-sectional teacher survey data to measure school climate, we utilize data from survey items that are consistently available throughout the period of study to support a longitudinal analysis—nine survey items in total, listed in table 2. The nine items are mapped onto four conceptually distinct elements based on NYCPS's framework for the NYC School Survey: (1) one item for the subcategory "School Commitment" among teachers included under the broader "collaborative teachers" category; (2) one item for the subcategory "Safety" included under the broader "supportive environment" category; (3) six items for "Effective School Leadership"; and (4) one item for "Teacher-Teacher Trust." See Luis A. Rodriguez, Richard O. Welsh, and Chelsea Daniels, "School Climate, Teacher Characteristics, and School Discipline: Evidence From New York City," *AERA Open* 10 (2024): 23328584241263860 for further details.

55. Rudasill et al., "Systems View of School Climate"; Beth E. Schueler et al., "Measuring Parent Perceptions of School Climate," *Psychological Assessment* 26, no. 1 (2014): 314–20, https://doi.org/10.1037/a0034830; Jayanti Owens, "Parental Intervention in School, Academic Pressure, and Childhood Diagnoses of ADHD," *Social Science & Medicine* 272 (2021): 113746; Rodriguez and Welsh, "The Ties That Bind."
56. Schueler et al., "Measuring Parent Perceptions of School Climate."
57. The New York City School Survey data provide over 518,000 parent responses across the five years under study (2014–2015 through 2018–2019). In addition, four items measuring parents' perception of school leadership and an additional two items measuring safety and order within a school serve as supplementary metrics of school climate. We began our analysis in the 2014–2015 academic year, considering that the parental guardian survey remained relatively consistent and unchanged after that year. Individual parent responses were linkable to the eldest child who was a student in a given NYC public school during a particular year, as parents were asked to fill out the survey about their oldest child within one school and separate surveys for children attending separate schools. The percentage of secondary school students whose parents answered the survey ranged from 34 to 37 percent during the years of our study but 50 to 53 percent among middle school students, although school-level response rates varied quite considerably. We limited our analysis exclusively to schools serving any combination of traditional middle school grades (grades 6–8) due to the low parental response rates to the NYC School Survey in high schools and the unavailability of discipline records for elementary grades. We conducted principal component analysis to reduce the dimensionality of the set of conceptually similar variables measuring each of the four areas of school-family relations as well as school leadership and safety/order. See Rodriguez and Welsh, "The Ties That Bind" for further details.
58. Catherine P. Bradshaw et al., "Altering School Climate Through School-Wide Positive Behavioral Interventions and Supports: Findings from a Group-Randomized Effectiveness Trial," *Prevention Science* 10, no. 2 (2009): 100–115, https://doi.org/10.1007/

s11121-008-0114-9; Gage et al., "Student Perceptions of School Climate as Predictors of Office Discipline Referrals"; Mitchell, Bradshaw, and Leaf, "Student and Teacher Perceptions of School Climate."

59. Wang and Degol, "School Climate."
60. Huang and Cornell, "The Relationship of School Climate with Out-of-School Suspensions."
61. Heilbrun, Cornell, and Konold, "Authoritative School Climate and Suspension Rates in Middle Schools."
62. Gregory et al., "An Examination of Restorative Interventions and Racial Equity in Out-of-School Suspensions."
63. Peer student behavior increases from –3 (three standard deviations below the average climate, i.e., extremely negative school climate) to 3 (i.e., an extremely positive school climate), the predicted probability of suspension declines by 4 percent for Black students, 4 percent for Latinx students, and 3 percent for White students. Racial disparities in exclusionary discipline can be conceptualized both as absolute (e.g., Black rate – White rate) or relative differences (e.g., Black rate/White rate), which may not necessarily give the same picture of racial disparities. The absolute difference in predicted probabilities across student groups may not substantially change as a function of the peer student behavior school climate measure—for instance, the Black–White gap in the predicted probability of suspension is 4 percent when peer student behavior is –3 and is 3 percent when peer student behavior is 3. However, the relative gap does grow for more positive values in the peer student behavior measure of school climate—the predicted probability of suspension is 1.6 times higher for Black students compared to White students when peer student behavior is –3 but is 2 times higher when peer student behavior is 3. Erik J. Girvan, Kent McIntosh, and Keith Smolkowski, "Tail, Tusk, and Trunk: What Different Metrics Reveal About Racial Disproportionality in School Discipline," *Educational Psychologist* 54, no. 1 (2019): 40–59, https://doi.org/10.1080/00461520.2018.1537125; Luis A. Rodriguez and Richard O. Welsh, "The Dimensions of School Discipline: Toward a Comprehensive Framework for Measuring Discipline Patterns and Outcomes in Schools," *AERA Open* 8 (2022): 23328584221083669, https://doi.org/10.1177/23328584221083669.
64. The differential associations for Asian students and other race students are less clear. Asian students appear to have a significantly larger reduction in likelihood of ODR and suspension in schools with better peer student behavior compared to White students; however, for the school environment construct, the opposite relationship (a smaller reduction in likelihood compared to White students) is found for student ODR and no significant differential relationship is found for student suspension. The disciplinary outcomes of other race students appear to have no significant differential association with school climate, except for having a smaller reduction in risk of suspension associated with a more positive school environment than White students.
65. Shafiqua J. Little and Richard O. Welsh, "Rac(e)ing to Punishment? Applying Theory to Racial Disparities in Disciplinary Outcomes," *Race Ethnicity and Education* 25, no. 4 (2022): 564–84, https://doi.org/10.1080/13613324.2019.1599344; Richard O. Welsh, "Schooling Levels and School Discipline: Examining the Variation in Disciplinary Infractions and Consequences Across Elementary, Middle, and High Schools," *Journal of Education for Students Placed at Risk* 27, no. 3 (2022): 270–95, https://doi.org/10.1080/10824669.2022.2041998; Richard O. Welsh and Shafiqua Little, "The School Discipline Dilemma: A Comprehensive Review of Disparities and Alternative

Approaches," *Review of Educational Research* 88, no. 5 (2018): 752–94, https://doi.org/10.3102/0034654318791582.

66. Vicki Nishioka, Becca Merrill, and Havala Hanson, *Changes in Exclusionary and Nonexclusionary Discipline in Grades K–5 Following State Policy Reform in Oregon* (Washington, DC: Institute of Education Sciences, Regional Educational Laboratory Northwest, February 2021), https://eric.ed.gov/?id=ED610682; Rebecca A. Cruz, Allison R. Firestone, and Janelle E. Rodl, "Disproportionality Reduction in Exclusionary School Discipline: A Best-Evidence Synthesis," *Review of Educational Research* 91, no. 3 (2021): 397–431, https://doi.org/10.3102/0034654321995255; Welsh, "Administering Discipline."
67. Anyon, Zhang, and Hazel, "Race, Exclusionary Discipline, and Connectedness to Adults in Secondary Schools."
68. I use student responses from the annually administered New York City School Survey to examine the relationship between student perception of school climate and school personnel, drawing on a longitudinal student-level sample for public middle and high schools for the years 2011–2012 to 2018–2019 (n = 3,988,020 student-years). The overall student survey completion rate in our sample was approximately 73 percent, ranging from 71 to 74 percent across the years 2011–2012 to 2018–2019. The overall response rate was about 68 percent for Black students, 78 percent for White students, 72 percent for Latinx students, 81 percent for Asian students, and 56 percent for students with other racial backgrounds, with no substantial variation between years. Almost all student and school variables had small but statistically significant average differences between students who completed the survey and those who did not. The student and school characteristics with the largest standardized differences included students receiving special education services, the proportion of students at a school who received special education services, the average attendance rate, the graduation rate, and the math and English Language Arts (ELA) proficiency rates. Overall, students in our sample who responded to the survey were from backgrounds and attended schools where it was more likely that they would have better perceptions of school climate—for example, 25 percent of students who responded were Black compared to 33 percent of students who did not respond, and about 40 percent of Black students are in the lowest tercile of perceptions of climate—so it is possible that we slightly under sampled students with worse perceptions of school climate.
69. Using linear regression analyses to predict student perceptions of school climate, various student and school characteristics had small but statistically significant associations with student perceptions (all effect sizes < 0.1).The two measures of students' perception of school climate (i.e., student behavior and school environment) had significant relationships with several of the school personnel variables after controlling for student and school characteristics and including school and year fixed effects.
70. Catherine P. Bradshaw et al., "Addressing School Safety Through Comprehensive School Climate Approaches," *School Psychology Review* 50, no. 2–3 (July 3, 2021): 221–36, https://doi.org/10.1080/2372966X.2021.1926321; National Center on Safe Supportive Learning Environments, "SCIRP: Reference Manual on Making School Climate Improvements," Department of Education, Office of Safe and Healthy Students, 2017, https://safesupportivelearning.ed.gov/resources/scirp-reference-manual-making-school-climate-improvements; Janet VanLone et al., "A Practical Guide to Improving School Climate in High Schools," *Intervention in School and Clinic* 55, no. 1 (September 1, 2019): 39–45, https://doi.org/10.1177/1053451219832988.

71. Gordon P. Capp, Ron Avi Astor, and Hadass Moore, "Positive School Climate for School Staff? The Roles of Administrators, Staff Beliefs, and School Organization in High and Low Resource School Districts," *Journal of Community Psychology* 50, no. 2 (2022): 1060–82, https://doi.org/10.1002/jcop.22701; Troy A. McCarley, Michelle L. Peters, and John M. Decman, "Transformational Leadership Related to School Climate: A Multi-Level Analysis," *Educational Management Administration & Leadership* 44, no. 2 (March 1, 2016): 322–42, https://doi.org/10.1177/1741143214549966.
72. Bradshaw et al., "Addressing School Safety Through Comprehensive School Climate Approaches."
73. Adam Voight and Maury Nation, "Practices for Improving Secondary School Climate: A Systematic Review of the Research Literature," *American Journal of Community Psychology* 58, no. 1–2 (2016): 174–91, https://doi.org/10.1002/ajcp.12074.
74. Cade T. Charlton et al., "A Systematic Review of the Effects of Schoolwide Intervention Programs on Student and Teacher Perceptions of School Climate," *Journal of Positive Behavior Interventions* 23, no. 3 (July 1, 2021): 185–200, https://doi.org/10.1177/1098300720940168; Kent McIntosh et al., "Effects of an Equity-Focused PBIS Approach to School Improvement on Exclusionary Discipline and School Climate," *Preventing School Failure* 65, no. 4 (August 2, 2021): 354–61, https://doi.org/10.1080/1045988X.2021.1937027.
75. Rodriguez, Welsh, and Daniels, "School Climate, Teacher Characteristics, and School Discipline"; Matthew Shirrell, Travis J. Bristol, and Tolani A. Britton, "The Effects of Student–Teacher Ethnoracial Matching on Exclusionary Discipline for Asian American, Black, and Latinx Students: Evidence from New York City," *Educational Evaluation and Policy Analysis* 46, no. 3 (2024): 555–80.
76. Anyon, Zhang, and Hazel, "Race, Exclusionary Discipline, and Connectedness to Adults in Secondary Schools"; Bottiani, Bradshaw, and Mendelson, "A Multilevel Examination of Racial Disparities in High School Discipline"; Voight et al., "The Racial School Climate Gap."
77. Cohen et al, "School Climate"; Thapa et al., "A Review of School Climate Research."
78. Rami Benbenishty et al., "Testing the Causal Links Between School Climate, School Violence, and School Academic Performance: A Cross-Lagged Panel Autoregressive Model," *Educational Researcher* 45, no. 3 (2016): 197–206.
79. Yolanda Anyon et al., "'It's All About the Relationships': Educators' Rationales and Strategies for Building Connections with Students to Prevent Exclusionary School Discipline Outcomes," *Children and Schools* 40, no. 4 (2018): 221–30; Richard O. Welsh, "Navigating Tensions in School Discipline: Examining School Leaders, Teachers, and the Conversion of Referrals into Suspensions," *American Journal of Education* 129, no. 2 (2023): 237–64; Richard O. Welsh and Neha Sobti, "Moving from Pathology to Politicized Care: Examining Black School Leaders' Perspectives on School Discipline," *Journal of School Leadership* 33, no. 6 (2023): 579–606.

Chapter 5

1. Melanie Leung-Gagné et al., *Pushed Out: Trends and Disparities in Out-of-School Suspension* (Palo Alto, CA: Learning Policy Institute, 2022), https://doi.org/10.54300/235.277.
2. Renee Ryberg et al., *Despite Reductions Since 2011–12, Black Students and Students with Disabilities Remain More Likely to Experience Suspension* (Bethesda, MD: ChildTrends, 2021), https://www.childtrends.org/publications/despite-reductions-black-students-and-students-with-disabilities-remain-more-likely-to-experience-suspension; Leung-Gagné

et al., *Pushed Out*; Edward J. Smith and Shaun R. Harper, *Disproportionate Impact of K–12 School Suspension and Expulsion on Black Students in Southern States* (Philadelphia: University of Pennsylvania, Center for the Study of Race and Equity in Education, 2015).

3. Nicholas A. Gage et al., "Exploring Disproportionate Discipline for Latinx Students with and Without Disabilities: A National Analysis," *Behavioral Disorders* 47, no. 1 (2021): 3–13, https://doi.org/10.1177/0198742920961356; Richard O. Welsh, "Student Mobility, Segregation, and Achievement Gaps: Evidence from Clark County, Nevada," *Urban Education* 53, no. 1 (2018): 55–85, https://doi.org/10.1177/0042085916660349; Richard O. Welsh, "Schooling Levels and School Discipline: Examining the Variation in Disciplinary Infractions and Consequences Across Elementary, Middle, and High Schools," *Journal of Education for Students Placed at Risk* 27, no. 3 (2022): 270–95, https://doi.org/10.1080/10824669.2022.2041998.
4. Jesse Margolis and Eli Groves, "Resilience: Will Urban Schools That Beat the Odds Continue to Do So During the COVID-19 Pandemic?," MarGrady Research, 2020, http://margrady.com/wp-content/uploads/2020/06/Resilience-Beat-the-Odds-Full-Report.pdf; Michael DeArmond et al., *Measuring Up: Educational Improvement & Opportunity in 50 Cities* (Seattle, WA: Center on Reinventing Public Education, 2015), https://eric.ed.gov/?id=ED560764; Jennifer L. Jennings et al., "Do Differences in School Quality Matter More Than We Thought? New Evidence on Educational Opportunity in the Twenty-First Century," *Sociology of Education* 88, no. 1 (2015): 56–82, https://doi.org/10.1177/0038040714562006; Daniel Muijs et al., "Improving Schools in Socioeconomically Disadvantaged Areas: A Review of Research Evidence," *School Effectiveness and School Improvement* 15, no. 2 (2004): 149–75, https://doi.org/10.1076/sesi.15.2.149.30433; Mark A. Partridge and Sharon Koon, *Beating the Odds in Mississippi: Identifying Schools Exceeding Achievement Expectations*, REL 2017-213 (Washington, DC: Regional Educational Laboratory Southeast, 2017), https://eric.ed.gov/?id=ED572606.
5. Neha Sobti and Richard O. Welsh, "Adding Color to My Tears: Toward a Theoretical Framework for Antiblackness in School Discipline," *Educational Researcher* 52, no. 8 (2023): 500–511, https://doi.org/10.3102/0013189X231191448; Richard O. Welsh, Luis A. Rodriguez, and Blaise B. Joseph, "Beating the School Discipline Odds: Conceptualizing and Examining Inclusive Disciplinary Schools in New York City," *School Effectiveness and School Improvement* 34, no. 3 (2023): 271–97, https://doi.org/10.1080/09243453.2023.2182795.
6. Richard O. Welsh and Walker A. Swain, "(Re)Defining Urban Education: A Conceptual Review and Empirical Exploration of the Definition of Urban Education," *Educational Researcher* 49, no. 2 (2020): 90–100, https://doi.org/10.3102/0013189X20902822.
7. Linsey Edwards, "Homogeneity and Inequality: School Discipline Inequality and the Role of Racial Composition," *Social Forces* 95, no. 1 (2016): 55–76, https://doi.org/10.1093/sf/sow038; Kelly Welch and Allison Ann Payne, "Racial Threat and Punitive School Discipline," *Social Problems* 57, no. 1 (2010): 25–48, https://doi.org/10.1525/sp.2010.57.1.25.
8. Anne Gregory, Russell J. Skiba, and Kavitha Mediratta, "Eliminating Disparities in School Discipline: A Framework for Intervention," *Review of Research in Education* 41, no. 1 (2017): 253–78.
9. Rebecca A. Cruz, Allison R. Firestone, and Janelle E. Rodl, "Disproportionality Reduction in Exclusionary School Discipline: A Best-Evidence Synthesis," *Review of Educational*

Research 91, no. 3 (2021): 397–431, https://doi.org/10.3102/0034654321995255; Anne Gregory et al., "Good Intentions Are Not Enough: Centering Equity in School Discipline Reform," *School Psychology Review* 50, no. 2–3 (2021): 206–20, https://doi.org/10.1080/2372966X.2020.1861911; Richard O. Welsh, "Up the Down Escalator? Examining a Decade of School Discipline Reforms," *Children and Youth Services Review* 150 (2023): 106962, https://doi.org/10.1016/j.childyouth.2023.106962; Richard O. Welsh, "Navigating Tensions in School Discipline: Examining School Leaders, Teachers, and the Conversion of Referrals into Suspensions," *American Journal of Education* 129, no. 2 (2023): 237–64, https://doi.org/10.1086/723064.

10. Leung-Gagné et al., *Pushed Out*; Welsh, "Schooling Levels and School Discipline"; Welsh, "Up the Down Escalator?"
11. Lora Henderson Smith et al., "The Discipline Gap in Context: The Role of School Racial and Ethnic Diversity and Within School Positionality on Out-of-School Suspensions," *Journal of School Psychology* 98 (June 1, 2023): 61–77, https://doi.org/10.1016/j.jsp.2023.02.006.
12. Edwards, "Homogeneity and Inequality"; Smith et al., "The Discipline Gap in Context"; Kathryn E. Wiley, "A Tale of Two Logics: School Discipline and Racial Disparities in a 'Mostly White' Middle School," *American Journal of Education* 127, no. 2 (2021): 163–92, https://doi.org/10.1086/712084.
13. Christine A. Christie, C. Michael Nelson, and Kristine Jolivette, "School Characteristics Related to the Use of Suspension," *Education and Treatment of Children* 27, no. 4 (2004): 509–26; Jason Jabbari and Odis Johnson, "The Collateral Damage of In-School Suspensions: A Counterfactual Analysis of High-Suspension Schools, Math Achievement and College Attendance," *Urban Education* 58, no. 5 (2023): 801–37, https://doi.org/10.1177/0042085920902256.
14. Ashleigh Kysar-Moon, "Adverse Childhood Experiences, Family Social Capital, and Externalizing Behavior Problems: An Analysis Across Multiple Ecological Levels," *Journal of Family Issues* 43, no. 12 (2022): 3168–93, https://doi.org/10.1177/0192513X211042849; Jennifer L. Miner and K. Alison Clarke-Stewart, "Trajectories of Externalizing Behavior from Age 2 to Age 9: Relations with Gender, Temperament, Ethnicity, Parenting, and Rater," *Developmental Psychology* 44, no. 3 (2008): 771–86, https://doi.org/10.1037/0012-1649.44.3.771; Luis A. Rodriguez and Richard O. Welsh, "The Ties That Bind: An Examination of School-Family Relationships and Middle School Discipline in New York City," *Educational Researcher* 53, no. 2 (2023): 85–99, https://doi.org/10.3102/0013189X231203696; Steven B. Sheldon and Joyce L. Epstein, "Improving Student Behavior and School Discipline with Family and Community Involvement," *Education and Urban Society* 35, no. 1 (2002): 4–26, https://doi.org/10.1177/001312402237212; Richard O. Welsh and Shafiqua Little, "Caste and Control in Schools: A Systematic Review of the Pathways, Rates and Correlates of Exclusion Due to School Discipline," *Children and Youth Services Review* 94 (2018): 315–39, https://doi.org/10.1016/j.childyouth.2018.09.031.
15. Kysar-Moon, "Adverse Childhood Experiences, Family Social Capital, and Externalizing Behavior Problems"; Miner and Clarke-Stewart, "Trajectories of Externalizing Behavior from Age 2 to Age 9"; Rodriguez and Welsh, "The Ties That Bind"; Russell J. Skiba et al., "Parsing Disciplinary Disproportionality: Contributions of Infraction, Student, and School Characteristics to Out-of-School Suspension and Expulsion," *American Educational Research Journal* 51, no. 4 (2014): 640–70, https://doi.org/10.3102/0002831214541670; Richard O. Welsh, "Administering Discipline: An

Examination of the Factors Shaping School Discipline Practices," *Education and Urban Society* (2023): 1–34, https://doi.org/10.1177/00131245231208170; Welsh, "Navigating Tensions in School Discipline."

16. F. Chris Curran et al., "Do Interactions with School Resource Officers Predict Students' Likelihood of Being Disciplined and Feelings of Safety? Mixed-Methods Evidence from Two School Districts," *Educational Evaluation and Policy Analysis* 43, no. 2 (2021): 200–232, https://doi.org/10.3102/0162373720985904; Welsh, "Schooling Levels and School Discipline"; Richard O. Welsh, "Economics of Urban Education: Race, Resources, and Control in Schools," in *Handbook of Urban Education*, ed. H. Richard Milner and Kofi Lomotey, 2nd ed. (New York: Routledge, 2021).
17. Welsh, "Schooling Levels and School Discipline."
18. Curran et al., "Do Interactions with School Resource Officers Predict Students' Likelihood of Being Disciplined and Feelings of Safety?"
19. I created four separate dichotomous variables to indicate whether a district was in the bottom quartile for each discipline measure. These four metrics (two relating to prevalence and two relating to disparities) were then combined to identify IDD districts that satisfy all four criteria.
20. Next, I replicated the principal component analysis (PCA) approach of Sartain and colleagues, using all of our defining characteristics for IDD districts and then selecting approximately the lowest quartile of values for the new PCA variable to identify IDD districts and then the highest quartile of values for the HDD districts. Using the PCA approach, all of the IDD and HDD districts previously identified are classified in the same way, but there are also substantially more schools included in both the IDD and HDD categories as a result. There is a correlation between the two variables of about 0.9. If we were to use the PCA approach, we would capture our current set of districts plus some additional districts with closer to average disciplinary outcomes. In other words, the PCA approach captures a broader set of districts than our IDD criteria. The PCA approach captures districts closer to the median and is less discerning for identifying school discipline exemplars. Lauren Sartain, Elaine M. Allensworth, and Shanette Porter, *Suspending Chicago's Students: Differences in Discipline Practices Across Schools* (Chicago: University of Chicago, Consortium on Chicago School Research, September 2015).
21. To contextualize these patterns, there are clear demographic and economic differences between regions: on average, the Midwest and West regions have similar income, poverty, and unemployment, whereas the Northeast has higher income and lower poverty and unemployment, and the South has lower income and higher poverty and unemployment. The Midwest and Northeast have similar proportions of Black residents, whereas the South has by far the greatest proportion of Black residents and the West has the lowest.
22. Francis A. Pearman II, "Gentrified Discipline: The Impact of Gentrification on Exclusionary Punishment in Public Schools," *Social Problems* 70, no. 1 (2023): 164–84, https://doi.org/10.1093/socpro/spab028.
23. Maithreyi Gopalan, "Understanding the Linkages Between Racial/Ethnic Discipline Gaps and Racial/Ethnic Achievement Gaps in the United States," *Education Policy Analysis Archives* 27, no. 154 (2019), https://eric.ed.gov/?id=EJ1237382; Man Hung et al., "Exploring Student Achievement Gaps in School Districts Across the United States," *Education and Urban Society* 52, no. 2 (2020): 175–93, https://doi.org/10.1177/0013124519833442.

24. Welch and Payne, "Racial Threat and Punitive School Discipline"; Kelly Welch and Allison Ann Payne, "Latino/a Student Threat and School Disciplinary Policies and Practices," *Sociology of Education* 91, no. 2 (2018): 91–110, https://doi.org/10.1177/0038040718757720.
25. Imani Perry, *South to America: A Journey Below the Mason-Dixon to Understand the Soul of a Nation* (New York: HarperCollins, 2022); Kristen L. Buras, "'Thank God for Mississippi!' How Disparagement of the South Has Destroyed Public Schooling in New Orleans—and Beyond," *Peabody Journal of Education* 90, no. 3 (2015): 355–79; Benjamin Schwarz, "The Idea of the South," *The Atlantic*, December 1997, https://www.theatlantic.com/magazine/archive/1997/12/the-idea-of-the-south/377028/.
26. Edward J. Smith and Shaun R. Harper, *Disproportionate Impact of K–12 School Suspension and Expulsion on Black Students in Southern States* (Philadelphia: University of Pennsylvania, Center for the Study of Race and Equity in Education, 2015).
27. Jerome E. Morris and Carla R. Monroe, "Why Study the US South? The Nexus of Race and Place in Investigating Black Student Achievement," *Educational Researcher* 38, no. 1 (2009): 21–36.
28. Mohamad Moslimani et al., "Facts About the U.S. Black Population," Pew Research Center, January 18, 2024, https://www.pewresearch.org/social-trends/fact-sheet/facts-about-the-us-black-population/#:~:text=The%20South%20is%20also%20the,9%25%20live%20in%20the%20West.
29. Morris and Monroe, "Why Study the US South?"; National Center for Education Statistics, "State Nonfiscal Public Elementary/Secondary Education Survey" (v.1a) [Data set], Institute of Education Sciences, 2022.
30. Erik J. Girvan et al., "The Relative Contribution of Subjective Office Referrals to Racial Disproportionality in School Discipline," *School Psychology Quarterly* 32, no. 3 (2017): 392–404, https://doi.org/10.1037/spq0000178; Skiba et al., "Parsing Disciplinary Disproportionality"; Richard O. Welsh and Shafiqua Little, "The School Discipline Dilemma: A Comprehensive Review of Disparities and Alternative Approaches," *Review of Educational Research* 88, no. 5 (October 1, 2018): 752–94, https://doi.org/10.3102/0034654318791582; Welsh, "Administering Discipline."
31. Cruz, Firestone, and Rodl, "Disproportionality Reduction in Exclusionary School Discipline."
32. Eric Booth et al., "Comparing Campus Discipline Rates: A Multivariate Approach for Identifying Schools with Significantly Different Than Expected Exclusionary Discipline Rates," *Journal of Applied Research on Children: Informing Policy for Children at Risk* 3, no. 2 (2012), https://doi.org/10.58464/2155-5834.1093; Christie, Nelson, and Jolivette, "School Characteristics Related to the Use of Suspension"; Gathogo Mukuria, "Disciplinary Challenges: How Do Principals Address This Dilemma?," *Urban Education* 37, no. 3 (2002): 432–52, https://doi.org/10.1177/00485902037003007; Sartain, Allensworth, and Porter, *Suspending Chicago's Students*.
33. Booth et al., "Comparing Campus Discipline Rates"; Mukuria, "Disciplinary Challenges"; Sartain, Allensworth, and Porter, *Suspending Chicago's Students*.
34. Welsh, Rodriguez, and Joseph, "Beating the School Discipline Odds."
35. The proportion of IDSs in NYC is much lower compared to the low exclusionary discipline practices (EDP) schools in Chicago in Sartain et al. and results from Booth et al. This may be partly due to differences in defining criteria across the studies. My criteria for IDS mean that I limit my selection to schools that are in the top quartile of inclusive disciplinary outcomes on a number of measures (suspension and ODR both overall and

for Black students, racial disparities, and chronic discipline). This identification criteria for IDS or equivalent contrast with the approach of Sartain et al., who select the top third of all schools using an aggregated measure of multiple discipline outcomes, and Booth et al., who find that approximately one-quarter of schools have lower suspension rates than would be expected given their composition. For this reason, my selection process results in a much smaller proportion of schools but enables me to analyze the characteristics of positive outlier schools in terms of discipline outcomes. When disaggregated by schooling level, the proportion of schools that are IDSs is 2 percent for grade 6–12 schools, 2 percent for high schools, and 4 percent for middle schools. In contrast, the proportion of schools that are HDSs is 4 percent for grade 6–12 schools, 5 percent for high schools, and 2 percent for middle schools. Booth et al., "Comparing Campus Discipline Rates"; Sartain, Allensworth, and Porter, *Suspending Chicago's Students*.

36. By NYC borough location, 36 percent of IDSs are in Manhattan, 30 percent in Queens, 17 percent in Brooklyn, 14 percent in the Bronx, and 3 percent in Staten Island (the share of IDSs for both Manhattan and Queens are substantially above their overall share of schools, while the IDS share for both Brooklyn and the Bronx are below their overall share, and Staten Island's IDS share is in line with its overall share). There appears to be some clustering of IDSs in certain districts: district 2 in Manhattan (sixteen distinct IDSs), district 10 in the Bronx (six distinct IDSs), and districts 24 and 30 in Queens (five and six distinct IDSs, respectively), although taken together, these are still less than one-third of all IDSs. These districts tend to serve communities with below-average proportions of Black students and overall Black population and with above-average income and below-average poverty and unemployment (with the exception of district 10 in the Bronx, which serves a relatively low-income, high-poverty neighborhood).
37. National Center for Education Statistics, *More Than 80 Percent of U.S. Public Schools Report Pandemic Has Negatively Impacted Student Behavior and Socio-Emotional Development*, Annual Report, July 6, 2022, https://nces.ed.gov/whatsnew/press_releases/07_06_2022.asp; David Naff et al., "The Mental Health Impacts of COVID-19 on PK–12 Students: A Systematic Review of Emerging Literature," *AERA Open* 8 (2022), https://doi.org/10.1177/23328584221084722.
38. Welsh, "Navigating Tensions in School Discipline."
39. Christie, Nelson, and Jolivette, "School Characteristics Related to the Use of Suspension"; Jabbari and Johnson, "The Collateral Damage of In-School Suspensions"; Skiba et al., "Parsing Disciplinary Disproportionality."
40. Christie, Nelson, and Jolivette, "School Characteristics Related to the Use of Suspension."

Conclusion

1. Shafiqua J. Little and Richard O. Welsh, "Rac(e)ing to Punishment? Applying Theory to Racial Disparities in Disciplinary Outcomes," *Race Ethnicity and Education* 25, no. 4 (2022): 564–84, https://doi.org/10.1080/13613324.2019.1599344.
2. Mark Dery, "Black to the Future: Interviews with Samuel R. Delany, Greg Tate, and Tricia Rose," in *Flame Wars: The Discourse of Cyberculture*, ed. Mark Dery (Durham, NC: Duke University Press, 1994), 179–222; Alondra Nelson, ed., *Social Text 20.2* (Durham, NC: Duke University Press, Summer 2002), 1–146.
3. Stephanie R. Toliver, "It Will Take Nations of Billions to Obstruct Our Dreams: Extending BlackCrit Through Afrofuturism," *Journal for Multicultural Education* 18, no. 3 (2024): 230–44.

4. fahima ife, "A Run//on Black Study," *Research in the Teaching of English* 57, no. 1 (2022): 8–22, https://doi.org/10.58680/rte202231999; Stephanie R. Toliver, "Afrocarnival: Celebrating Black Bodies and Critiquing Oppressive Bodies in Afrofuturist Literature," *Children's Literature in Education* 52, no. 1 (2021): 132–48, https://doi.org/10.1007/s10583-020-09403-y; Chezare A. Warren and Justin A. Coles, "Trading Spaces: Antiblackness and Reflections on Black Education Futures," *Equity & Excellence in Education* 53, no. 3 (2020): 382–98, https://doi.org/10.1080/10665684.2020.1764882.
5. Toliver, "It Will Take Nations of Billions to Obstruct Our Dreams."
6. Jason A. Okonofua, Gregory M. Walton, and Jennifer L. Eberhardt, "A Vicious Cycle: A Social–Psychological Account of Extreme Racial Disparities in School Discipline," *Perspectives on Psychological Science* 11, no. 3 (2016): 381–98.
7. Dorothy E. Hines and Jennifer M. Wilmot, "From Spirit-Murdering to Spirit-Healing: Addressing Anti-Black Aggressions and the Inhumane Discipline of Black Children," *Multicultural Perspectives* 20, no. 2 (2018): 62–69, https://doi.org/10.1080/15210960.2018.1447064; Jason A. Okonofua, David Paunesku, and Gregory M. Walton, "Brief Intervention to Encourage Empathic Discipline Cuts Suspension Rates in Half Among Adolescents," *Proceedings of the National Academy of Sciences* 113, no. 19 (2016): 5221–26, https://doi.org/10.1073/pnas.1523698113; Jason A. Okonofua et al., "A Scalable Empathic-Mindset Intervention Reduces Group Disparities in School Suspensions," *Science Advances* 8, no. 12 (2022): eabj0691, https://doi.org/10.1126/sciadv.abj0691.
8. David Aguayo et al., "Centering Students' Voices in the Exploration of In-Classroom Culturally Responsive Practices," *Journal of School Psychology* 105 (2024): 101317, https://doi.org/10.1016/j.jsp.2024.101317.
9. Carl A. Grant, Ashley Woodson, and Michael Dumas, eds., *The Future Is Black: Afropessimism, Fugitivity, and Radical Hope in Education* (New York: Routledge, 2021); Daniel Solorzano, Miguel Ceja, and Tara Yosso, "Critical Race Theory, Racial Microaggressions, and Campus Racial Climate: The Experiences of African American College Students," *Journal of Negro Education* 69, no. 1/2 (2000): 60–73; Chezare A. Warren, *About Centering Possibility in Black Education* (New York: Teachers College Press, 2021); Warren and Coles, "Trading Spaces."
10. Tyrone Howard, "Examining Our Past to Imagine a Better Future: Recognition and Redress of Racial Injustice in Education" (AERA Annual Meeting in Philadelphia, April 13, 2024).
11. Dafina-Lazarus Stewart, "Language of Appeasement," *Inside Higher Ed*, March 29, 2017, https://www.insidehighered.com/views/2017/03/30/colleges-need-language-shift-not-one-you-think-essay; Dafina-Lazarus Stewart, "Ideologies of Absence: Anti-Blackness and Inclusion Rhetoric in Student Affairs Practice," *Journal of Student Affairs* 28 (2019): 15–30.
12. Stewart, "Ideologies of Absence."
13. Thomas A. DiPrete and Brittany N. Fox-Williams, "The Relevance of Inequality Research in Sociology for Inequality Reduction," *Socius* 7 (2021): 23780231211020199, https://doi.org/10.1177/23780231211020199.
14. Prudence L. Carter et al., "You Can't Fix What You Don't Look At: Acknowledging Race in Addressing Racial Discipline Disparities," *Urban Education* 52, no. 2 (2017): 207–35, https://doi.org/10.1177/0042085916660350; Rebecca A. Cruz and Allison R. Firestone, "On Reducing Disparities in Office Discipline Referrals: A Systematic Review of Underlying Theories," *Whiteness and Education* (2023): 1–23, https://doi.org/10.1080/23793406.2023.2174449; Rebecca A. Cruz, Allison R. Firestone, and Janelle E.

Rodl, "Disproportionality Reduction in Exclusionary School Discipline: A Best-Evidence Synthesis," *Review of Educational Research* 91, no. 3 (2021): 397–431, https://doi.org/10.3102/0034654321995255.

15. Russell J. Skiba, Suzanne E. Eckes, and Kevin Brown, "African American Disproportionality in School Discipline: The Divide Between Best Evidence and Legal Remedy," *NYLS Law Review* 54, no. 4 (2009): 1071.
16. Skiba, Eckes, and Brown, "African American Disproportionality in School Discipline."
17. Carter et al., "You Can't Fix What You Don't Look At"; Anne Gregory et al., "Good Intentions Are Not Enough: Centering Equity in School Discipline Reform," *School Psychology Review* 50, no. 2–3 (2021): 206–20, https://doi.org/10.1080/2372966X.2020.1861911; Russell J. Skiba et al., "Race Is Not Neutral: A National Investigation of African American and Latino Disproportionality in School Discipline," *School Psychology Review* 40, no. 1 (2011): 85–107, https://doi.org/10.1080/02796015.2011.12087730; Richard O. Welsh, "Economics of Urban Education: Race, Resources, and Control in Schools," in *Handbook of Urban Education*, ed. H. Richard Milner and Kofi Lomotey, 2nd ed. (New York: Routledge, 2021).
18. Gloria Ladson-Billings, "From the Achievement Gap to the Education Debt: Understanding Achievement in U.S. Schools," *Educational Researcher* 35, no. 7 (2006): 3–12, https://doi.org/10.3102/0013189X035007003.
19. Olivia Rios, Madison Watts, and Sarah Woll, *Building a Better Behavior Management Strategy for Students and Teachers: Key Findings from EAB's Student Behavior Survey* (Washington, DC: EAB, 2023), https://pages.eab.com/rs/732-GKV-655/images/EDIL-Student%20Behavior%20Executive%20Briefing-PDF.pdf; Richard O. Welsh, "Navigating Tensions in School Discipline: Examining School Leaders, Teachers, and the Conversion of Referrals into Suspensions," *American Journal of Education* 129, no. 2 (2023): 237–64, https://doi.org/10.1086/723064.
20. *Parents Involved in Community Schools v. Seattle School Dist. No. 1*, No. 05-908 (US Supreme Court 2007); Amy Howe, "Affirmative Action Appears in Jeopardy after Marathon Arguments," *SCOTUSblog*, October 31, 2022, https://www.scotusblog.com/2022/10/affirmative-action-appears-in-jeopardy-after-marathon-arguments/.
21. Skiba, Eckes, and Brown, "African American Disproportionality in School Discipline."
22. Howe, "Affirmative Action Appears in Jeopardy after Marathon Arguments."
23. Howe, "Affirmative Action Appears in Jeopardy after Marathon Arguments."
24. Skiba, Eckes, and Brown, "African American Disproportionality in School Discipline."
25. Carter et al., "You Can't Fix What You Don't Look At"; Gregory et al., "Good Intentions Are Not Enough"; Skiba et al., "Race Is Not Neutral"; Russell J. Skiba, "Interventions to Address Racial/Ethnic Disparities in School Discipline: Can Systems Reform Be Race-Neutral?," in *Race and Social Problems: Restructuring Inequality*, ed. Ralph Bangs and Larry E. Davis (New York: Springer, 2015).
26. Mark J. Chin et al., "Bias in the Air: A Nationwide Exploration of Teachers' Implicit Racial Attitudes, Aggregate Bias, and Student Outcomes," *Educational Researcher* 49, no. 8 (2020): 566–78, https://doi.org/10.3102/0013189X20937240; Miles Davison, Andrew M. Penner, and Emily K. Penner, "Restorative for All? Racial Disproportionality and School Discipline Under Restorative Justice," *American Educational Research Journal* 59, no. 4 (2022): 687–718, https://doi.org/10.3102/00028312211062613; Amanda E. Lewis, and John B. Diamond, *Despite the Best Intentions: How Racial Inequality Thrives in Good Schools*, Transgressing Boundaries (New York: Oxford University Press, 2015).

27. Adai A. Tefera et al., "Disrupting Disparities in School Discipline," *Phi Delta Kappan* 105, no. 7 (2024): 32–37, https://doi.org/10.1177/00317217241244903.
28. Bruce Schreiner, "Kentucky Governor Signs Student Discipline Bill into Law," *AP News*, March 23, 2023, https://apnews.com/article/kentucky-legislature-school-student-discipline-law-9cb93b82039639fc81b2a6e35fbfefa9.
29. Emily G. Owens, "Testing the School-to-Prison Pipeline," *Journal of Policy Analysis and Management* 36, no. 1 (2017): 11–37, https://doi.org/10.1002/pam.21954; Emily K. Weisburst, "Patrolling Public Schools: The Impact of Funding for School Police on Student Discipline and Long-Term Education Outcomes," *Journal of Policy Analysis and Management* 38, no. 2 (2019): 338–65, https://doi.org/10.1002/pam.22116.
30. Asher Lehrer-Small, "Four Houstonians Got Suspended from School While Homeless. Here's How It Changed Their Lives," *Houston Landing*, May 23, 2024, http://houstonlanding.org/texas-homeless-student-suspension-stories/; Asher Lehrer-Small, "Texas Schools Illegally Suspended Thousands of Homeless Students—and Nobody Stopped Them," *Houston Landing*, May 23, 2024, http://houstonlanding.org/texas-homeless-student-suspension-school/.
31. Safia Samee Ali, "Teachers Get More Power to Remove Unruly Students in Some States," *NewsNation*, June 6, 2024, https://www.newsnationnow.com/us-news/education/teachers-power-remove-unruly-students-states/.
32. Richard O. Welsh and Luis A. Rodriguez, "The Plight of Persistently Disciplined Students: Examining Frequent Flyers and the Conversion of Office Discipline Referrals into Suspensions," *Educational Evaluation and Policy Analysis* 46, no. 1 (2023): 160–70, https://doi.org/10.3102/01623737231155155; Richard O. Welsh, "Administering Discipline: An Examination of the Factors Shaping School Discipline Practices," *Education and Urban Society* (2023): 1–34, https://doi.org/10.1177/00131245231208170.
33. Erik J. Girvan et al., "The Relative Contribution of Subjective Office Referrals to Racial Disproportionality in School Discipline," *School Psychology Quarterly* 32, no. 3 (2017): 392–404, https://doi.org/10.1037/spq0000178; Richard O. Welsh, "Schooling Levels and School Discipline: Examining the Variation in Disciplinary Infractions and Consequences Across Elementary, Middle, and High Schools," *Journal of Education for Students Placed at Risk* 27, no. 3 (2022): 270–95, https://doi.org/10.1080/10824669.2022.2041998.
34. Welsh and Rodriguez, "The Plight of Persistently Disciplined Students"; Welsh, "Administering Discipline."
35. Girvan et al., "The Relative Contribution of Subjective Office Referrals to Racial Disproportionality in School Discipline"; Welsh, "Schooling Levels and School Discipline."
36. Alex Zimmerman, "Will NYC School Restorative Justice Programs Tumble over the Fiscal Cliff?," *Chalkbeat*, May 14, 2024, https://www.chalkbeat.org/newyork/2024/05/14/nyc-school-restorative-justice-programs-face-federal-fiscal-cliff/.
37. Jennifer Smith Richards and Jodi S. Cohen, "An Illinois School District's Reliance on Police to Ticket Students Is Discriminatory, Civil Rights Complaint Says," *ProPublica*, June 4, 2024, https://www.propublica.org/article/federal-civil-rights-complaint-rockford-illinois-schools.
38. Rachel M. Perera and Jon Valant, "The Biden Administration's Updated School Discipline Guidelines Fail to Meet the Moment," Brookings, June 28, 2023, https://www.brookings.edu/articles/the-biden-administrations-updated-school-discipline-guidelines-fail-to-meet-the-moment/.

39. Office of Civil Rights, *Resource on Confronting Racial Discrimination in Student Discipline* (Washington, DC: US Department of Education, 2023), https://www2.ed.gov/about/offices/list/ocr/docs/tvi-student-discipline-resource-202305.pdf.
40. Melanie Leung-Gagné et al., "Pushed Out: Trends and Disparities in Out-of-School Suspension," Learning Policy Institute, September 30, 2022, https://doi.org/10.54300/235.277.
41. Zachary Schermele, "Civil Rights Complaints Are Plaguing Schools at Record Rates. Is the Solution in Congress?," *USA TODAY*, June 6, 2024, https://www.usatoday.com/story/news/education/2024/06/06/civil-rights-complaints-office-biden/73959910007/.
42. Richard O. Welsh, "Assessing the Quality of Education Research Through Its Relevance to Practice: An Integrative Review of Research-Practice Partnerships," *Review of Research in Education* 45, no. 1 (2021): 170–94, https://doi.org/10.3102/0091732X20985082.
43. Caitlin C. Farrell et al., *Research-Practice Partnerships in Education: The State of the Field* (New York: William T. Grant Foundation, 2021); William R. Penuel and Douglas A. Watkins, "Assessment to Promote Equity and Epistemic Justice: A Use-Case of a Research-Practice Partnership in Science Education," *Annals of the American Academy of Political and Social Science* 683, no. 1 (2019): 201–16, https://doi.org/10.1177/0002716219843249; Vivian Tseng, John Q. Easton, and Lauren H. Supplee, "Research-Practice Partnerships: Building Two-Way Streets of Engagement," *Social Policy Report* 30, no. 4 (2017): 1–17, https://doi.org/10.1002/j.2379-3988.2017.tb00089.x; Welsh, "Assessing the Quality of Education Research Through Its Relevance to Practice"; Laura Wentworth, Christopher Mazzeo, and Faith Connolly, "Research Practice Partnerships: A Strategy for Promoting Evidence-Based Decision-Making in Education," *Educational Research* 59, no. 2 (2017): 241–55, https://doi.org/10.1080/07391102.2017.1314108.
44. Cynthia E. Coburn, Meredith I. Honig, and Mary Kay Stein, "What's the Evidence on Districts' Use of Evidence?," in *Research and Practice in Education: Towards a Reconciliation*, ed. John Bransford et al. (Cambridge, MA: Harvard Education Press, 2009); Vivian Tseng, *Research on Research Use: Building Theory, Empirical Evidence, and a Global Field* (New York: William T. Grant Foundation, 2022), https://eric.ed.gov/?id=ED620212; Tseng, Easton, and Supplee, "Research-Practice Partnerships."
45. Caitlin C. Farrell et al., "Conceptions and Practices of Equity in Research-Practice Partnerships," *Educational Policy* 37, no. 1 (2023): 200–224, https://doi.org/10.1177/08959048221131566; Neha Sobti and Richard O. Welsh, "Adding Color to My Tears: Toward a Theoretical Framework for Antiblackness in School Discipline," *Educational Researcher* 52, no. 8 (2023): 500–511, https://doi.org/10.3102/0013189X231191448.
46. Caitlin C. Farrell et al., "Learning at the Boundaries of Research and Practice: A Framework for Understanding Research–Practice Partnerships," *Educational Researcher* 51, no. 3 (2022): 197–208, https://doi.org/10.3102/0013189X211069073.
47. Farrell et al., "Conceptions and Practices of Equity in Research-Practice Partnerships."

Acknowledgments

This book is a labor of love. A journey of joys and pains, trials, and tribulations. I've been accompanied and aided on this journey by many individuals. I aim to give them their due, but space constraints won't allow me to fully articulate the universe of relationships and interactions that have shaped and inspired my scholarship. I'm grateful to each and every soul I've encountered on my path to insights on school discipline. I thank you and remain forever indebted to you, even if I don't call your name.

With that caveat in mind, I will start with the book itself. When Jayne Fargnoli reached out to gauge my interest in writing a book, I was honored and humbled. She patiently guided me through a robust proposal process. Of course, Reviewer 2 pushed my thinking and forced me to clarify the contributions and audience of the book before I put pen to paper. Thank you for believing in me, Jayne. And thank you for the opportunity and support to bring my scholarship to the grand stage that is Harvard Education Press (HEP).

Jayne left me in quite capable hands when she stepped away from HEP. Jess Florillo, Molly Cerrone, Matthew Browne, Michael Higgins, and the entire HEP crew—thank you for your patience as emails went unanswered for months on end. I appreciate your support.

Several district and school leaders welcomed me into their space and allowed me to sit at their feet to learn the ins and outs of school discipline. There are far too many to name, but my Clarke County School District family warrants special mention: Dr. Dawn Meyers, James Barlament, Dr. Demond Means, Dr. Jennifer Scott, Dr. Robbie Hooker, Dr. Lakeisha Gantt, and Dr. Beverly Ford. Sir Jabari Cobb and Sir Eric Thigpen drove me around their districts and taught me so much from our conversations and interactions. I thank you all for teaching me and supporting my scholarship. I can't forget my New York family, particularly the folks at the Research Alliance for New York City Schools. James Kemple, Cheri Fonscali, and Chelsea Farley have always had my back and ensured I had data access and opportunities to amplify the impact of my work. I thank you.

Dr. Luis Rodriguez and I met at a Think coffee shop on Mercer Street on August 27, 2019. We sketched out four papers to work on together. But our collaboration has mushroomed into much more. Several of the chapters in this book draw on our work. And my thinking and ways of being as a scholar have been shaped in immeasurable ways by working with you. Thank you for the support my brother.

Blaise Joseph, Neha Sobti, and Kathryn James McGraw are my superstar graduate research assistants that have helped in indelible ways to bring this book to life. I appreciate you all.

Before I started developing my research agenda on school discipline, there was a period of training and development. My Stanford days were invaluable, and I owe gratitude to Dr. Peter Henry, who first put the PhD bug in my ears and gave me my first job as a research assistant. Dr. Henry was also a living example of how to function and contribute as a scholar. I also owe much credit to Dr. Dominic Brewer. From our first phone call exploring whether I was a good fit for the University of Southern California (USC), Dom has been supportive. I remember as I approached graduation and had my doubts about the next steps, your pep talk again lit my path—"If not you, then who?" I love you Dom, and thank you for everything you have done for me. This book is a testament to your mentorship. I would be remiss to reminisce on my USC days without a big up to Rochelle Hardison. It is not easy being a Black academic at predominantly White institutions, and your guidance and love showed me how to move in a room full of vultures. I thank you and will never forget what you did for me.

Fast-forward to my first tenure track position at the University of Georgia (UGA). Dr. Sheneka Williams, I will never forget our conversation on my job market visit after my first day. You saw what my career may look like before I even believed I would have a career in the academy. I appreciate you world without end. My UGA years were quite formative, and there are many folks that I interacted with that I owe gratitude. I'm especially indebted to Dr. Elizabeth DeBray, Dr. Kathleen DeMarrais, Dr. Karen Bryant, Dr. April Peters-Hawkins, Dr. Jori Hall, and Dr. Walker Swain for making me the person and scholar I am today.

After UGA, I came to New York University (NYU) just in time for the COVID-19 pandemic. Dr. Noel Anderson and Dr. Lisette Nieves made me feel at home in the big city and inspired me to do great things as I saw y'all doing great things. I appreciate you both world without end.

I came back to the South to Vanderbilt University after my New York sojourn. Dr. Rich Milner has been an exemplar of how to teach people how to treat Black scholars. You're truly an inspiration, and I appreciate all the ways you've supported me along the journey. Dean Camilla Benbow believed and invested in my talent and encouraged me to take my scholarship to the next level. My esteemed colleagues in the Department of Leadership, Policy, and Organizations ensured that tenure did not turn off my turbines with the quantity and quality of scholarship they produce. Thank you all my Vandy family.

I conclude my acknowledgements with those who knew me before I entered the game of the academy. My day one folks and family. Bronson McDonald, Matthew Smellie, and Kareem Tomlinson are brothers that have held me down for decades.

Friends who are family. I love you my brothers and thank you for keeping it real and letting me know when I was doing too much.

For all my Campion Ol' boys and girls—you know who you are, and there are too many to name. The link will forever be stink. That is it!

Rose-Patricia Boland and Lloyd Allan Welsh combined to give birth to me and raised me to be the man I am today. I am because of you, my parents. Words will never capture my love and appreciation. Everything I do always represents you. In the same breath, Michelle Welsh and Maudrie Tyrell (Princess) have been second moms to me. I love you and thank you.

My siblings, especially Bim (Kimberly Welsh), Outlaw (Christopher Welsh), Javvy (Javone Welsh), Kong (Kirk Welsh), Nancy (Karen Welsh), and Dimmy (Dimetri Bourne)—one team, one dream. Y'all have been my rocks and put up with my youthful exuberances and have been the wind beneath my wings. I appreciate you, and we shall continue to make the Founder proud.

Last but certainly not least, my ride or die, my better half, the love of my life, my wife, Kimberley Danielle McKinson. We've been on this journey of life together—adulting, parenting, and finding our way through thick and thin. There is no one I would rather share this journey with. Your greatness inspires me and compels me to be a better man for you and our children.

Bubba (Solomon Lloyd Welsh) and Mimi (Amina Karlene Patricia Welsh), my heart walking outside my body. I pray for long life so I can continue to witness your growth and greatness. I'm here for you forever—the good, the bad, and the ugly.

I didn't intend for my acknowledgements to be a chapter. But the world should know I did not write this book on my own. For my thoughts, perspectives, and resilience have been shaped by a village I've been blessed to call mentors, colleagues, friends, and family. I thank you all. With love. One love. And of course, Jamaica to di worl!

Richard Osbourne Welsh
June 2024

About the Author

Richard O. Welsh is an associate professor of education and public policy in the Peabody College of Education and Human Development at Vanderbilt University. His research is focused on understanding and transforming inequality in K–12 education. He is the founding director of the School Discipline Lab.

Index